INSIGHT GUIDES

The world's largest collection of

JERUSALEM

This edition produced by Simon Griver
Original edition written by Norman Atkins
Principal photography: Richard Nowitz

Editorial Director: Brian Bell

Discovery
CHANNEL

APA PUBLICATIONS

Part of the Langenscheidt Publishing Group

INSIGHT GUIDES

Jerusalem

CONTACTING THE EDITORS: Although every effort is made to provide accurate information in this publication, we live in a fast-changing world and would appreciate it if readers would call our attention to any errors or outdated information that may occur by writing to us at Apa Publications,
P.O. Box 7910, London SE1 8ZB, England.
Fax: (44) 171-620-1074.
e-mail: insight@apaguide.demon.co.uk.

First Edition 1990
Third Edition (updated) 1999

Distributed in the United States by
Langenscheidt Publishers Inc.
46–35 54th Road
Maspeth
NY 11378
Fax: (718) 784 0640

Distributed in the UK & Ireland by
GeoCenter International Ltd
The Viables Centre, Harrow Way
Basingstoke, Hampshire RG22 4BJ
Fax: (44) 1256-817988

Worldwide distribution enquiries:
APA Publications GmbH & Co. Verlag KG
(Singapore branch)
38 Joo Koon Road
Singapore 628990
Tel: 65-8651600
Fax: 65-8616438

Printed in Singapore by
Insight Print Services (Pte) Ltd
38 Joo Koon Road
Singapore 628990
Fax: 65-8616438

Discovery CHANNEL

This guidebook combines the interests and enthusiasms of two of the world's best known information providers: Insight Guides, whose range of titles has set the standard for visual travel guides since 1970, and Discovery Channel, the world's premier source of nonfiction television programming.

The editors of Insight Guides provide both practical advice and general understanding about a destination's history, culture, institutions and people. Discovery Channel and its Web site, www.discovery.com, help millions of viewers explore their world from the comfort of their own home and also encourage them to explore it firsthand.

Griver

The often disputed status of Jerusalem, a city holy to Jews, Christians and Muslims, has been in the news constantly since the historic peace accord between Israel and the Palestine Liberation Organization. The subsequent headlines have sounded alarming, sometimes even apocalyptic, yet it's easy to forget that this eternal city has been through far worse crises over the past 3,000 years than its current political troubles. Even so, there has been enough change recently to merit publishing this thoroughly revised edition of *Insight Guide: Jerusalem*, produced authoritatively by Insight Guides' Israel-based correspondent, **Simon Griver**.

Atkins

Jerusalem excites religious passions among pilgrims, but more surprisingly the Holy City has the ability to captivate non-religious visitors too. For above and beyond the fascinating religious history and archaeology, Jerusalem's breathtaking mountain views, graceful gardens and elegant architecture can stir the soul of the most cynical atheist. Spirituality aside, the city is also a sensual, romantic place, perhaps lacking the verve and vigour of nearby Tel Aviv but nevertheless having a vibrant nightlife with the restaurant and pub district crowded well into the early hours of the morning.

However, Jerusalem is first and foremost the cradle of monotheism – sacred to Jew,

Davis

Nowitz

Braun

Christian and Muslim. It was here that King David established the capital of the ancient Israelites 3,000 years ago and his son King Solomon built the resplendent Temple. It was here that Christ, according to tradition, was sentenced to death, crucified, buried and rose from the dead. And it was from here Muslims believe that the prophet Mohammed ascended to heaven.

Such a destination lends itself especially well to the approach taken by the 190-title *Insight Guides* series, and Jerusalem was one of the first cities to be given an entire book to itself. The original edition, on which this current edition is built, was written wholly by **Norman Atkins**, a New York-based journalist whose work has appeared in publications ranging from *Rolling Stone* to the *Washington Post*. During a long stay in Israel, he studied at a Jerusalem *yeshivah*, and, although he did not become *frum* (Orthodox), he emerged with a profound regard for the tradition and the guru-rabbis who are its curators.

As with all the books in this series, *Insight Guide: Jerusalem* encourages readers to celebrate the essence of a place rather than try to tailor it to their expectations and is edited in the belief that, without proper insight into a people's character and culture, travel can just as eadily narrow the mind as broaden it.

The book is carefully structured: the first section covers the city's history, and then analyzes its culture in a series of magazine-style essays. The main Places section provides a full run-down on the things worth seeing and doing. Finally, a listings section contains useful addresses, telephone numbers and opening times.

Revising the book for this edition, **Simon Griver** wrote the chapters on "Jerusalem Today" and "Architectural Heritage" as well as several essays in the "People" section. He brought the "Travel Tips" section compre-

hensively up to date. Griver, a writer who was born in England, never really felt he had found his true home until he settled in Israel. The experience is typical of many immigrants and enabled Griver to contribute valuable insights on everyday life.

The essays in the "People" section on Jews, Arabs and Christians came from **Helen Davis**, a New Zealand-born journalist who moved to Israel. The chapter on Hebrew was written by London-born **Asher Weill**, who moved to Israel in 1958, later becoming editor of *Israel Scene* and *Ariel*.

Mordechai Beck, who expertly delineated the various faiths in "Varieties of Religion". attended art school, yeshiva and university in London and made his *aliyah* to Israel in 1973.

Credit for researching and copy-editing the first edition of the book goes to **Angie Kritz**, who was in the process of organizing an Israeli jewellery import business. Having graduated from Yale University and studied in St Petersburg, she brought her fluent Hebrew and Russian to Jerusalem to work for the Soviet Jewry Education and Information Centre. During this book's production, Atkins and Kritz were married and had a baby son.

An outstanding feature of *Insight Guides* series is the striking photography. Maintaining the tradition in this book was **Richard Nowitz**, whose 12 years working in Jerusalem put him among the ranks of the nation's top photographers. He has now moved back to the United States but keeps close ties with Israel.

Also providing striking photographic material was **Werner Braun**, who was born in Germany and emigrated to Palestine in the mid-1940s. Braun has gained wide renown as one of the Israel's leading photographers and has had numerous exhibitions around the world.

The final editing work was completed in Insight Guides' London editorial office, where the book was proofread and indexed by **Pam Barrett**.

CONTENTS

Introduction

The Challenge
of Jerusalem 17

History

The City of David 23
The City of Jesus 31
The City of Islam 37
Perpetual Conquest 41
Zionism and the Arab-
Israeli Conflict 45
Jerusalem Today 51

People

Introduction 59
Secular Jewry 60
Orthodox and Ultra-
Orthodox Jewry 62
Russian Jews 64
Ethiopians 66
Christians 68
Israeli Arabs 71
Palestinians 72
Aliya: A Constant
Renewal 76

Features

Culture 80
Food 82
Varieties of Religion 85
The Hebrew Language 88
Archaeology 91
The Architectural Heritage 92

Places

Introduction 101
Old City Sites 106
Via Dolorosa 126
Church of the Holy
Sepulchre 133
Mount Zion 135
The Mount of Olives 138
East Jerusalem 145
The New City 152
Ein Kerem 189

Excursions

Tel Aviv – Jaffa 194
The Diaspora Museum ... 204
Bethlehem 208
Jericho and the Dead Sea 213
Masada 217

Maps

Israel 100
Northern Israel 102
Jerusalem 103
The Old City 108
Tel Aviv 196
Masada 217

Preceding pages: arch in the Christian Quarter; a *chamsha* or lucky charm to ward off the "evil eye".

Getting Acquainted

The Place 222
History 222
Government & Economy 222
People 223
Climate 223
Business Hours 224
Public Holidays 224

Planning the Trip

Passports and Visas 225
Customs 225
Health 226
Money Matters 226
What to Bring 227
Tourist Offices 227
Getting There 227

Practical Tips

Media 228
Communications 229
Embassies and Consulates 230
Travelling with Children 230
Student Travel 230
Senior Citizens 230
Disabled Travel 231
Security & Crime 231
Medical Services 231
Etiquette 232
On Departure 232

Getting Around

By Road 233
Public Transport 233
Taxis 235
Domestic Flights 235
Driving 235

Where to Stay

Kibbutz Guest Houses 237
Christian Hospices 237
Bed & Breakfast 237
Hotels 237
Holiday Flats & Apartotels 238
Camping and Youth Hostels 239

Eating Out

What to Eat 239
Where to Eat 241

Culture

Archaeological Sites 243
Religious Sites 243
Museums 243
Cultural Centres 244
Art Galleries 244
Music Dance Theatre 244
Cinema 244
Nightlife 245

Festivals

The Sabbath & Jewish
Holy Days 245
Muslim Holy Days 245
Druze Holy Days 245

Attractions

Parks & Gardens 246
Zoos 246
Hiking 246

Shopping

What to Buy 246
Shopping Areas 246
Shopping Hours 247

Sport & Leisure

Participant 247
Spectator 247

Language

Hebrew 248
Arabic 248

Further Reading

General 250
Other Insight Guides 250

Art/Photo Credits 251
Index 252

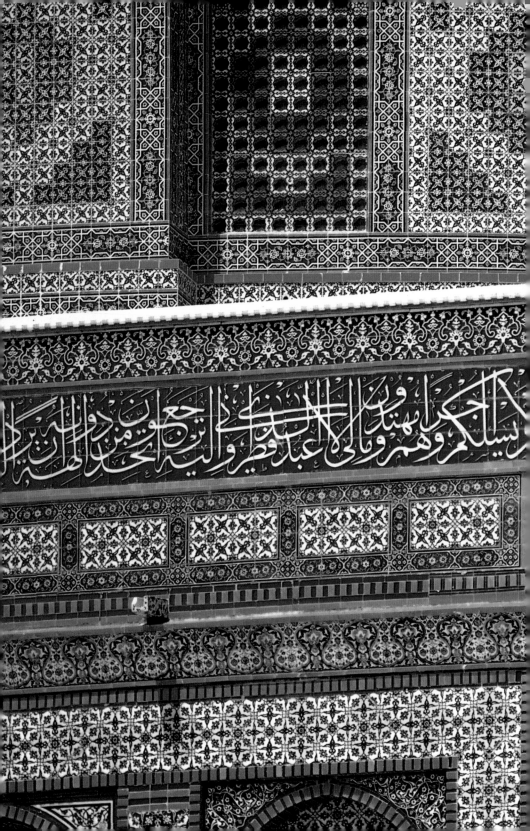

In a slim but wise volume called *Abroad*, Paul Fussell distinguishes between three types of journey: first comes adventure, then travel, and finally tourism. Most trips today are lucky enough to be considered even travel, and normally end up as mere tourism. But the urge to travel is as old as humanity itself, and over the course of history, no destination has been more obvious or attracted more tourists than the city of Jerusalem.

That has become clear once again in recent times. Ever since the Israeli army vanquished Jordan in 1967 and reunited the city, visitors have flocked here from every corner of the earth. For the modern secularist, Jerusalem is the stuff of legends, a place that was once considered the geographic centre of the world.

For Muslims, Jerusalem (after Mecca and Medina) is the third most important pilgrimage site, and during the Islamic festival of *Ramadan*, they crowd the famed shrines, the Dome of the Rock and the Al-Aksa Mosque. For Christians, Jerusalem is *the* mecca, the single most important place of worship, and many would not think of dying before visiting the "Holy Sites" of Jesus. The Talmud (which comprises all of Jewish oral law) says that when 10 measures of beauty came upon the world, "nine were taken by Jerusalem – and one by the rest of the world."

For the Jews, there is a commandment not merely to visit the city, but if at all possible to settle there and an increasing number have made that commitment since 1967. In that time the Israeli government has tried to make the city hospitable to these and still other visitors and residents, with no small financial rewards accruing to the state's booming tourist industry.

Yet, unlike Rome, Athens, or other ancient capitals, Jerusalem is *not* a tourist town. It is not cute, quaint, or easy. To be sure, you will

Preceding pages: a youngster tries his hand at Talmud; detail from the Dome of the Rock; view from the Dominus Flevit Church; a Yemenite Jew. **Left**, acrobat teeters over the Valley of Hinnom. **Right**, an Orthodox Jew at prayer.

find swinging sidewalk cafés, shopping stores and swimming pools on roofs or overpriced hotels (in abundance). But this city is not about any of those things. No matter what your intentions may be in embarking upon your journey, once you have arrived Jerusalem will show you that rare bird, an adventure. It will not let you get away with simply clicking snapshots from tour bus windows.

"You see that arch from the Roman period?" writes the city's poet laureate Yehudah

Amichai. "It is not important but next to it... there sits a man who bought fruit and vegetables for his family." Amichai has captured the city's ethos. For it liberates you from strictly sightseeing and lets you squeeze the vegetables and get to know that man and his family. Everyone you meet here, from the bus driver to the mayor, seems to have lived a thousand lives and can fill your ears with stories that defy the imagination. Moreover, they're constantly asking *you* questions: What are your politics? Do you believe in God? Where are you *really* from? If you permit yourself, Jerusalem will engage you, force you to marvel at the sweep of all human history, and prod you to confront your own identity, whatever it may be.

In a passage of his book *To Jerusalem And Back*, the Nobel Prize-winning Jewish writer Saul Bellow has written about this inexplicable mystical grip: "The air, the very air, is thought nourishing in Jerusalem, the Sages themselves said so… The universe interprets itself before your eyes in the openness of the rock-jumbled valley ending in dead water. Elsewhere you die and disintegrate. Here you die and mingle."

The city is a challenge. Even getting there can be an adventure. By air, you arrive at Ben

Gurion airport near Tel Aviv, or perhaps you come overland from Jordan, across the Allenby Bridge. But, by whichever port of entry, you are instantly struck by the tight security that greets you, the way your bags are rifled, your passport photo scrutinized for an extra minute, or your Swiss army knife confiscated. Visitors are often irritated (and the Palestinians embittered) by such inconvenience, not to mention the rudeness that the Israeli soldiers almost invariably display. But the Israelis themselves are actually comforted by the trouble. They figure it's a small price to pay for safety.

Jerusalem, you must remember, is geographically situated at the fulcrum between Asia and Africa, in the heart of Israel, a tiny nation itself in the heart of the Middle East, a disturbed, fractured, increasingly fanatic, and increasingly powerful region. The city is prized, the object of much resentment and longing. The Palestinian Authority (PA) would like to see Jerusalem become the capital of an independent Palestinian state. But, even after the historic peace accord between Israel and the PLO, the Israelis have remained adamant that the issue of Jerusalem is politcally closed, though they will take into account the needs of the various religious beliefs.

One cannot easily even understand what people are saying in the midst of this heated discourse, so strange is the mélange of languages. Indeed, it is easy to imagine that every language that has ever been spoken is spoken on any average day in Jerusalem. The city itself has the character of each part of the world from which these languages sprang – Russian ghetto, Armenian village, Fez souk. Passing from one neighbourhood to the next can feel like being spirited from one universe to another.

Amos Oz, the famed Israeli novelist who was born in the city, wrote in his celebrated book *My Michael* about the strange admixture of fire, angles, and light that characterize the place: "Jerusalem is a burning city. But a closer glance reveals an immeasurable weightiness. The overpowering arbitrariness of the intertwining alleys. A labyrinth of temporary dwellings, huts and sheds leaning in smouldering anger against the grey stone that takes on now a blue, now a reddish tinge. Rusting gutters. Ruined walls. A harsh and silent struggle between the stonework and the stubborn vegetation. Waste-plots of rubble and thistles. And, above all, the wanton tricks of light: if a stray cloud comes for a moment between the twilight and the city, immediately Jerusalem is different."

Take this landscape and throw into it the oddest and most diverse collection of geniuses, exiles, dreamers, and freaks on the face of the earth. A city with so many joyously pious or genuinely spiritual pilgrims is also a magnet for its fair share of charlatans, faith healers, and false messiahs patrolling the streets in search of the gullible. It is not always easy to distinguish one from the other, but to be too cautious about whom you talk to or whose dinner invitation you accept is to deny yourself the city's richest resource.

Perhaps, for example, you will find yourself in the forbidding neighbourhood of Mea Sharim, face to face with a bearded, dandruff-infested Hassidic Jew, whose family came from some Russian ghetto somewhere in the Pale of Settlement. Perhaps, if you are lucky, he will talk to you. Perhaps, if you are luckier still, he will tell you a story such as this one, which has for the visitor to Jerusa- who could neither light a fire, nor say the prayer, saved his people because at least he could find the special place in the forest. After many years, yet another disciple said to God, 'I do not know how to light the fire. I do not know how to say the prayer. I cannot even find the place in the forest. All I can do is tell the story, and this must suffice.' And, you know something, it did suffice because, so it is related, God made human beings because He loves stories."

Jerusalem may be a mystical place, but the people who reside there are so far removed from the lives of Abraham, David, Moham- med, Jesus, and the other historical and pro-

lem a special significance.

"The founder of Hassidism was the Baal Shem Tov. It is said that when he saw misfortune threatening his people, he would find a special place in the forest where he would meditate, light a fire, say a prayer, and the misfortune would be avoided. Some time after, one of his disciples found that special place, but he did not know how to start a fire; so he said the prayer and again the danger was averted. Later still, another disciple,

Left, model of ancient Jerusalem at Holyland Hotel. **Above**, soldiers on the Mount of Olives.

phetic personages who made the city what it is. Jerusalemites today only have the stories, and even that is a miracle. For the modern visitor, the challenge is not to see the greatest number of shrines and monuments, many of which are described herein. The challenge is to open oneself to meeting the disciples, of whichever faith and no matter how many generations removed, and hear the stories of how the city – and all the world – came to be what it is. Whether one goes away convinced that one, several, or no stories are the truth hardly matters. For, as the Hassidic tale says, God loves stories.

Some 4,000 years ago Abraham (so the Bible tells us) ventured 2,000 miles from his native Ur to the Land of Canaan. Thereupon this sheikh-like Chaldean shepherd emerged as a prosperous trader, a skilful warrior, and the undisputed leader of his family clan.

At a time when idolatry was common and polytheism was the rage, Abraham was smashing his father's idols. Abraham swore fealty to *one* God.

So fervently did he worship God that one day he journeyed to Mount Moriah and prepared to sacrifice his son simply because the Lord willed it. When Abraham had bound Isaac and laid him across the altar, however, God intervened. "Do not raise your hand against the boy," said an angel of the Lord. "For now I know that you fear God, since you have not withheld your son, your favoured one, from me."

Thus did Abraham emerge not only as the patriarch of the Jewish people and the progenitor of monotheism but also as a prophet venerated by Christians, Muslims and even modern philosophers. In the context of the history of Jerusalem, this particular revelation resulted in the city's origin as the world's great spiritual centre, and it is a belief that has transcended time.

In the time of Abraham, the town was a small Canaanite city-state settled in the middle of the Bronze Age, perhaps around 2500BCE (BCE stands for Before Common Era and is the term used by non-Christians in numbering years Before Christ). The town was ruled by the Amorites, Hittites, and Jebusites. The former supposedly followed a lord named "Shalem", from which the city ("yerah") got its name "Yerushalayim". Shalem (or "Shalom") also means peace, and hence Jerusalem is more commonly called "The City of Peace", an encomium not wanting in irony.

One may wonder why so many wars have

been fought in the past 3,000 years over an area which the city's historians delight in cataloguing its inadequacies: Jerusalem sits at the head of no generous river or harbour; no vital trade route or highway cuts though it; it conspicuously lacks mineral riches; and it has never represented a crucial domino in the sport of empire conquest. In short, the city has no more military, topographic, or economic value than any other average Bedouin base camp.

No wonder Abraham's descendants, the Jews, upon escaping from Egypt and sweeping into Canaan didn't bother to conquer Jerusalem. Even after settling the land around it, they left the city to the Jebusites perhaps because these 12 tribes of Israel were preoccupied with their own civil wars until the time of King David.

Now David was a stunningly handsome farmer who had become fairly famous while still a lad, so the legend goes, by defeating the enormous Philistine champion Goliath in combat. The southern tribes of Israel, known as Judah, gathered around David, and he

Preceding pages: the ancient Madaba map. Left, ruins of the City of David. Right, menorah adorns window at Hechal Shlomo.

ascended to the throne in the capital of Hebron. As he grew in power, the weaker northern tribes came to Hebron and recognized David, anointing him their monarch as well in about 1000BCE.

King David is remembered for destroying the Philistine armies and finally securing the borders of the land that God had promised the children of Abraham. But he is remembered best of all for his decision to conquer and take as his new capital Jerusalem.

This was not as foolish as it may have seemed. In terms of the land apportioned to the 12 tribes, Jerusalem was centrally located. Since no tribe in particular held any historical claim to it, all could be brought together under its aegis without inspiring the normal amount of rivalry.

As the conquest and achievement of King David, Jerusalem came to symbolize the new monarch ("The City of David") and acted as a focus for unifying the nation. In addition, the city was strategically well positioned for defending itself against foreign foes because mountains fortified it on three sides. Although lacking the ideal water supply, it was conveniently located near the spring of Gihon, a surprising water source in the otherwise barren, soil-poor Judean hills. Those hills must initially have looked inhospitable, but the Jews soon learned to make the best of a bad situation and subsequently pioneered mountain agriculture and reared sheep and goats.

To Jerusalem David brought the Ark of the Covenant. It was reputed to be the mobile shrine that the Jews built during 40 years of wandering to hold the tablets of law which God gave Moses and all of Abraham's descendants on Mount Sinai. Once in Jerusalem, David built a tabernacle to cover the shrine, and went in search of land upon which a permanent home could be established. To this end he purchased for 50 shekels of silver the threshing floor of Araunah the Jebusite on a hill just outside the settled part of the city.

This very hill brings us back to the story of Abraham. In the oral tradition of the Jews,

David did not select this spot arbitrarily, God showed it to him. The Lord is to have revealed it as Mount Moriah, the very place where Abraham offered his son Isaac in sacrifice. This meant that Jerusalem was the holiest ground of all.

David may have found the land, but the tradition says he could not build the Temple because he was a warrior, his hands too bloody. Shortly before he died in 960BCE, David anointed his youngest son Solomon to be his successor. Solomon was known for being both a splendid poet and statesman, both wise and rich. He forged treaties with a number of former adversaries, taking their

daughters for wives. He was even linked romantically with fabled queen of Sheba. But the culmination of Solomon's rule was fulfilling the mission set forth by his father, building the Temple. It was dedicated at *Sukkot* (the feast of the tabernacles) in 953BCE. At that moment, Jerusalem became the religious as well as the political centre of the Jewish people.

Upon Solomon's death in 922BCE, the 10 northern tribes, unhappy with rule from Jerusalem, seceded to establish their own state, the Kingdom of Israel. The southern two tribes – Benjamin and Judah – continued to

Left, a model of Herod's Temple. **Right**, a replica of an ancient mosaic of Chanukah menorah.

follow the House of David and formed the Kingdom of Judah, with the capital remaining in Jerusalem. There followed over the next two centuries an on-again, off-again civil war between these two kingdoms. For the city, the war with the northern tribes meant a loss of trade and taxes.

In 722BCE, King Sargon II of then powerful Assyria conquered Samaria, where the northern tribes had their capital. He exiled them to the furthest reaches of the empire, where many presumably assimilated. Thus they are called the Ten Lost Tribes of Israel. By all logic, the other two tribes should have met the same destiny and would have were it

could neither penetrate the wall, nor survive outside it for very long without water.

When King Hezekiah died in 687BCE, he had done much to save the city. His son Manasseh, who succeeded him, proceeded to undo much of that work, making Judah the virtual vassal of Assyria, adopting idol-worship, and regularly permitting the sacrifice of children in the valley of Hinnom, customarily regarded ever since as the geographic site of Hell. Manasseh's grandson, King Josiah (640–609BCE) was considered considerably more righteous, and during his rule child sacrifices were abolished and a religious revival took place under the influence

not for Judah's King Hezekiah, the unsung hero of Jewish history.

He prepared the city for siege first by rallying the previously doomsayers' populace. With the support of the prophet Isaiah, he repaired the temple, destroyed all idols, and outlawed pagan-worship.

Then he mobilized the Jews to build a massive wall around the city and a 1600-ft (500-metre) tunnel through which water could be drawn from the Gihon Spring to the Siloam pool just inside the city walls. In 701BCE, Assyrian King Sennacherib came with his armies to Jerusalem. His forces

of the prophet Jeremiah. During this period, the cycle of three yearly pilgrimages to Jerusalem began.

Although Josiah was able to annex the northern territories, by 602BCE the Kingdom of Judah was torn asunder in the midst of war between Babylon and Egypt. At first Josiah's son, a treacherous ruler named Zedekiah, ruled Jerusalem as a Babylonian puppet. When he finally tried to resist and forge an alliance with Egypt, Babylonian King Nebuchadnezzar came to Jerusalem and turned away the Egyptians. Although the Jews barricaded themselves inside the city for many months, even as they were on the verge of starvation in 587BCE the city walls were breached.

Zedekiah fled to Jericho, but was soon captured, forced to watch his family butchered before his own eyes were ripped out and he was carried off to Babylon in chains. No kinder fate awaited the rest of the Jews. By 586BCE Nebuchadnezzar toppled the city, burned down the Temple, killed off part of the population, and hauled the rest of the people off into exile.

Fifty years later, the Persian king Cyrus reduced Babylon and allowed the exiles to return. A benevolent dictator, Cyrus even

Ataxerxes I to make him governor of the land and he immediately returned to a home he had never seen.

Nehemiah led the third and decisively important wave of returning exiles in 440BCE. It is said that under his guidance, the walls of the city were built in 52 days, the Temple significantly refurbished. Meanwhile, Ezra the Scribe led a group of priestly types from Babylon to Jerusalem to revitalize the study of Jewish law. The community in exile had practised a far more rigid observance of the tradition than the community of returnees. Ezra is remembered best of all for compiling the canon of Jewish Torah (or Bible), which

donated money from the royal coffers for reconstruction of the Temple, which was finished in 515BCE. Despite this good fortune, many Jews had remained in Babylon, where they had become well established in business and in the Persian administration. One such high-ranking official was Nehemiah. And when a delegation of Jews from Jerusalem visited him and told of the terrible conditions of their city, he persuaded King

Left, a medieval portrayal of King Solomon and the Queen of Sheba. **Above**, the ruins of the steps leading to the Temple.

has been followed ever since.

The Persians continued to control Jerusalem until 333BCE when the young and indominatable general Alexander the Great annexed it to the Greek empire. At first, the Greek Ptolemies of Egypt did not interfere with the established Judean theocracy and the city prospered. They did, however, haul off a substantial number of Jewish prisoners to the Egyptian city of Alexandria, which hence became an important early centre of diaspora Jewry.

The Greeks of Egypt were finally ousted by the Greeks of Syria, the Seleucids, in

198BCE. If they were benevolent initially, by 175BCE. Seleucid King Antiochus IV, whose chief goal was to transform Jerusalem into a Greek city, made observance of Judaism punishable by death. He built a Hellenistic fortress on the Temple mount, rededicated the Temple itself to Zeus, and sacrificed swine across its altars.

In a recurring pattern throughout their history, many Jews accepted idol worship and assimilated to Hellenism. Others passively resisted, continuing their Jewish prayers and observance in private. Others still preferred death. By 167BCE, the Jews began a National War of Resistance against the Greeks. It was led by five brothers from the House of Hasmon, the eldest of whom was called Judah the Maccabbee because he was as powerful as a hammer.

The Hasmoneans fought a guerrilla war from the Judean mountains, culminating in the reconquest of the Temple mount in 164BCE. When they reached the Temple, it was terribly befouled and (so the Talmud tells us), there was only enough pure oil to last one day. But, by the miracle of God, it lasted eight days until a new supply of oil became available. That is why on the yearly Jewish celebration of Chanukah, which commemorates the Maccabbean victory, the Jews light eight candles.

Within a few years, from the Temple Mount base, the Hasmoneans beat back the Seleucids and controlled Jerusalem once again. Judah the Maccabbee died in 160BCE, but he was succeeded first by his righteous brothers Jonathan and Simon and finally by his fascistic nephew John Hyrcanus, who ruled from 135 to 104BCE.

Not happy with mere independence, Hyrcanus dreamed of building a Jewish kingdom and – in an act thoroughly out of line with Jewish law or tradition – he forcibly circumcised and converted a conquered people called the Idumeans.

Opposed to Hyrcanus was an ideological faction of Jews called the Pharisees. They cared more about the Torah than the kingdom and were more concerned with religious observance than imperial conquests. The Sadducees, a competing faction representing the priestly and monied caste, supported the combined political and religious leadership of Hyrcanus. The rift between these two groups coupled with less than inspired leadership from the heirs to Hyrcanus left Jerusalem ripe for the picking when the Rome's conquering hero Pompey arrived in 63BCE.

Within 25 years, the Romans had decisively established their control with the appointment of Herod as king of Judea. Herod was descended from the aforementioned Idumeans. He reigned for 35 years, during which time the city prospered and underwent massive repairs.

Rome considered him an ally, but Herod disturbed many of his so-called subjects the way he flaunted the latest foreign styles and fashions. In Jerusalem itself, for instance, he constructed a Greek Hippodrome near the Temple mount.

Herod was so paranoid a ruler that he had his own wife and two sons killed because he feared they would destroy him. This, along with his disregard for Jewish dietary law, prompted one of the king's admirers, Emperor Augustus Caesar to quip: "I would rather be Herod's pig than Herod's son."

It's impossible to say, however, whether the Jews could have mistrusted Herod as much as he imagined. In any event, he decided to try to ingratiate himself by leading the reconstruction of the Temple. According to the historian Josephus, Herod's Temple was built by 10,000 workmen and 1,000 priests. It took eight years to complete the courtyard and another couple of years for the Temple itself. When it was finished, it was widely regarded as one of the wonders of the world. The Talmud says that one who had not seen Herod's Temple had not seen a beautiful building.

Herod came to a bloody end in 4BCE, upon which a Jewish revolt was put down by Roman legions, and soon Judah was annexed by Rome and ruled by procurators. It was into this chaotic world and time that a certain child named Jeshua, or Jesus, was born, and that world, as they say, has never been the same.

Right, David playing the harp, as depicted by Marc Chagall for the Knesset.

The Jews believe that there is a man in every generation who has the potential to be the Messiah, and since the Roman era seemed to call urgently for divine intervention, there were repeated claims around town that one or another zealous type was, in fact, the Messiah who had come to save the Jews from the tyranny of their rulers. It is probably true that such a claim was made on behalf of Jesus as much or more than for any other man of his time.

When Jesus was born in Nazareth, not so far away, the population of Jerusalem was nearly a quarter of a million and it swelled to about a million during festival times. Pilgrims would come from all across the land and the Diaspora to make sacrifices and worship at the Temple for the three festivals: *Pesach* (Passover), which marked the celebration of the Jews' exodus from Egypt; *Shavuoth* (Feast of Weeks), the wheat harvest festival; and *Sukkot* (Feast of the Tabernacle), in which the Jews give thanks for God's bountiful nature.

Jesus's parents, Joseph and Mary (so we learn from Luke), were in the habit of making this pilgrimage from their native Galilee on *Pesach* every year. When Jesus was 12 years old, they brought him along. On their way home after the festival, however, they lost track of the boy and had to search for him for days. They went back to Jerusalem and finally found him still inside the Temple, completely absorbed with the teachings of Pharisee rabbis, engaged in a dialogue that greatly impressed his elders.

Like the Pharisees, Jesus was contemptuous of Roman authority and scorned the priestly administrators of the Temple, the way they valued ceremony over spiritual substance. He was bothered by the materialism of the wealthy Jerusalemites and the fact that they exploited the poor. He denounced the rampant hate that had spread across the town, and expounded upon the Gold Rule of

Rabbi Hillel: "Don't do unto your neighbours that which you find offensive."

As Jesus got older, it was apparent he wasn't the typical yeshivah *bucher* (student). It would be said later about him that he was indeed the Messiah, a direct descendant of the House of David, that he had performed certain miracles, and that he had thrown off the formalistic religious observance of the Pharisees. Still, in terms of his criticism of the Roman rule and the decadence of his

contemporaries, his concerns were shared by a growing number in Jerusalem.

Because of this widespread discontent, the Roman Procurator Pontius Pilate, who governed between 26 and 36CE (CE stands for Common Era and is the term used by non-Christians in numbering years After Christ) attempted to diminish the significance of the city by shifting the capital to Caesaria on the Mediterranean coast. But Pilate was so deeply concerned about the rumblings in Jerusalem that he came to watch at festival time just to make sure the vast influx of pilgrims were not roused to revolt. It was in this spirit Pilate

Left, Crusader crosses in the Church of the Holy Sepulchre. Right, the 1683 floorplan of the church.

arrived on the eve of Passover in the year 33CE.

Jesus and his disciples had also come from the Galilee to celebrate the festival. A large *Pesach* meal (a *seder*) was prepared for them on Mount Zion, and they drank the customary four full cups of wine. Then they crossed the Kidron Valley to the Mount of Olives, and to the garden of Gethsemane. If Jesus sensed he was in danger, his disciples were of little help, falling asleep from all the wine. It is said that Jesus wept that night when he beheld the city because he presaged its ultimate destruction and the fall of the great Temple. Shortly thereafter, he was arrested

resistance was building. When the lunatic Roman Emperor Caligula attempted to have his own image carved into the Temple, he helped instigate the ultimate revolt, which came in AD66. The war of the Jews Against the Romans, as it was called, lasted five years. At first, the Jewish zealots seized Masada, Herod's old fortress, and eventually triumphed in Jerusalem, to which the Romans responded by butchering the entire Jewish population of Caesaria.

Emperor Vespasian set out to restore Roman rule in Jerusalem, dispatching his son Titus to quash the insurrection. In AD70, Titus routed the Jews, though the Temple

and brought before a Jewish court and then before Pilate himself. Jesus was found guilty of some trumped-up charges of crimes against the state and the procurator sentenced him to the death penalty, customarily carried out by crucifixation in those times. After suffering on the cross, he was given a proper Jewish burial, and, although his disciples went into deep mourning, with the exception of this small cadre of followers, his death was scarcely remarked upon for the next two centuries or so.

The Romans may have executed so-called revolutionary leaders like Jesus, but Jewish

remained a last holdout a month longer. Finally, Titus's armies broke through and burned the Temple to the ground. This happened, hauntingly enough, on the 9th day of the Hebrew month of Av, on the very anniversary of the day the First Temple was destroyed by the Babylonians. It is worth noting that the Talmud does not say that the Temple fell because the Romans were better armed or stronger than the Jews, but because of causeless hate among the Jews themselves. Interestingly enough, Jesus, among other zealots of his time, had dedicated their lives to preaching causeless love.

After the destruction of the Temple, the Jews worshipped on its ruins. Emperor Hadrian saw in the rubble a Jewish nationalism that frightened him. So he outlawed the observance of the Sabbath, circumcision, and resolved to turn Jerusalem into a Roman city, replete with a temple to Jupiter on the old Temple mount. This touched off yet another rebellion and, improbably enough, the Jews actually won their city back for three years, AD 132–135.

They were led by the brilliant general Simmon Bar Kochba, whom Rabbi Akiva, one of the great sages of all Jewish history, thought to be the Messiah. In this rare case,

except on the 9th of Av, the anniversary of the Temple's destruction. It was in the wake of this decree that followers of Jesus made a certain decision. Up until this time, they were considered a small Jewish sect, who followed all Jewish laws and customs, except that they believed Jesus was the Messiah and were awaiting a second coming. Now, however, to distinguish themselves from the Jews, and gain admittance to Jerusalem, they would change certain traditions – for instance, starting to observe the Sabbath on Sunday instead of Saturday.

In the Greek town of Antioch, this group of followers acquired the derogatory name

the rabbi was gravely mistaken and the Jews lost a grip on Jerusalem. Akiva was cruelly murdered in front of his community.

Hadrian intended to wipe out any trace of the former Jewish city and he renamed it Aelia Capitolina, built the temple to Jupiter, and placed an equestrian statue of himself in front of it. He further decreed that, upon penalty of death, no Jew could enter the city

Left, original pavement showing ancient Roman dicing game. Above, Byzantine carving from the door of the Holy Sepulchre Church, now in the Rockfeller Museum.

"Christians" because they believed Jesus was Christos, the anointed one. Still this was such an obscure group that Jesus would certainly have faded from memory were it not for Saul of Tarsus, a tentmaker, rabbinic student, and zealously observant follower of Jewish law. Of Saul, the historian Cecil Roth has written: "Few Jews have ever influenced the world to the same extent." Saul scoffed at the Messianic claims made by Jesus's followers until one day, as he was approaching the city of Damascus, it hit him in a flash that they were right.

At first, he set about proselytizing in Jewish circles, at synagogues throughout Diaspora, but he wasn't too successful. Some say he was embittered by the experience and began throwing off Jewish traditions altogether. Others say that he realized that Christianity wouldn't go over too well so long as it clung to the adherence of so many rigorous rules, including the rite of circumcision. Whichever the case, when Saul began his wide-ranging missions in the non-Jewish world, Christianity began spreading like wildfire and the words of Apostle Paul – as Saul became known – were widely quoted.

Of those who had been profoundly influenced by Paul's teachings, by far the most

important was Constantine the Great (AD288–337). Constantine by this time ruled the Roman empire, a good chunk of the world that included Jerusalem, from his capital of Byzantine. Soon Christianity became the official faith of the empire and Constantine dispatched his enthusiastic mother, Queen Helena, on a mission to Jerusalem to locate the: "Holy Places" – where Jesus tarried and where he'd been buried. Escorted around town by Jerusalem's Bishop Micarius, Queen Helena had one stroke of good fortune after another. When she found a Roman temple to Venus, she determined it was the place where

Jesus had actually been crucified. Hadrian built it there, she surmised, to wipe out any memory of the Jewish martyr. Constantine replaced it with the fabulous Church of the Holy Sepulchre, an earlier version of the very one you find in Jerusalem today.

Under Constantine, Christianity gained many adherents. Jerusalem emerged as a holy city for a whole new and larger group of people, and pilgrims flocked there from all over the world. Monasteries, hospices, churches were built across the city, and the Christians comprised a majority of the population. Meanwhile, Judaism was regarded as a dangerous rival to Christianity – so much so that marrying a Jew at this time could make one liable for the death penalty. And under Emperor Theodosius II (AD408–50) – "the first Christian Inquisitor" – anti-Jewish discrimination became part of the fabric of the European attitude and jurisprudence. In AD610, Emperor Heraclius went so far as to order that all Jews be baptized.

So when the majestic Byzantine Jerusalem was sacked by the Persian armies in AD614, it is not surprising that the Jews of Galilee jumped to their assistance. The city was taken in 20 days, and the Jews expected that Jerusalem would henceforth be given back to them. But this was no more than a pipe-dream. The situation worsened when in AD629 Heraclius turned back the Persians and reconquered Jerusalem. Predisposed to despise the Jews, Heraclius was especially incited against them by charges that they had beaten and killed Christians during Persian rule. He, in turn, permitted a new wave of Jew killing. Those who survived the massacres were banished and forced to live at least 3 miles (5 km) outside the city limits.

Heraclius's own days were numbered, the Byzantine reconquest short-lived. For within 10 years, the Arabian army of Caliph Omar, inspired by a new religion called Islam, besieged Jerusalem until the Byzantines threw out the white flag. Once a Jewish city, then a Christian city, Jerusalem now became a centre of the Muslim religion.

Left, the Cenacle, where Jesus ate the Last Supper. Right, pilgrims flock to Jerusalem from all over the world.

With the dispersion of the Jews and the spread of Christianity, Jerusalem's religions reached many a far-flung land. In Arabia, a young religious student named Mohammed studied with a group of *banifs*, teachers of both brands of worship. It is said that one night, on a spiritual quest of his own, this Mohammed walked into a cave, and, when he finally emerged, he was reciting aloud an Arabic literature such as none before had ever heard. (*The Koran*, which is the written version of Mohammed's message, literally means recital.)

Mohammed had placed himself squarely on Abraham's shoulders, his principal idea simply expressed in a new and more widely spoken language: *La-Allah-il-Allah* ! ("The only God is God!"). Mohammed did far more than Abraham to bring monotheism to the masses. So it was not altogether inappropriate for his followers to add, *Mohammed rasoula*! ("And Mohammed is His prophet!")

Like the Apostle Paul, Mohammed first hoped his message would attract many Jews, especially with his emphasis on the rite of circumcision and the strict Jewish dietary laws. For a year and a half, he even instructed worshippers to face Jerusalem during their prayers. But the stiff-necked Jews turned away from the new prophet and the Muslims, a situation which has created tension between the two groups to this very day.

None of this would have touched the history of Jerusalem quite the way it has were it not for the Islamic tradition of Mohammed's "Night Journey." Mohammed had a legendary wonder horse named el-Burak, which had wings, a woman's face, and the tail of a peacock. It was upon this trusty steed that the prophet (so the *Koran* tells us) rode one night from Mecca to "The Farthest Mosque." He met there the Angel Gabriel, and was accompanied through the seven heavens, where he

Left, an 1898 portrait of a Palestinian Arab. Right, an idyllic representation of Jerusalem in the 18th century.

prayed with all the old Jewish and Christian prophets and finally with God Himself. The Muslims identified "The Farthest Mosque" with a heavenly place, but later said that it was on the Temple Mount of Jerusalem, which they called *el Quds* ("The Holy").

It's doubtful whether Mohammed's successor, Caliph Omar, had any of this in mind when he led the invasion on the Byzantine and Persian empires not long after the prophet himself died. Omar conquered Jerusalem in

AD638, greatly assisted by Jewish armies. He believed he came to power because of his relationship with the Jews, and he allowed them to return to Jerusalem, even granting them permission to rebuild the Temple on the mount.

Shortly thereafter, the Caliph must have changed his mind. According to Muslim tradition, he was so disgusted by the way the Byzantines befouled the Temple Mount, he forced the Christian Patriarch to crawl on his hands and knees through the dung heaps. Then he poured his purse full of gold and silver on the mounds of garbage as reward to the poor for cleaning it up. The Temple Mount, called by the Arabs *Haram esh-Sharif* ("Noble Sanctuary"), was rededicated as a place of Muslim worship.

The fabulous shrine known as the Dome of the Rock was built by a later Caliph, Abd al-Malik in AD691 on the site where the Temples of Solomon and Herod once stood. The Muslims, agreeing with the Jewish tradition, said this Rock (*as Sakhra*) was the one upon which Abraham prepared his son for sacrifice. They also believe it is the precise spot from which Mohammed rose to the heavens during his "Night Journey".

Abd al-Malik, however, may not have

erected the magnificent edifice solely for spiritual reasons. As the ruler of the Umayyad Dynasty in nearby Damascus, he may have felt it necessary to put up something that could compete with Mecca and thus keep local pilgrims from patronizing the rival caliph there. Also, he may have wanted to outdo the Christian shrine of the Holy Sepulchre; if so, it is ironic that he relied on Byzantine architects to help him accomplish the task.

In the early part of the 8th century, Al-Malik's son, Al-Walid built the Al-Aksa Mosque on the southern end of the Temple Mount. It was subsequently said about this mosque: "One prayer in Mecca is equal to ten thousand (anywhere else); one prayer in Medina equals one thousand; and one prayer in Jerusalem equals five hundred." It was thus that Jerusalem came to be known as the third city of Islam.

The city never served as the capital of the Umayyad Dynasty, but during this time it underwent great restoration and revival. After the Baghdad-based Abbasid Dynasty seized control of Jerusalem in AD750, the city declined in importance over the next two centuries, with most Muslims making pilgrimages to Mecca. The Jewish and Christian populations maintained communities without interference from the distant rulers and the Abbasids still found pilgrimages profitable. One ruler actually permitted Charlemagne to endow and maintain a centre for European pilgrims.

All that changed with the rise of the Fatimid Dynasty. The Fatimids had stormed through Mecca, Medina, Egypt, Palestine, and Syria, assisted by the Bedouins. When they conquered Jerusalem, the Egyptian-based "Mad Caliph" Al-Hakim had all synagogues and churches destroyed. It was said that he more than any other figure during Muslim rule, paved the way for the coming Crusaders. What was especially tragic about this episode was that it was widely rumored back in Europe that the Jews instigated the Caliph's fanaticism, and there followed in Christian towns across the northern continent the massacre of Jews.

The Fatimids lost a grip on Jerusalem when in 1071 the Seljuks – Asian slaves-cum-Muslim converts – overtook Syria and Palestine. The Seljuks wildly went about vandalizing Jerusalem and persecuting Jews and Christians alike. The Christians were sufficiently angered to prepare an invasion of their own from the north. The Fatimids reconquered Jerusalem before the turn of the century; but, as they were doing so, the Crusader armies were on their way.

Left, the Al Aksa Mosque, where every Islamic ruler of Jerusalem has traditionally come to worship. **Right**, the Dome of the Rock, where Mohammed rose to heaven.

By the second half of the 11th century, pilgrims returned from Jerusalem to Christian Europe with horror stories about the way the Muslims were treating the Holy Places. Pope Urban II finally exhorted the Christians to recover control of the Holy Land.

The campaign culminated in 1097 when Godfrey de Bouillon led combined forces of the German and French Knights (the Crusaders, as they were called), into Jerusalem. The streets of the city, it is said, ran with blood, and nearly every one of the 40,000 inhabitants (Jews and Muslims) were killed. Any Jew who survived was either sold into bondage or ransomed to the Jewish community in Alexandria. By 1099, the Crusaders' newly established Latin Kingdom declared that Jerusalem was its capital.

Subsequently, as many as 10,000 Christian pilgrims journeyed to Jerusalem each year. Churches and monasteries were built frenetically, each in some way connected to the life of Jesus and his disciples. Christian Arabs were brought in from the East to settle the Jewish Quarter, and in addition the Syrian and Armenian Quarters were firmly established.

All told, the city was greatly fortified, which made the Crusader defeat by the Egypt-based sultan Saladin all the more impressive in 1187. Saladin did not seek retribution against the Christian population for the massacre of the Muslims. In fact, he encouraged Eastern Christians, as well as Jews, to settle in Jerusalem, especially if they were likely to be allies in the ongoing war against the Crusaders.

The Crusaders, however, retook Jerusalem through the back door in 1241. After Saladin died, his sons divided up the empire and then went into battle against each other. To outmatch the Damascus heir, the Egyptian heir brokered a deal with Frederick II of Germany. In exchange for an alliance, the

Crusader emperor could have all of Jerusalem except the Temple Mount (which remained in Muslim hands). The Pope, meanwhile, withheld his blessing since he believed one must battle Muslims, not bargain with them.

After three years, the Crusaders were expelled once more, this time by an army of nomad Turks, who were the paid mercenaries of the new Egyptian Sultan. And shortly thereafter in 1258, the Mamelukes seized

power from Saladin's successors. The Mamelukes ruled from Cairo, where they had been brought originally to serve as a special guard of the sultans. They eventually rebelled against their masters and established an empire of their own.

During their rule, Jerusalem was relegated to minor importance, serving primarily as the Siberia of its time, a place of exile for dangerous or disgraced government officials. The Mamelukes levied heavy taxes on the local populations, which depressed the economy. Despite this, they did bring to the city an exotic and beautiful style of archi-

Left, every conqueror has maintained control of the Old City from the Citadel of David. Right, a Mameluke fountain.

tecture that (though not showcased) can be seen in the city to this very day.

Eventually the Mameluke Empire disintegrated, and the powerful Ottoman Empire succeeded it in 1516. Within a year, Jerusalem was in Turkish hands. The first ruler, Selim I, was responsible for imposing yet another stiff tax on all non-Muslims. Selim's son, Suleiman the Magnificent, who ruled from 1520 to 1566, is generally considered a brilliant and benevolent ruler.

Suleiman brought to Jerusalem a new era of prosperity and took as his mission rebuilding the walls of the city, which are the very ones you see today. He also reconstructed,

with much flourish, the Damascus Gate and fortified the Tower of David.

After Suleiman's death and for the following three centuries, the city fell to pieces. The rulers from Constantinople cared not a whit about the place. They made themselves scarce and their custodians were corrupt. They extracted bribes from each of the Christian sects squabbling for the right to control various Holy Places.

Toward the Jews the Turks were just as arbitrary. They proved particularly capricious in 1799 after Napoleon had beseeched the Jews of Africa and Asia to follow him to Jerusalem and rebuild the city. Of course the Emperor never made good on his whim, but the Turks, riled by the putative connection between Napoleon and the Jews, allowed thieves to run rampant looting and destroying Jewish homes.

In 1831, the Jews and Christians received a temporary respite during the fabulous and surprising rule of the Egyptian army officer Mohammed Ali. Ali assumed control of Egypt and expelled the Ottoman Empire from Jerusalem and all of Palestine. He embodied the modern ruler and was largely responsible for initiating a series of economic and governmental reforms in the city.

Ali's greatness was also recognized by the European powers. In 1840, when Ali tried to attack Istanbul, the European states assisted the Turks in turning him back.

Ottoman control resumed, but each sultan thereafter was reduced to obsequiousness before European leaders. When the Sultan's guest, the German Kaiser Wilhelm, made his grand entrance through the city walls at the turn of the 20th century, it was as if he were conquering the place.

The British also made their presence known in Palestine. Fighting both the Germans and the Turks in World War I, the British General Edmund Allenby waltzed into Jerusalem on 11 December 1917, and inaugurated a 41-year rule by yet another imperial power.

British rule was both positive and negative. The British Mandate has been credited with overseeing Jerusalem's economic renewal and at the same time preserving the city's special historical character through a rigorous set of architectural planning guidelines. However, the Mandate's legacy is also known for sowing the seeds of the Arab-Israeli conflict. In 1917, even before the start of the Mandate, Britain's Lord Balfour signed a declaration that the Jewish Zionists subsequently regarded as their Magna Carta: "His Majesty's Government view with favour the establishment in Palestine of a National Home for the Jewish people."

Left, Jaffa road awaits the visit of Kaiser Wilhelm II in 1898. **Right**, the present city walls, built by Suleiman the Magnificent in the 16th century.

Even with the Balfour Declaration, who could have imagined the Jewish rise to statehood from the ashes of destruction and exile? Ever since the Second Temple was destroyed, Jews in exile the world over have cried out in messianic hope: "Next year in Jerusalem!" And yet throughout this Diaspora, many have maintained that the Messiah would not come until the Jews stopped waiting on Him and instead returned to Jerusalem and began rebuilding the city.

Though small, there has been a continuous presence of this community in Jerusalem ever since the Crusaders were turned back in the 13th century. At that time, Rabbi Mocco ben Nachman (Nachmanides) led the return of Spanish Jews. Upon reaching the city, Nachmanides wrote to his family: "What shall I say of this land? Great is its desolation. The more holy the place, the greater the desolation. Jerusalem is the most desolate of all... The only Jewish residents are two brothers, dyers by trade. The city has no master and he that wishes may take possession of the ruins. May you, my son and your brothers, and the whole of our family, see the salvation of Jerusalem."

By the early 19th century, the city was not so bleak as when Nachmanides lived there, but still most of its precious sites lay in shambles. Two thousand Jews or one fifth of Jerusalem's population were crammed into the filthy, disease-ridden Jewish Quarter. Most were elderly, poor and religious. It was not until the second half of the century, with the advent of Zionism, that Jews began to actively resettle Jerusalem.

Zionism comes from the Hebrew word *tzion*, a Biblical name for at times Jerusalem (site of Mount Zion) and the entire land of Israel. It developed as a decidedly secular, nationalist movement, advocating the rebuilding Jerusalem and not to hasten the coming of the Messiah. Zionism was an

attempt to give the Jewish people a home, making them a nation like all others.

The early movement: The idea first came up in a 1862 book *Rome and Jerusalem*, by Moses Hess, the father of German Social Democracy. He advocated the establishment of a truly socialist nation-state in Palestine. The argument, however, failed to gain much credence until another book, *Auto-Emancipation* by the Russian Jew Leo Pinsker, was published in 1882. Pinsker, arguing forcibly

that Jews remained vulnerable to anti-Semitism precisely because they lacked a nation of their own, soon wielded enormous influence. He inspired the formation of young Zionist clubs in Russia, where pogroms against Jews were becoming commonplace.

It's doubtful, however, that Zionism based solely on the enthusiasm of Russian Jewish youth would have endured. What gave the movement structure and popularity was the tireless work of a Viennese journalist named Theodore Herzl. Herzl, a thoroughly assimilated, liberally educated and affluent Jew, was an archetypal product of the European

Left, Theodore Herzl, one of Zionism's founding fathers. **Right**, a young David Ben-Gurion, wearing a Turkish fez.

Enlightenment. It was not until he witnessed the rampant anti-Semitism in France while covering the Dreyfus Affair that he realized that Enlightenment was a false promise – Jew-hate was deep-seated and ineradicable.

Herzl popularized Pinsker, wrote books of his own, met with Jewish and foreign leaders, and convened the first International Zionist Congress in Switzerland in 1897. He didn't care about preserving Jewish culture, much less religion. His goal was to find a place where Jews could gather.

By the time of Herzl's death in 1904, there was no Zion, though Zionism was catching on. Jews were leaving behind the pogroms of

improved and in the beginning the British helped the Jewish Agency with immigration and land purchases.

Britain's first civilian governor, Sir Herbert Samuel, a Jewish Zionist, attempted to gain acceptance from Arabs as well as Jews. He even appointed a young, radical Arab nationalist, Hajj Amin al-Husayni, to be *mufti* (chief Muslim legal officer) of Jerusalem. The *mufti*, extreme though he might have been, gave full expression to the mainstream and burgeoning Palestinian consciousness. He later became such an influential leader that the British deported him in 1937, and he signed on with Hitler's propaganda machine.

Russia and moving to Palestine. The population in and around Jerusalem reached nearly 60,000, with more than 60 percent Jews. In the 10 years following the failed Russian revolution of 1905, there was another huge influx of Jews on the shores of Palestine.

The British presence: Jerusalem's development was slower than some of the new towns on the Mediterranean coast. But after World War I – the Palestine Mandate having been approved by the newly-formed League of Nations – the British set up its administrative capital there and rapidly modernized the city. Jerusalem's infrastructure was vastly

Samuel encouraged Jews and Arabs to establish their own institutions, which the former did with a fervour (the inauguration of Hebrew University on Mount Scopus in 1925 was considered a landmark in Zionist development) and the Arabs did hardly at all.

For a time it appeared the Jews and Arabs might live in peace. The number of Jewish settlers shrank; from 1926 to 1928 as many Jews were leaving Jerusalem as entering it. Some say a symbiotic relationship developed between the two people – Jewish capital and Arab labour, and Jewish technical expertise and Arab knowledge of the land.

That flickering hope of peaceful coexistence was put out forever in 1929 when a feud between Arabs and Jews over access to the holy sites at the Temple Mount erupted into violence and spread from Jerusalem to the rest of the country, leaving more than 200 dead. Although most of them were Jews, a British White Paper blamed the systematic Jewish land purchases from Arab peasants for creating the tinderbox of tensions that had been sparked.

By the early 1930s, with the rise of Hitler, the worldwide depression and the strict immigration quotas in America, more and more Jews sought refuge in Palestine. In Jerusa-

British government despatched the Peel Commission to Palestine to study the causes and nature of the conflict. The commission's report first spelled out the idea of partitioning the land. The Jews would gain a small patch of land in the north and the Arabs the rest, except for an enclave in and around Jerusalem, over which the British would retain control. Meanwhile, Jewish immigration would be drastically restricted.

The policy adopted by the British was clearly anti-Zionist and tensions between Jews and Arabs increased. The Jews of the Old City lived exclusively in the Jewish Quarter. The Jewish underground and Zion-

lem the large number of immigrants strained the limits set by the British and the Arabs naturally began to wonder when they would become a small minority.

In 1936, al-Husayni, the Jerusalem mufti, took control of the Arab Higher Committee, which represented almost all Palestinian Muslims and Christians in the land. He then called for a large Arab strike-cum-rebellion which lasted three years. In response, the

Left, British soldiers in Jerusalem, 1917. **Above,** crowds of illegal immigrants gaze out in hope from a British troop ship.

ist defence force, the Haganah, engaged in terrorist acts. Some Arabs hoped the Germans would liberate Palestine from the Jews. However, the Jews supported a cease-fire during World War II and joined the allied forces to fight Hitler.

Arab conflicts: When the war ended in 1945, the civil war resumed in Palestine. In Jerusalem, the Zionist underground Irgun, led by future Prime Minister Menachem Begin, blew up part of the King David Hotel, where the British administration and army had set up offices. The next year, in 1947, the British beseeched the United Nations to resolve the problem. The United Nations voted to partition Palestine and to make Jerusalem itself a separate international municipality.

For the Jews, the proposed borders were bad from a military and political point of view, but they accepted them as the first step to statehood. The Arabs, however, refused them altogether. During the next half year, the Jewish underground and Arab partisans fought. Jerusalem became a battle zone – a city in siege. In April 1948, the Irgun massacred a peaceful Arab village called Dir Yasin on the outskirts of Jerusalem, killing more than 200 and an Arab terrorist group ambushed a Jewish bus on its way to Mount

Scopus to the Hadassah Hospital, killing 75 professors, doctors, and nurses. The British took no action until 15 May 1948, when they finally evacuated Jerusalem.

The Jews immediately took over the British administration buildings and the State of Israel was declared. The Zionists called on Arab inhabitants "to preserve the ways of peace" and asked the surrounding Arab nations to cooperate with their rule. Whether this was a sincere plea or diplomatic propaganda, one could hardly expect the Palestinian Arabs to trust the Zionists. Many fled their homes during the early fighting and looked to the Arab nations for assistance.

The next day, five Arab states sent troops to Palestine to fight Israel. Forces from Iraq and Egypt easily reached the Jerusalem border and on 28 May, after weeks of furious fighting, the Jewish Quarter of the Old City finally fell to the Jordanian Legion. For the first time in its history, Jerusalem was now divided. The Jews controlled West Jerusalem and the Jordanians controlled East Jerusalem, including the Old City.

Because West Jerusalem was virtually surrounded by hostile Arab territory, Israel initially established its capital in Tel Aviv. When the United Nations proposed to internationalize the city, in utter defiance, Israel moved its capital to Jerusalem. While West Jerusalem underwent continued urbanization, East Jerusalem was neglected by its Jordanian caretakers.

For the next 19 years, a border of minefields and barbed wire ran through city. In June 1967, Jordan's King Hussein ignored Israel's pleas not to interfere in the war with Egypt. Some say the King wanted to join Arab forces and push Israel into the Mediterranean; some say he purposely sought to relinquish the burden of Jerusalem. Whichever is the case, in response to his advances, the Israelis moved swiftly inside the Old City and captured it. The soldiers, moved by the fact that Jerusalem was finally back in Israeli hands, instinctively rushed to pray at the Wailing Wall.

The territories that Israel controlled after the Six Day War were placed under military rule and, to the chagrin of the Palestinians, were regarded as temporarily "occupied territories." But the treatment of Jerusalem was less tentative: on 28 June 1967, East Jerusalem was officially annexed and the city reunified. Rebuilding of the Jewish Quarter and other sites quickly began. New hotels began to rise, a modern university campus was built at Mount Scopus, and Jewish suburbs were created. The aim was clear: repartition should be made next to impossible.

Left, Israeli soldiers see the Wailing Wall for the first time in 1967's Six Day War. Right, the menorah in front of the Knesset was a gift from Great Britain.

48

On the surface, the status of Jerusalem seems to be the most intractable issue within the plethora of disagreements plaguing the Israeli-Palestinian conflict. Yasser Arafat has repeatedly declared that Jerusalem will be the capital of the Palestinian state, while Israeli leaders from left and right have insisted that Jerusalem will remain united under Israeli sovereignty.

This dual claim over Jerusalem often seems to threaten the entire peace process. The opening of the Hasmonean tunnel in 1996 and construction in 1997 at Har Homa, a neighbourhood south-east of Jerusalem, both resulted in violence and the suspension of the peace talks.

However, beneath the posturing there is room for optimism. Israeli Prime Minister Benjamin Netanyahu's election campaign in 1996 was fought around the slogan that "Peres Wants To Divide Jerusalem." Yet not long after Netanyahu's election victory, the far right began a campaign around the slogan "Netanyahu Wants To Divide Jerusalem," after it became clear that he was willing to divide Hebron.

Nor has Netanyahu been able to carry out his election pledge to close down Palestinian institutions in East Jerusalem such as New Orient House where Palestinian leader Faisal Husseini meets visiting foreign dignitaries.

The fact is that Jerusalem is already divided. True, the city was physically reunited in 1967 when the walls were torn down during the Six Day War. But socially the city remains divided today as if the walls were still there. Indeed, it is probably more split that it was in the honeymoon years following 1967.

Then the Palestinians were fascinated by the liberalism, democracy and western ways of Israel and naively believed that it would automatically fulfil their nationalist aspirations. For their part, Jews fell in love with the hustle and bustle of the Old City's Arab market and on Saturdays Israelis came from afar

Left, young women serve in the military. **Right**, shop window in the Old City.

to pack the alleyways of the Muslim quarter.

Jerusalem's former mayor, Teddy Kollek, built on this goodwill. He provided the former Jordanian-controlled half of the city with basic water and sanitation utilities, and the standard of living of Jerusalem's Arabs rose dramatically. Because Jerusalem had been annexed by Israel, while the West Bank and Gaza remained under military administration, Jerusalem's Arabs were able to enjoy greater freedom, establishing more than a dozen

daily newspapers and weekly magazines that served the Palestinian people, as well as a range of human rights organisations. Ironically, Israel's annexation of East Jerusalem enhanced the city's status as the principal Palestinian city.

Even during the years of amiable relations, the Palestinians never acknowledged Israeli sovereignty over the city. They refused to assume Israeli citizenship and vote in Knesset elections. They preferred to set up their own universities in the West Bank rather than study at the Hebrew University. Even municipal elections were boycotted, although the

Viennese-born mayor Kollek, a liberal socialist who established a tradition of racial and religious harmony in the city, was popularly admired.

The romance between Jews and Arabs in Jerusalem lost its lustre after 1978 when the Likud came to power. The Palestinians began to realise that they were under siege as massive Jewish suburbs surrounded the city. Some extremist Jews even moved into the Old City's Muslim Quarter. The Intifada in 1987 further soured relations. It was almost as if the wall had been rebuilt. Israelis stopped shopping in East Jerusalem and Palestinians stayed away from the night spots of West Jerusalem.

The Israel-PLO accord in 1993 eased social tension but also created new facts as Jerusalem's Palestinians began flying flags, displaying pictures of Arafat and opening national institutions. A brutal Hamas terrorist bombing campaign further accentuated the divisions between Jew and Arab. However, even in the worst years of the Intifada, there was relatively little rioting in Jerusalem. For there has been an underlying pragmatic consensus shared by Jew and Arab that harmony and prosperity are more important than uncompromising nationalism.

To be sure, this spirit of conciliation has helped the city flourish. Since 1967 Jerusalem has been transformed from squalor into one of the world's most lovely cities. Kollek, who ruled it from 1965 to 1993, imposed a style of good aesthetic taste as he resurrected a British edict that all new buildings must be faced with local stone, and bullied property speculators into leaving prime land for parks rather than real estate development.

Kollek's successor as mayor, Ehud Olmert, who comes from the liberal wing of the nationalist Likud party, has refrained from fanning sectarian flames. His liberal critics, however, feel that he has been too accommodating of his ultra-orthodox Jewish coalition partners. Indeed, many Israelis view Jerusalem's ultra-orthodox community, who comprise one-quarter of the city's residents, as a greater threat to the city than the Palestinians. But while it is true that few ultra-orthodox Jews serve in the army, and many are even anti-Zionist, the ultra-orthodox Jews have no separatist nationalist claims.

Of course the Palestinians do have such claims. But, despite extremist rhetoric, a new status quo isn't difficult to envisage. Even hawkish Israelis acknowledge that the neighbourhoods in which the city's 200,000 Palestinians live are essentially foreign to them. Even stridently nationalist Palestinians insist that walls should never again divide the city.

In all likelihood, parts of Jerusalem will eventually be allowed a degree of autonomy, though perhaps not as much as that given in the West Bank and Gaza. It may take 20 years rather than two, and a great deal of compromise and sacrifice on both sides, but since 1967 the vast majority of the city's Jews and Arabs have repeatedly shown that they have no stomach for the alternative scenario of bloodshed and violence.

Sometimes they can even laugh at their dilemma. Both communities, for example, were able to enjoy the vicious satire of the irreverent TV show *Hartzufim*. Based on Britain's *Spitting Image*, it showed puppets of Arafat and Netanyahu cuddling up together suggestively but, time and again, miserably failing to reach a climax.

Left, study time at Hebrew University. Right, a typical "Sabra" (an Israel-born person).

The majority of Jerusalem's 620,000 residents are either Arab (30 percent) or ultra-orthodox Jews (25 percent). Nevertheless, the reins of power are held firmly by the secular and modern orthodox Jews who comprise about 45 percent of the city's population. Both the current mayor, Ehud Olmert, from the right-wing Likud, and his left-wing predecessor, Teddy Kollek, who ruled the city from 1965 to 1993, are staunchly secular figures who built successful coalitions with the ultra-orthodox Jewish political parties. The city's Arabs, who have had the right to vote since Jerusalem was annexed by Israel in 1967, have consistently refused to do so, claiming that they are Palestinian rather than Israeli citizens.

But it would be over-simplistic to speak of the city's population solely in terms of its Arab, ultra-orthodox and modernist groupings. Teddy Kollek was fond of referring to the city as a delicate mosaic with each community knowing its place, shape and colour in the scheme of things and eager to perpetuate its traditions.

Of the city's 200,000 non-Jews, some 85 percent are Muslims. This is a relatively homogeneous population, showing allegiance to the Palestinian national movement but ranging from Muslim fundamentalists through to secular but very conservative family-oriented Arabs. The main divisions are political rather than religious, with the fundamentalists supporting *Hamas* and mainstream Palestinians opting for the PLO's *Fatah*. Though heavily politicised, Jerusalem's Palestinians take a more pragmatic approach towards co-existence with Israel, and the city sees little violence which is perpetrated by East Jerusalem Arabs. Unlike their cousins in Gaza and the West Bank, the city's Arabs come into daily contact with Jews who are not soldiers and tend to demonize them less. Much of the wealthy middle class is dependent on tourism, which clearly suffers when political tensions escalate.

The city's 30,000 indigenous Christians also identify with the Palestinian national movement but will privately say they are of Greek or Armenian rather than Arab origin. The Greek Orthodox church, with a community of more than 20,000 has the largest number of adherents. There are 2,000 Armenians living in Jerusalem's Old City and nearly 6,000 Catholics, not only Latins but autonomous sects like the Greek Catholics, Armenian Catholics and Maronites. Inter-marriage among the Christian sects and with middle-class Muslims is not uncommon.

In addition to the indigenous Christian community, tens of thousands of other Christians reside in Jerusalem, usually attached to the various churches, monasteries and seminaries, and there are thousands of long-stay believers. The number of sects is vast, making Jerusalem an ecumenical nightmare.

<u>Preceding pages</u>, **Muslim women at festival time; Orthodox Jews in Mea She'arim.** <u>Left</u>, **a Yemenite Jew.**

For many non-Jews the term secular Jewry would seem to be a contradiction in terms. Many Jews, too, argue that Judaism is a religion and not a nationality and, therefore, Jews can be Orthodox or not Orthodox but never secular. Such semantic discussions overlook the realities of everyday Israeli life. The fact is that most Israeli Jews define themselves as both secular and Jewish.

It is difficult to ascertain who is a secular Jew. By and large European Jews clearly identify themselves as either secular, Orthodox or ultra-Orthodox and tend to be more extreme in their allegiances. It was Ashkenazi secular Jews from Europe who were the architects of the state in the early 1900s. Oriental Jews, who in the main came later in the 1940s and '50s are more traditional. Many non-religious Oriental Jews have assimilated European Jewish contempt for Orthodoxy but most remain more respectful and even deferential.

Indeed the divide between Ashkenazi and Oriental Jewry remains today. But intermarriage is common and most Oriental Jews have made it out of the poor apartment buildings constructed for them when they arrived. In the most senior positions in the current government Foreign Minister David Levy was born in Morocco, while Defence Minister Yitzhak Mordechai comes originally from Iraq and Deputy Prime Minister Moshe Katzav hails from Iran.

But virtually all of the most impoverished Jewish Israelis are Oriental Jews, and it is this sector that is antagonistic to Ashkenazi Jewry. This deprived sector of society also tends to have strong religious leanings and is hostile to the secularism of Ashkenazi Jewry.

Politics and religion: Israel's secular Jews share the liberal, universalist views of their North American and Western European counterparts. Democracy, freedom of expression and minority rights are the sacred values. They would not mind if their daughter wanted to marry a non-Jew and would quite likely be more bothered if she brought home a black-hatted ultra-Orthodox Jew. Though secular Jews firmly hold the reins of political power, there is an almost paranoid belief that they are slipping out of their hands.

Secular Jewry, especially in Jerusalem, feels it is a besieged community, threatened demographically by both the Arab minority and ultra-Orthodox Jewry, both of whom have much higher birth rates.

Secular Jewry often complains about the existence of Orthodox religious parties, but the fact is that it is impossible in Israel to separate politics from religion. The left-wing Meretz faction, which together with allies on the left of the Labour Party probably commands the support of a third of Israelis,

spearheads the political fight against orthodox attempts to legislate over the definition of a Jew, social issues like abortion or the import of un-kosher meat and pig rearing, or practical matters such as the closing of roads on the Sabbath.

But it would be a mistake to assume by reading the political map from left to right that secular Jewry only commands minority support. There is often as much support on the right for secular causes. Prime Minister Benjamin Netanyahu himself, like most of the Likud leaders, is a staunchly secular figure. His personal lifestyle has never endeared him to his religious bedfellows in his coalition government. He is currently married to his third wife, and his second wife was not Jewish.

Indeed the Tzomet bloc within the Likud, led by Rafael Eitan, is known for its anti-clerical leanings. But political expediency has led to an alliance between the essentially anti-religious Likud and religious elements. The Likud is reluctant to relinquish the West Bank and Gaza for security and nationalistic reasons, while the religious cherish the biblical concept of the Land of Israel. Moreover,

the Likud has traditionally relied on support from the Oriental Jewish communities, who incline towards tradition.

Sentimental attachment to Judaism: If non-Jews and sometimes Diaspora Jews are surprised by the extent to which Israel's secular majority disregards religious practice, it can be misleading to think that Israelis have no regard for religion. It is difficult for outsiders to know where lines are drawn between the acceptable and unacceptable. Take dietary laws, for example. McDonald's, the multi-

Left, informal study on the Mount Scopus campus of the Hebrew University. **Above**, kibbutzniks.

national hamburger chain, undertook detailed market research before moving into Israel. The result: bacon Macmuffins were non-starters, but cheeseburgers were introduced successfully even though kosher laws prohibit the mixing of meat and milk. But bread is not permissible during Passover, so McDonald's serves cheeseburgers in potato flour buns.

On more substantive issues such as marriage and burial, opinion polls consistently show that the majority of Israelis support the Orthodox monopoly of these rites. This has greatly anguished the Reform and Conservative movements, imported to Israel from America, which attempt to adapt Judaism to the modern age, and in particular to integrate women into the synagogue service.

The fact is that secular Israelis have Zionism, which remains an ideology capable of drawing a high level of commitment to the building of the state and is closely linked to conservative family values. And even the most outwardly secular of Jews still tends to have an inner belief in the essential Jewish values – belief in God and a divine plan. This fills the spiritual vacuum. In the wake of Yitzhak Rabin's assassination young Israelis were able to cope with their grief over the death of a loved leader.

Family values: Like the post-Christian West so post-Jewish Israel suffers from rising crime, violence, drug addiction and inner-city poverty. But despite a growing divorce rate family ties remain strong and there is a deep respect for symbols of state as well as a high motivation to serve in the army.

Deceptively, secular Israel is at once both radical and conservative. The long-haired teenager with an earring through his nose, for example, is happy to have a short back and sides and submit to army discipline at the age of 18. The divisions in Israeli society, though real, are misleading. The assassination of Yitzhak Rabin, a left of centre, secular Ashkenazi, by Yigal Amir, a right-wing religious Jew from a Yemen-born family, seems to epitomise enmities. But this violent deed was an astounding, exceptional event. When the chips are down Israelis have a surprising capacity to join ranks.

To the non-Orthodox Jew these two groups have much in common. Both strictly observe the all-encompassing world of *halacha* – Jewish Orthodox practice. This means that the men keep their heads covered and pray at least three times a day. Kosher dietary laws are strictly followed and the Sabbath is a day for absolute abstention from work, including "lighting a spark", thus making travelling, cooking, switching on a light and even smoking prohibited activities.

The diverse head coverings of the men often indicate degrees of Orthodoxy. Generally, the larger the *kippa* (skull cap) the more Orthodox the wearer. The *kippot* range from the small knitted variety, worn by the modern Orthodox, to the large knitted and black *kippot* of the mainstream Orthodox and the large black skull caps beneath even larger black hats of the ultra-Orthodox.

It is usually the clothes of the woman rather than the size of the man's *kippa* which hints at the Orthodox Jew's lifestyle. A man with a small knitted *kippa* is likely to be accompanied by a woman with "immodest" jeans or other tight clothing. Women in the large knitted *kippa* community will wear long dresses and keep their arms covered but may not be wearing wigs or head scarves.

Women in the ultra-Orthodox communities are literally kept under wraps. Not a square inch of flesh is seen other than the face and hands, and female visitors to the ultra-Orthodox quarters of Mea Shearim in Jerusalem and Bnei Brak near Tel Aviv should heed warnings not to wear immodest dress. Those in violation of this edict may be sworn and spat at and even stoned.

The ultra-Orthodox woman cannot be in an enclosed room with men other than her immediate relatives. At weddings and parties women will sit in a separate area.

Ultra-Orthodox Jewish society comprises a collection of sects as much medieval Eastern European as biblical in their origins. On Saturdays and festivals the men wear fur hats more suitable for a Russian winter than a Middle Eastern summer.

From anti-Zionism to Ultra-Zionism: Historically Jews were by definition Orthodox and three or four centuries ago all of Eastern

European Jewry would have followed a moral code similar to that of Mea Shearim today. Growing secularism in 19th-century Christian Europe compelled Jews to find other outlets of cultural expression, and Zionism emerged as a secular movement. Therefore, at first all Orthodox Jews were anti-Zionist, opposed to the use of Hebrew, the holy tongue, for everyday use and the notion that a Jewish state could contemplate any degree of separation between synagogue and state.

However, in the 1990s a strong national

religious movement emerged, combining the nationalistic values of Zionism with the tenets of Orthodoxy. With its own kibbutzim and workers' movements, it was bolstered by the mass immigration of Oriental Jewry which had deeper ties with Jewish tradition.

Commanding the political support of about 10 percent of the population, the national religious movement, which historically contained strong elements of liberalism, veered sharply to the right after 1967. Holding the Land of Israel to be sacred, the Gush Emunim settlers' movement sprung up from the national religious movement. It has come to be perceived as the fiercest opponent of territorial compromise. The national religious movement has its own religious schools distinct from their secular counterparts.

Ultra-Orthodox Jewry, known in Hebrew as Haredim, also has its own education system. These black-clad communities are at best critical of Zionism and at worst still opposed to the Jewish State. Each sect has its own rabbinical leaders and most of them sit in New York rather than Jerusalem.

The largest and best known Haredi sect is the Lubatvitchers. Under the late Rabbi

Schneerson, who was revered by his followers as a messianic figure, the Lubavitchers took a pro-Israel hawkish stand supporting continuation of Jewish control of the West Bank. The Satmar, on the other hand, also a New York headquartered sect, refuses to recognise the government of Israel as legitimate representatives of the Jewish people.

An extreme Jerusalem based sect called Netorei Karta even supported the PLO when its charter called for the destruction of the Jewish state. Netorei Karta believes that the

Left, at the Western Wall. Above, an Orthodox Jew blows a ram's horn for the new year.

Zionists are worse than the Nazis, for while the Nazis sought to destroy the Jews physically, the Zionists are spiritually destroying the Jewish people.

Prayer power: All these sects, even those with pro-Zionist leanings, tend to have contempt for the institutions of modern Israel – the flag, the army, the Supreme Court, etc. Few ultra-Orthodox Jews serve in the army and those who do will often end up in the Rabbinical corps checking that kitchens are kosher. Even the right wing Lubavitchers will argue that praying for the strength of Israel is as important as fighting for it.

As a result secular Jewry detests ultra-Orthodox Jewry for its lack of patriotism, while ultra-Orthodox Jewry holds secular Jewry in contempt for its non-religious lifestyle. Orthodox Jewry is often caught in the middle justifying and condemning both sides.

Individual prejudice aside, secular Israel is tolerant towards Orthodoxy. This is mainly because the ultra-Orthodox parties hold the balance of power between left and right. Moreover, many Jews believe that to harass the ultra-Orthodox communities could leave them open to charges of anti-Semitism.

Oriental Jewry: Religious Jews from Asian and African countries have never fitted comfortably into the European pattern of sects, though Israel's European religious establishment did succeed in imposing black hats and suits on large numbers of Jews from the Yemen and North Africa.

But ultimately religious leaders like the charismatic former Sephardi Chief Rabbi Ovadia Yosef, who wears oriental robes rather than a black hat, have prevailed. His Shas political party today controls nearly 10 percent of Knesset seats. Much of Shas's support comes from traditional rather than Orthodox Oriental Jews indicating that the divide between observant and non-observant Oriental Jews is narrower than between their European counterparts.

Overall, an estimated 20 percent of Israeli Jews are Orthodox. This number has remained constant over the past decade for, though Orthodox Jewry has a much higher birth rate, the overwhelming majority of new Jewish immigrants from Russia are secular.

"Let My People Go" was the slogan coined by campaign activists pushing for the right of Soviet Jewry to emigrate freely. Nobody believed it would ever actually happen even in the era of détente in the 1970s when nearly 400,000 Soviet Jews were allowed out of the Soviet Union, about half of them reaching Israel while the rest headed for the US.

But as glasnost gained momentum in the late 1980s the right to emigrate was suddenly granted to Soviet Jewry during the final months of the decade. For Israel the event

keeping their options open with an anxious eye on political developments.

Transforming Israel: During the 1990s, Russian-speaking Jewry surpassed Moroccans as Israel's largest immigrant group. By 1999 more than 800,000 had arrived in the latest wave of immigration, making more than a million Soviet-born Israelis, when combined with the émigrés from the 1970s and Soviet veterans from earlier in the century.

As a result, Israel's urban landscape has a decidedly Slavic feel. Cyrillic shop signs

was as momentous as the breaching of the Berlin Wall. It was like a dam bursting. During the course of 1990 more than 200,000 Jews reached Israel, while in 1991 more than 170,000 arrived. After the break up of the Soviet Union the pace slackened with some 60,000 Jews emigrating to Israel each year from the former Soviet republics.

Not every Russian-speaking Jew has wanted to come to Israel. The US has allowed in about 40,000 every year, while Germany, Canada and other Western countries have taken in tens of thousands more. Moreover, more than a million Jews remain by choice in the former Soviet Union,

abound, vying for space with Hebrew, English and Arabic lettering. News-stands are bursting with Russian-language publications, and in some suburbs of Tel Aviv and Haifa, Russian is the lingua franca.

The full political and economic potential of Russian-speaking Jewry is yet to be realised. True, it was these new immigrants who, despite their hawkish tendencies, voted in the more dovish Labour Party in 1992 as a protest against Likud neglect of their economic needs. Then, disillusioned by both Labour and Likud, the renowned refusnik Natan Scharansky, who had spent years in Soviet prisons fighting for the right to emigrate, set up his own immigrant party, Yisrael Ve'Aliyah, and gained an impressive seven seats (6 percent of the vote) in the 1996 Knesset elections. Scharansky joined Prime Minister Benjamin Netanyahu's right-wing government haggling over the negotiations in Russian with Yvette Liberman, the Russian-born director of Netanyahu's office.

The newcomers may also cause crowding in the professions. Generally speaking, the latest wave of Russian immigrants has a high educational profile. They are academically trained scientists and engineers, musicians and teachers. Even before this immigration started, Israel had the world's highest proportion of doctors per capita. With 15,000 more doctors among the newcomers, many have not been able to qualify for medical licences or get jobs in their professions.

But it takes time to master Hebrew and adjust to the more assertive behaviour of a Western society. Too often, Russian-speaking newcomers expect to be given jobs, housing and other benefits, and it takes them time to realise they must get these for themselves. It usually takes a year of sweeping streets or washing dishes before an immigrant finds a job in his or her profession.

Such immigrants have changed the demographic balance of Israel. Before their arrival, Israel had a small Oriental Jewish majority. Russian Jewry has tipped the scales back in favour of Ashkenazi Jewry, although some 10 percent of these newcomers are Oriental Jews from the ancient Persian-speaking communities in Georgia, Azerbaijan and the Russian Caucasus as well as Uzbekistan.

Kosher and un-kosher: In the main Russian-speaking newcomers are Ashkenazi and secular, if they are Jewish at all. Between 20 and 40 percent of newcomers are not halachically Jewish. They qualify for Jewish citizenship by virtue of having one Jewish grandparent but do not meet the Orthodox Jewish requirement of having a Jewish mother.

Even those Jews who are rabbinically kosher know little about their Jewish herit-

age after growing up under the Soviet regime. Israel was already a highly secular society before the newcomers arrived. Once acculturated, these immigrants are bound to push for more secular legislation, disturbing the delicate religious–secular status quo. At present a large number of Russian-speaking newcomers cannot be buried in Jewish cemeteries or have a Jewish marriage ceremony.

Nor are these newcomers Zionists. The immigrants of the 1970s risked imprisonment in order to leave for Israel. The major-

ity of those who reached Israel in 1990 and 1991 had a profound sense of Jewish identity; they simply put out their wings and migrated with the flock at the first opportunity. But recent arrivals have a less clear agenda. They seek a more secure economic life amid the greater opportunities of Israel.

The latest wave of immigrants represents over 20 percent of the Jewish population. Undoubtedly they and their children will assimilate Zionist norms of allegiance to the state, service in the army, and fluency in Hebrew. In parallel, influenced by the secularism of these immigrants, Israel is likely to move further away from traditional Judaism.

Left, Russian immigrants arrive at Lod Airport in the early 1960s. **Right**, Russian-language newspapers are now available in Israel.

The dramatic airlifts of Ethiopian Jews from the heart of Africa to the Promised Land in 1984 and 1991 captured the world's imagination. For centuries, Ethiopian Jews cherished the dream of one day returning to Jerusalem. The dream came true, but the reality has been somewhat different from their expectations.

Before they came to Israel, most Ethiopian Jews were semi-literate subsistence farmers who had lived in simple villages, usually without electricity. Suddenly they were thrust

ties to recognise the unequivocal Jewishness of the Ethiopians. Thus Ethiopian Jews are required to undergo symbolic conversion to Judaism by being immersed in a ritual bath. In addition the *kessim* are not permitted to officiate at marriages.

The younger generation (half the community is younger than 18) has been adept at assimilating Israeli values. The vigour with which they have protested their grievances through demonstrations, the media and political lobbying bodes well for the future. For

into a fast-moving, high-tech society, which was very traumatic for them, especially for those people who were over 30 when they arrived.

Some of Israel's 70,000-strong Ethiopian Jewish community have done well. Adisu Massala, for example, was elected to the Knesset in 1996 as a Labour Party delegate, and Belaynesh Zevadiah became Israel's vice-consul in Chicago. These success stories are both children of the *kessim*, the community's religious leaders.

Alienation: The sense of alienation felt by many Ethiopians has been exacerbated by the reluctance of Israel's rabbinical authori-

their part, the Israeli establishment has allocated major resources for the education of the young generation and has introduced positive discrimination measures, such as more generous mortgages than those available to other new immigrants.

While racism against the Ethiopians is rare (the most anti-Ethiopian racist sector in Israeli society is probably found among the new immigrants from Russia), the community sometimes suffers as a result of excessive political correctness. For example, the Health Ministry decided that Ethiopians were not suitable blood donors because of a higher incidence of Aids, tuberculosis and other diseases. However, instead of the decision being announced publicly, a secret memo was sent to blood donation staff asking them to accept Ethiopian blood but then to throw it away. The discovery of the policy provoked a storm of protest. An enquiry found that the policy was justified but that its underhand method of implementation was totally inappropriate.

The Ethiopians began reaching Israel via Sudan in the early 1980s and Operation Moses in 1984 saw 7,000 airlifted to Israel.

(invaders), they are believed by some scholars to be remnants of Dan, one of the 10 lost tribes. The Ethiopians themselves claim to be the descendants of King Solomon and the Queen of Sheba.

Cut off from world Jewry for two millennia, the community has sustained traditions remarkably similar to mainstream Judaism. There are distinctions, though; for example, the Ethiopians took with them into exile the Five Books of Moses and the stories of the Prophets, but have no knowledge of the Oral

Most had trekked hundreds of miles across the desert to the Sudanese border and many had died en route. Even more dramatically, 14,000 Ethiopians were flown to Israel in Operation Solomon in a 24-hour period in 1991. These Jews had gathered in Addis Ababa over the course of a year but had been prevented from leaving by the Marxist regime. The Israeli Air Force rescued them just as the regime was toppled by rebels.

The origins of Ethiopian Jews are shrouded in mystery. Known in Ethiopia as *falashas*

Left, an Ethiopian Jewish soldier guards a tomb at Hebron. **Above**, Ethiopian crafts.

Law, which was codified only after the fall of the Second Temple in AD 70.

In modern times Ethiopian Jewry has been located in two regions of Africa. Those Jews who reached Israel in the early 1980s came primarily from Tigre, while the subsequent wave of immigrants originated principally from Gondar. The two groups use the same Amharic alphabet but speak different Ethiopic languages.

All but several hundred Ethiopian Jews have now left Africa. Israel has also brought over the Falash Mura, who claim they converted to Judaism in the 19th century, and who had wanted to emigrate to Israel.

Nowhere in the world is the observant traveller more aware of the rich and fascinating diversity of Christianity than in the Holy Land. On a morning's stroll through the Old City of Jerusalem, you might encounter Greek Orthodox or Syrian Orthodox monks, Ethiopian and Coptic clergymen, Armenian priests, Catholic priests and, without knowing it, clerics and scholars from virtually every Protestant church in Christendom.

There is no mystery to the extraordinary variety of Christian congregations in the Holy Land. From the time of the Byzantines (AD 324–636) through the era of the Crusader kingdoms (l099–1291) and 400 years of Ottoman rule (1517–1917) until today, churches sought to establish – then struggled to retain – a presence in the land where their faith was born.

The result is a plethora of denominations served by 2,500 clergy from almost every nation on earth. The Greek Orthodox, Russian Orthodox, Roman Catholics, Syrian Catholics, Maronites, Greek Catholics, Armenian Catholics, Chaldean Catholics, Armenian Orthodox, Syrian Orthodox (Jacobites), Copts, Ethiopian Orthodox – all have secured claims, sometimes competing claims, to revered holy sites.

The "younger" churches – the Anglicans, the Church of Scotland, the Seventh Day Adventists, the Pentecostals, the Church of Christ, the Baptists, the Brethren, the Menonnites and the Jehovah's Witnesses – also maintain institutions and congregations.

The founding of Israel provoked unease among the Christians, who were uncertain what to expect from the new Jewish state and were deeply suspicious of Jewish intentions (the Vatican still does not recognise Israel). Nevertheless, Israel's Declaration of Independence spelt out the state's attitude to the diverse faiths within its borders, pledging to "guarantee the freedom of religion, conscience, education and culture (and) safeguard the holy places of all religions."

The Six Day War of 1967, which left Israeli forces in control of the old city of Jerusalem, revived religious misgivings. Yet, the Israeli government has been scrupulous in its attitude towards the rights and prerogatives of the churches, adhering to the intricate balance created by the Ottoman rulers and British Mandatory authority in apportioning responsibility for the holy places.

As a result, relations have been good – or at least correct – between the Jewish state and the churches. Indeed at times, the Israeli government has found itself a reluctant referee of intra-Christian rivalries.

A recent phenomenon that is having an impact on the face of the Holy Land and Christian–Jewish relations is the world-wide

growth of Christian Zionism, which regards the birth of the State of Israel as a fulfilment of biblical prophecy. Over the past decades, theological and ecumenical institutions have mushroomed to cater to this movement and enable young Christians to study in Israel.

The "Christian Embassy" in Jerusalem – the focus of much Christian–Zionist activity – has delighted and intrigued many Israelis. But it has dismayed others who fear that the real intention of their proclamations of friendship is the conversion of Jews.

This deeply held suspicion was given expression in vociferous opposition to a Mormon project on 4 acres (1.6 hectares) of prime land overlooking the Old City – a likely precursor of other Christian groups which are seeking a toehold in the Holy Land. Among them, the Apostolic Church of Switzerland, Nigeria's Celestial Church of Christ, the Korean Evangelical Church and the Hope of Israel Church in California.

The work of Christian-Jewish reconciliation is, however, not the sole preserve of the "new" churches. The Roman Catholic order of the Sisters of Zion, established in Jerusalem in 1855 by French Jewish converts to

Christianity, has been working towards such understanding for many years.

Every year, some 250,000 pilgrims visit the order's Ecce Homo Convent next to the Second Station of the Cross on the Via Dolorosa and many stay to hear the sisters speak of Jesus the Jew and of Judaism as the wellspring of their faith. The sisters study Jewish history and the Talmud and sometimes celebrate Mass in Hebrew. They hold classes for Jews and Arabs wanting to learn each other's

Above, Greek Orthodox Christians celebrate Christmas amid the rich surroundings of their church in Bethlehem.

languages, and have set up a department of adult education at the Hebrew University with a convent sister as its administrator.

The Hebrew University boasts yet another Catholic of note: Father Marcel Dubois, a Dominican monk, is chairman of the university's philosophy department.

The grassroots language of Christianity in Israel is Arabic. The great majority of Israel's 100,000 Christians (including the 13,700 Christians of East Jerusalem) are Arabs and the parish clergy who serve them are either Arabs or Arabic-speaking.

The allegiances of Christian Arabs in Israel clearly favour the established Patriarchates: there are 35,000 Greek Catholics; 32,000 Greek Orthodox; and 20,000 Catholics. There are small communities of Anglicans and Lutherans (both churches are stronger on the West Bank than in Israel proper), and despite more than 100 years of missionary work by more than 50 organisations, there are no more than 1,000 local Arab adherents of evangelical churches. There are also about 2,000 Messianic Jews, mostly immigrants from Eastern Europe.

The Roman Catholic Church has established indigenous orders, such as the Rosary Sisters and the Sisters of St Joseph, and at its seminary in Jerusalem trains Arab priests from both Israel and Jordan.

Arab Christians, while growing in numbers and flourishing economically – particularly those living in areas that attract Christian tourism – have been hesitant about asserting themselves politically to press issues of specific Christian concern. As a group, the Christian community displays many of the characteristics of a marginal minority trying to maintain a balance between its Christian identity, Arab nationalism and its delicate relations with its Muslim neighbours – all within the context of a Jewish society.

Nonetheless, an Anglican Arab clergyman is prominent in the Arab–Jewish Progressive List for Peace, a political party which supports the establishment of a Palestinian state on the West Bank. Israel's Greek Orthodox community, on the other hand, traditionally supports the oddest political bedfellow: the Communist Party.

Not all the Arab inhabitants of Palestine heeded the call of the surrounding states (and "promptings" from the nascent Israeli army) to flee their homes when Israel was established, with the promise that they would return within weeks once the Jewish state had been snuffed out by the invading armies.

About 150,000 remained and numbers have since grown to their present 1,100,000. Half of Israel's Arab population is urbanised in the towns and villages of the Galilee. There are large Arab communities in Nazareth, Haifa, Ramle, Jaffa and Jerusalem.

Israeli Arabs – 77 percent are Muslim, 13 percent Christian and 10 percent are Druze and Bedouin – present the real paradox of being at once Arab, with linguistic, historic, cultural, religious and familial ties to the Arab world, and also citizens of a state which, for 38 years, has been in conflict with that world. And yet, Israel's Arabs have managed to walk the tightrope.

The only legal discrimination against Israeli Arabs is that they are not liable to military conscription – although they may volunteer – because it is thought to be unreasonable to ask them to fight against their co-religionists and kinsmen (only the small Druze community is subject to the draft – and that at their own request).

But exemption from military service is a double-edged sword. The army is, after all, the great equaliser, the shared national experience, the common thread that unites Israelis from wildly different backgrounds. Exclusion from it inevitably involves social handicaps. In a more tangible form, it renders Israeli Arabs ineligible for certain jobs and state benefits.

In spite of this and other disabilities, the Arabs of Israel have flourished, making great strides in health, education and generally improved living standards.

One indicator of the process of change is education. Arab illiteracy has plunged from 95 percent in 1948 to just 5 percent today. While in 1948, only 32.5 percent attended grade school, by 1982, 92 percent had five to eight years of education, and more than 30 percent nine to 12 years, reflecting the growing numbers of Arabs enrolling in Israeli institutes of higher learning.

Most Israeli Arab parents choose to send their children to Arabic-language schools, which combine instruction in Arab history and culture with that of the Jews.

Today around 6,000 Arabs are studying at Israeli universities. Others travel abroad to study, but not, like the Arabs from the West Bank and Gaza, to the Arab world because they carry Israeli passports.

The impact of education and involvement with Israel's vigorously open and democratic society has been profound. These days most young Arabs live with their own Western-style nuclear families and are economically independent of their elders. There is still, to be sure, strong attachment to traditional values and customs, but these are tinged with a clear preference for the comforts of the affluent West.

Israeli laws granting women equal rights have helped to liberalise attitudes towards women in Arab society. The changing aspirations of women (and their husbands) is reflected in the birthrate – down from an astonishing average of 8.5 children per family in 1968 to 5.5 in 1982 and expected to continue falling during the 1990s to the Jewish average of 3.2 children per family.

For all that, there is a strong trend towards polarisation of Jewish and Arab Israelis, though programmes to foster understanding between youngsters are arranged by Israel's Education Ministry.

A spiral of radicalism is not inevitable. A new breed of young Arab mayors and leaders – educated in Israel and at ease with the Israeli system – is emerging at a grass-roots level. They are demanding that facilities in their areas be brought up to the standard of their Jewish neighbours, and their style demonstrates a self-confidence that is at once proudly Arab and unequivocally Israeli.

The increasing Arab clout in the political arena is another significant development. At present, there are seven Arab members of the Knesset out of a total of 120, representing a broad spectrum of opinion.

Left, an Arab Jerusalemite presents a handsome profile to the city.

The birth of the Palestinian national movement was a reaction to Zionism. As Jews began buying up Arab land at the turn of the century so the indigenous Arab population was compelled to question its own identity. Historically that identity had revolved around the extended family, the village, the Arab people and Islam. But in the modern world of emerging nations such an identity was either too parochial or too broad.

Just as many Jews and non-Jews originally opposed the notion that the Jews constituted

Jews were unable to counter the militant rejectionism of Syria and Egypt and of local leaders such as Sheikh Haj Amin Husseini.

The tragedy of the Palestinian people was the stubborn inability of its leadership to accept the *fait accompli* of a Jewish state. Arab anger may be understandable, as European anti-Semitism drove Jews back to the Middle East and resulted in the loss of Palestinian land. But attempts to "drive the Jews into the sea" in 1948 and 1967 and the expulsion of over a million Jews from Arab

a nation, so the Palestinians found their legitimacy under fire from both friends and foes. Arabs within Palestine and without spoke of pan-Arabism and of one Arab nation encompassing North Africa and Asia Minor. Often such talk cloaked the expansionist ambitions of Syria, Jordan and Egypt.

Irreconcilable aims: For the Jews, of course, the Palestinian national movement which denied the right of a Jewish State to exist could never be reconciled with Zionist aspirations. Moderate Palestinian leaders as well as the Hashemite kings (King Abdullah and his grandson, King Hussein) who were amenable to national coexistence with the

countries simply saw Israel strengthened territorially and demographically.

The founding of the PLO in 1964 proved to be a crucial stage in the evolution of the Palestinian national entity. Even so, its leader from 1965, Yasser Arafat, found himself in prison in Damascus. The fact is that since the Muslim conquest Palestine had been ruled from Damascus and the region had become known as Lower Syria. Thus the modern Syrians saw Palestine – and for that matter Lebanon and Jordan – as an integral part of the modern Syrian nation.

The Six Day War of 1967, and the further expansion of Israel, saw the PLO come into its own. It was now in Syria's interest to encourage Arafat to regain Arab lands. Before 1967, the West Bank was in Jordanian hands, while Gaza was under Egyptian rule. But if the PLO and its many factions, each owing allegiance to a different Arab leader, were puppets designed to restore Arab sovereignty over as much of Israel as possible, Arafat – and most especially the Palestinians of the West Bank and Gaza – proved to be more independently minded than either Israel or the Arab world had anticipated.

Israel presumed that the Arabs of the West Bank and Gaza would prove as malleable as the Palestinian Arabs who had stayed behind in 1948 and taken up Israeli citizenship. But Israeli Arabs were mainly village people, while the Arabs of Gaza and the West Bank had a large urban intelligentsia who identified strongly with the Palestinian nationalism espoused by Arafat and the PLO. Many of them were Christians.

When given the right to assume Israeli citizenship, the 150,000 Arabs of East Jeru-

Occupation and acrimony: Israel, after its occupation of the West Bank and Gaza in 1967, enjoyed good relations with its newly conquered Palestinian subjects. The Arabs of the West Bank and Gaza, for their part, were beguiled by Israeli liberalism and other Western ways. A free press was set up, universities were established, elections were held for the local municipalities, and the economy flourished. (One reason it flourished, of course, was thanks to the menial work done cheaply by Palestinians in Israel.)

Left, group portrait in an Old City café. **Above**, a Palestinian policeman on duty.

salem refused the offer to a man. It took Israelis, even on the left, many years to appreciate that Palestinian nationalism was not going to go away, just as many progressive Palestinians thought that Zionism was a passing phenomenon.

But while rejecting Israeli hegemony, the Palestinian notables in the West Bank and Gaza also felt alienated from the PLO leadership. Arafat, who built his own organisational hierarchy, first in Jordan, then in Lebanon and finally in Tunis, was often viewed as a wealthy Diaspora leader who represented the millions of Palestinians living in Jordan, Syria, Lebanon, Egypt, the Gulf and elsewhere in the world, but was out of touch with the Palestinians on the front line of Israeli occupation.

The effects of the Intifada: PLO tactics in the 1970s and '80s were a mixture of terrorism and diplomacy. Brutal terrorism against civilians both in Israel and around the world, forced the Palestinian question onto the international agenda. Moreover, Arafat forged powerful alliances with the Soviet bloc and Third World which unswervingly supported the Palestinian cause. But while the PLO was able to cause Israel untold political and economic damage and create a climate of national insecurity, it was unable

to achieve its ultimate goal of an independent Palestinian state.

The momentum for change came from within the West Bank and Gaza. The Intifada began in December 1987 in the Gaza Strip as a spontaneous uprising spawned by resentment against Israeli occupation. Within days, it became an orchestrated campaign against Israeli troops characterised by the throwing of rocks and occasional Molotov cocktails. The rebellion spread to the West Bank.

From the start, the Intifada was designed to make Israeli liberals and the country's Western allies uncomfortable. The objective was to get the international media to show

Palestinian women and children defenceless against the might of the Israeli army. True, the defenceless Palestinians were throwing rocks, which can kill and maim, but this only heightened the biblical comparison with David and Goliath. The Palestinians had hit on a winning formula and it was only a matter of time before the Israeli Goliath would be felled.

Moreover, a new, young Palestinian leadership was emerging in the West Bank and Gaza. While it didn't discourage the throwing of stones at the Zionist enemy, it was also prepared to enter into dialogue with Israel. Faisal Husseini, nephew of the arch anti-Zionist Sheikh Haj Amin Husseini, learned fluent Hebrew as a gesture of goodwill towards Israel.

Arafat jumped on the Intifada bandwagon. But it was the local Palestinian leadership that was calling the tune, while Arafat and his entourage in Tunis were looking more and more remote from the Palestinians in the front line. Arafat put out diplomatic feelers, letting it be known that he was prepared to recognise Israel and discontinue terrorist tactics. But a brief flirtation with American diplomats in the late 1980s ended after Arafat was unable to prevent his own people from launching terrorist attacks against Israel. Nor was the right-wing government in Israel prepared even to contemplate an indirect dialogue with Arafat.

Arafat's stock fell even further after he threw his support behind Iraq's Saddam Hussein after the invasion of Kuwait in 1990. This decision isolated Arafat from many of his Arab allies and caused the mass expulsion of the affluent Palestinian communities of the Gulf. The collapse of the Soviet Union, the traditional superpower patron of the PLO, saw Arafat down and, many assumed, out.

Gaza via Madrid and Oslo: Arafat proved more resilient and compromising than many gave him credit for. He was allowed to attend the Madrid peace conference in 1991 as part of the Jordanian delegation. Furthermore, no Palestinian leader of any stature in the occupied territories had emerged to challenge Arafat's primacy during the Intifada.

After the election of the Labour government in Israel in 1992, Arafat seized the olive branch held out by Rabin's dovish advisors, and in less than a year he was shaking hands with the Israeli prime minister on the White

House lawn. In 1994 Arafat came in triumph to Gaza as Israeli troops withdrew from most of the Gaza Strip.

By 1998 the Palestinian Authority's jurisdiction, earlier confirmed through democratically held elections, comprised the major West Bank towns, excluding half of Hebron, and more than 2 million Palestinians.

The assumption of power brought Arafat international legitimacy, but it also brought problems in its wake. The Hamas, Islamic fundamentalists, stepped into the rejectionist vacuum left by the PLO's acceptance of Israel and carried out a vicious bombing campaign inside Israel that has threatened to

tion in which the Palestinians focus on economic and social development while putting Israel under diplomatic pressure is likely to ensue. Major terrorist acts, even if committed by Hamas, are likely to push the peace process backwards rather than ahead.

Such a period of consolidation will enable the Palestinian Authority to establish a stable regime and develop a viable economic infrastructure. Until the start of the Intifada, the Palestinian economy was largely dependent on workers travelling each day to employment in Israeli factories, and the Palestinians want to restart this economic relationship. (There are plans for a series of Israeli-owned

derail the peace process. Under Israeli pressure, Arafat has cracked down on Hamas to save the Oslo accords, and he has had some success in restraining them.

A ragged economy: The principal problems confronting the Palestinians are political and economic. Arafat realised it would be hard to wring more territorial concessions out of the Netanyahu administration, but the status quo was clearly unacceptable, and Arafat has stated that he wants independence by May 1999 . Nevertheless, a period of consolida-

and Palestinian-manned industrial parks on the border.) But good relations with Israel are a prerequisite for this economic symbiosis.

Palestine is in effect a state in the making. It has a flag, its own stamps and currency, it competes in the Olympics and World Cup, and it is a full member of the United Nations. But it has no control over its borders. The Israelis decide who comes in and who doesn't, thus denying entry to millions of Palestinians worldwide – although the Palestinians are not able to absorb so many refugees.

But the breakthrough has been made. Palestine exists. Progress is fraught with obstacles but the peace process is irreversible.

Left, making a point in Jerusalem. **Above**, Arafat-blessed souvenirs; a café in Bethlehem.

ALIYA: A CONSTANT RENEWAL

In the days before the great Temple was destroyed, long before Zionism, Jews spoke of making *aliya*, literally meaning "going up". By this they meant ascending the hills of Judea to Jerusalem and climbing the stairs of the Temple to offer a sacrifice at festival time. In the Diaspora, *aliya* always signified a return to Jerusalem, and thus it was only natural for Zionists to use the word to describe immigration to the Land of Israel.

The "First Aliya" came from Russia in the 1880s. Inspired by the publication of Leo Pinsker's Zionist manifesto, *Auto-Emancipation*, a Russian Jewish federation called *Chovevai Tzion* ("Lovers of Zion") began sending Jewish students to Palestine. Within two decades, some 40 new settlements were established in the land; many of the new *olim* ("ascenders") came to Jerusalem, where they began building the first neighbourhoods outside the Old City.

The "Second Aliya" represented an even larger emigration of Jews from Russia following the aborted 1905 revolution there. Most of these Jews migrated to the United States, lured by the belief that the roads were paved with gold. A small minority headed to Jerusalem and Palestine, an altogether more idealistic and adventurous lot.

The *olim* who arrived between 1905 and 1914 are largely credited as the founding fathers and mothers of the State of Israel, establishing many of its important education, business, and political institutions. By the outbreak of World War I in 1914, there were nearly twice as many Jews living outside the Old City as those residing within it. As a result of the Jewish *aliya*, an increasing number of Arabs were sent up to Jerusalem, attracted by the city's increasing prosperity and modernity.

Some 35,000 Jews from Eastern Europe accounted for the "Third Aliya" (1919–24). Many were grievously disappointed by the failures of the Bolshevik Revolution and placed their hope in a Jewish state. Such

hope was fuelled by the Balfour Declaration and its ratification by the League of Nations. The Zionist dream had actually been ratified by international law.

Fleeing the anti-Semitic repression in Poland, 68,000 Jews comprised the "Fourth Aliya" (1924–29). Over one third of them left shortly after their arrival. In the mid-1920s, an equilibrium was reached between the number of Jew leaving Jerusalem and the number coming in.

The "Fifth Aliya" (1930–39) coincided with the rise of Hitler. Given the British restrictions on Jewish immigration during and after World War II, it is common to speak of those who came in up until the creation of the state in 1948 as the "Aliya Bet" (illegal immigration).

All along, the Zionists had hoped Israel would provide a home for displaced Jews. In 1950, the Israeli parliament, the Knesset, unanimously passed the Law of Return, which said that every Jew in the world had a right to settle in Israel.

In the next 14 years, there was a mass *aliya*, the vast majority were Jews from Arabic countries: Iraq (126,000), Morocco (120,000), Egypt (75,000), Tunisia (30,000), Libya (35,000) and Syria (26,000). In a project called "Operation Magic Carpet," the entire Jewish population of Yemen (nearly 50,000) boarded Israeli airplanes and flew to a home they'd never seen. Some American and Western European Jews made *aliya* to Israel in the Zionist fervour that surrounded the 1967 war and reunification of Jerusalem.

From 1967, the *aliya* movement concentrated on fighting for the rights of oppressed Jews to emigrate, such as those in the Soviet Union. Nearly 200,000 Soviet Jews reached Israel in the 1970s, and then the gates burst open with more than 800,000 Jews immigrating to Israel from the former USSR between 1990 and 1999. The daring rescue of more than 70,000 Ethiopian Jews captured the imagination, but the entire migration remains one of the most remarkable stories of the late 20th century.

Left, a member of the most recent wave of *olim*.

In the Diaspora, Jews were always known as the "People of the Book" for the way in which they cleaved to the Torah. For religious Jews today, cultural life still centers around the *yeshivah,* where the Torah is passed down from one generation to the next. Although secular Israelis read Hebrew too, the Book has been replaced by books in general.

Jerusalemites especially are voracious readers, and as one can see from walking into

among them, S.Y. Agnon, the 1966 winner of the Nobel Prize and Chaim Bialik, the nation's first poet laureate.

Today, the Jerusalemite poet Yehudah Amichai best captures the nation's pathos – the sense of loss and war, the passion and the unflagging sense of humour. The best-read novelist is Jerusalem-born Amos Oz, who writes foreboding novels (such as *My Michael*) about the city and the land in the shadow of the Arab-Israeli conflict. Many of

any Stiematzky's book store, they have a wealth of Hebrew literature to choose from.

The revival of Hebrew as a modern language was, astoundingly enough, accomplished by one man, Eliezer Ben-Yehudah, an Eastern European Jew who came to Jerusalem in 1881. Compiling the modern Hebrew dictionary, Ben-Yehudah was a kind of Tower of Babel in reverse, presenting an exiled people of so many foreign tongues the language of their forefathers.

What is even more amazing is how the writers who came after Ben Yehudah built a castle of literature on thin air, most famous

these writers are of Ashkenazi origin, writing in Yiddish rhythms.

In the past 20 years, a group of Sephardic writers, such as A.B. Yehoushua and Amnon Shamosh, have brought to the language a distinctly Arabic flavor. Perhaps the book that represented the greatest triumph for Hebrew literature, however, was written by a Christian Arab, *Arabesque*, published in 1985 by Anton Shams. Said Oz, "If the Hebrew language is becoming attractive enough for a non-Jewish Israeli to write in it, then we have arrived."

If an Arab has put Hebrew to the service of

his story, Jews have long been setting Hebrew lyrics to Arabic melodies in their popular music. Israeli music has undergone a considerable change since the mid-1970s, when the scene was dominated by Ashkenazi intellectuals, such as David Broza and Arik Einstein, belting out folk songs in the manner of Bob Dylan.

The Arabic-influence music made by Sephardic Jews was once referred to pejoratively around Jerusalem as "bus station mu-

Henry Crown Symphony Hall on Marcus Street, or (even better) drive to Tel Aviv and catch the world renowned Israeli Philharmonic under the direction of Zubin Mehta. The largest concert hall is the Binyanei Ha-Uma, near the Holiday Inn hotel and the central bus station. Jazz sessions can be heard at the Pargod Theatre on Bezalel Street.

Jacobo Timmerman once wrote that while Israelis seems very coarse on the outside, one can only appreciate their sensitivity and

sic" for the milieu in which it was most often heard. Now it has become part of the mainstream culture in the work of Yehudah Poliker, Yehudit Ravitz and others.

Most older Jerusalemites – especially those from European countries – are avid classical music fans. In Jerusalem, one can hear the Jerusalem Symphony Orchestra play at the

Preceding pages: summer concert at Sultan's Poll, with the Citadel in the background. Left, the Jerusalem Symphony plays at the Citadel of David. Above, a dance performance at the Rubin Academy of Performing Arts.

emotions by watching them sing. For music is perhaps the only medium in which they truly feel comfortable. Every Shabbat the streets of Jerusalem fill with the songs – *nigguns* – of that inner spirit.

Each spring Jerusalem hosts a range of international festivals that transform the city into a bustling cultural center. The annual Israel Festival is a showcase of opera, symphony, and chamber music, theatre and dance from around the world, and a film festival highlights many rare movies. Each December there is a liturgical music festival, Liturgica.

The Jewish obsession with food is well documented in the Torah. The very first command God gives His people is a dietary or kosher law – he forbade Adam and Eve from eating of the Tree of Knowledge. The Torah then goes on to enumerate a large body of kosher laws (such as not eating certain animals or mixing milk with meat), which most Jews continue to observe (generally with more diligence than Adam and Eve). Most restaurants in West Jerusalem serve only kosher

vegetables – but is otherwise simple, relying on peasant staples of grains and beans. Although the Middle East has traditionally harvested oranges and olives, only recently – since the Israeli kibbutz system radically changed the face of the land – has such a variety of fruits and vegetables been made available.

A generally accepted kibbutz idea is that during each harvest season the national should try to produce a new fruit. So when Jeru-

food and they display a sign to this effect.

So you should not expect to have coffee and dairy dessert in the same restaurant where you eat a meat dish for dinner. Religious tradition also dictates that people wash before meals and pray after. Most Jerusalem restaurants provide a sink with a pitcher.

What people traditionally associate with "Jewish food" is actually Eastern European – *matzo* ball soup, *gefilte* fish, *latkes*, *cholent*. The main food Jews and Arabs eat in Jerusalem, however, is largely influenced by the Turks. Turkish cuisine can be sophisticated – a traditional Jerusalem specialty is stuffed

salemites shop at Mahane Yehudah market, they are always delighted to discover the annual treat – whether it be kiwis or strawberries. Jerusalemites take considerable pride in the farming process.

If you love lamb but find it too expensive in other places, in Jerusalem you'll find it's pretty cheap; *shashlik* is an especially popular dish. Beef is also popular, but of poor quality because there's not enough grass in the land to spare for grazing cattle. Cows here aren't slaughtered for the meat, they're just milked to death. Therefore, the traditional Israeli meat staple is chicken. Some say it's hard to find a meal in Jerusalem that doesn't include either chicken or eggs.

Jerusalemites start their days with a salad and a generous breakfast. Lunch, the biggest meal of the day is taken at 2pm, just like in Europe. Siestas are pretty common, especially in the hot summer. By 5pm, the cafés are packed with young people. At 8 or 9pm, usually a light dinner is served – for example, eggs and salads.

Most restaurants in West Jerusalem are

must not miss the sweet smells wafting across Jerusalem on the eve of Sabbath.

So too, in the evening one must not miss the sounds rolling down the city's streets of families singing at the dinner table. The meal actually starts with a blessing on the candles, the *challah* (bread) and the wine. The Saturday meal usually consists of extremely well cooked meat and beans – anything that you can put in the oven Friday afternoon and leave there indefinitely.

closed on Sabbath and tourists traditionally check out the many fine restaurants in East Jerusalem on this night. Others try to get themselves invited to a Jewish family's home for an incomparable experience. Sabbath, in short, is a weekly family food feast, and in this respect secular Jews observe the tradition as much as the Orthodox.

On Friday mornings, the man in the family customarily does the shopping, while by early afternoons women start cooking. One

Left, the Mahane Yehudah Market. Above, a corner store in the Bukharin Quarter.

Jerusalemites are also notorious for having a sweet tooth, putting three spoons of sugar in their coffee and wolfing down more pastries per capita than just about any nation in the world. As a result, café-hopping is a popular Jerusalem pastime. Favourite munchies include bagel-shaped sesame-sprinkled breads (served with *za'ata*, a wild oregano-based spice mixture), nuts and sunflower seeds. The ultimate Sabra snack has to be *felafel* (fried chickpea balls served in pitta bread with a variety of vegetable possibilities). And in Israel the variety of fruit and vegetables is truly legendary.

There's more than an even chance that day or night, someone, somewhere in Israel will be praying. Whether under a prayer shawl in a synagogue, beneath a cross in a church or on a mat facing Mecca, the faithful will be lauding the Creator of the Universe.

The sheer intensity of the religious ardour in this small country is overwhelming: in Jerusalem's Old City, Jews at the Western Wall, Muslims at the Dome of the Rock and Christians at the Church of the Holy Sepulchre may well be saying their prayers simultaneously, to say nothing of the myriad other synagogues, churches and mosques in the Old City alone.

Likewise, the diversity of religious experience here is of a category all its own. Hassidim in 18th-century *kapotas* and *shteimels* (coats and hats) rub shoulders with robed monks and nuns from every Christian denomination East and West, while Muslim *imams* in *tarboosh* and *galabiyah* walk unnoticed among secular Israelis and pilgrims to the Holy Land. Many of the holiest sites from the Bible have alternately hosted synagogues, churches and mosques over the centuries, and even today visitors of one faith may well find themselves paying respects to a chapter of their own history in the house of worship of another.

The Jewish presence: Jewish spiritual life revolves around the home, house of study (*cheder* for youngsters, *yeshiva* for adolescents and adults) and synagogue – of which the latter is the most accessible to the visitor. Jerusalem's 500 synagogues range from the humblest *shtible* and Sefardi community synagogue to the gargantuan Belzer Center (seats 3,500) and the "Great" along downtown King George Street. The Great's massive edifice gives people the idea that it might be the third Temple. Other large synagogues in Jerusalem include the Central, Yeshrun and Italian.

The Orthodox pray three times a day, but it is at weekends and festivals that the liturgy is at its most elaborate. This is a good time to catch the Hassidic services whose more modest premises are compensated for by the fervour of the prayers. Such groups exist in Safed, Bnei Brak and in Jerusalem's Mea Shearim and Geula districts.

Among the warmest and most approachable of the Hassidic groups is the Bratslav, whose Mea Shearim premises contain the renovated chair of their first and only rebbe Rabbi Nahman. He was famous for his delightful tales; one of his sayings, "the world is a narrow bridge; the main thing is not to be afraid at all," has endeared him to all Israelis.

At the other end of Mea Shearim is Karlin, whose devotees screech their prayers – unlike their Geula neighours, Ger, whose tightly-knit organisation is reflected in their operatic music and self-discipline: "A true Ger Hassid," says one, "never looks at his wife."

A similar outlook is espoused by Toledot Aharon, opposite Bratslav, whose purity of purpose is matched by their animosity towards political Zionism, which they view as usurping the divine process of redemption. In this they follow the line of Neturei Karta (Guardians of the City), which boasts its own government-in-exile in its campaign for political autonomy. Both, too, campaign against the Conservative and Reform Movements, which have their own centres and desegregated houses of prayer in Jerusalem (on Agron and King David streets, respectively).

The cycle of the Jewish year: The framework of Jewish piety is determined by the lunar cycle beginning around September and October with Rosh Hashona (the New Year) and Yom Kippur, the Day of Atonement – a rigorous fast of 25 hours duration. Synagogues are packed; services are long but moving. If you're Jewish and you hail from Minsk, Marrakesh or Manhattan, you're sure to find at least one service meeting your liturgical needs.

An unusual and controversial custom precedes Yom Kippur: Kaparot, which entails swinging a white chicken above the head of the penitent, after which the slaughtered fowl is sold or given to charity. The gruesome ceremony can be witnessed in most open market-places.

Succot, the Festival of Rejoicing, combines harvest gathering and prayers for winter rains and is celebrated on secular kibbut-

Left, a Torah scroll and its keeper.

zim as well as by the Orthodox. The celebrants live in a temporary hut for seven days. During the evenings, the pious let down their sidelocks to dance, somersault and juggle to live, intoxicating music. Some Hassidic sects cap off the ceremonies with a candlelight procession by their children.

More lights burn during Channukah, usually in December, when eight-branched candelabra shine in most homes. This celebration of the Maccabean victory over the Greeks some 2,300 years ago was preceded by a couple of centuries by one over the upstart Haman, whose sad fate is recorded in the Scroll of Esther and read on Purim (usually in March). Children and adults dress in cos-

mourning for the Temples, culminating in the day-long fast on Tisha B'Av.

New Jews and Messiahs: Orthodoxy is fashionable, no less so among the Jews, and in the past 15 years a whole wave of "returnees" have passed through special *yeshivot* for the uninitiated, eventually to weave themselves into the fabric of the local religious life. Their devotion takes expression in a variety of ways, from those Jews who integrate their Western careers or professions with a pious daily routine, to such phenomena as the Selah Torah Rock Band, now located at the Israel Center on Jerusalem's Strauss Street, which blends Jewish and Western styles with consummate ease.

tumes, shout, get drunk, and give each other presents of food or drink.

In April, everyone spring-cleans for Passover, the annual feast celebrating the Exodus from Egypt. Seven weeks later they celebrate Shavuot, the Feast of Weeks, when thousands congregate at the Western Wall for dawn prayers, having spent the night studying Israel's national book, the Torah. Between Passover and Shavuot, the Orthodox invest Independence Day and Jerusalem Unity Day with spiritual significance, creating new festivals.

The yearly cycle reaches full circle in high summer, with the three-week period of

The Christian presence: These messianic messengers are not always Jewish, but include long, blond-haired types with pre-Raphaelite faces. They may be part of the growing Evangelical presence in Israel whose belief in the redemption has made them enthusiastic supporters of Zionism. The Christian Embassy on Jerusalem's Brenner Street recently attracted over 5,000 people from 40 countries to participate in their Christian version of the Feast of the Tabernacles. Another sort of backing comes from Nes Ammim, a semi-collective village near Acco where Christians of various denominations work the land – in co-founder Christine

Pillon's words – "in returning to our sources and being subjected to a new kind of Reformation. Our principles include the rejection of proselytising and the call for respect for Judaism as a living, ongoing tradition."

Most of the traditional Christian communities in Israel – numbering in total roughly 120,000 souls – are more concerned with their own internal affairs. Many devote themselves to lives of prayer and meditation, and preserving the presence of their church in the Holy Land. Often the priests, monks or nuns watch over and maintain traditional shrines associated with figures in the New Testament: a cave where the Holy Family found refuge, or the site of one of Jesus's miracles. With the West Bank in its control, Israel holds nearly all of what is commonly known as the "Holy Land", and the devoted visitor can follow in the footsteps of Jesus from Virgin Birth in Bethlehem to early life at Nazareth, to Crucifixion at Golgotha, in Jerusalem.

Complicated by their variety, the Christian groups celebrate some 240 feasts and holy days in any year, using two separate calendars, the Julian and the Gregorian. This provides three dates for Christmas: 25 December for Western Christians, 7 January for Greek Orthodox, Syrians and Copts, and 19 January for the Armenians – as well as two sets of Holy Weeks.

Only genuine pilgrims are allowed into Bethlehem for Christmas, where the main events take place at the Church of the Nativity; just as, in Easter Week, there is a reenactment of Jesus's last days with readings and processions on the sites historically associated with the original events. These include walks from the Mount of Olives, complete with palm branches, and along the Via Dolorosa to the Church of the Holy Sepulchre. Here, two unique ceremonies take place: the Washing of the Feet (John 13; 1-18) on Maundy Thursday, and the Kindling of the Holy Fire (symbolising the coming world redemption), by the Orthodox and Eastern Churches on Holy Saturday.

The climactic carrying of the cross on Good Friday between the Praetorium and Calvary (Golgotha), along the Via Dolorosa, is repeated weekly by the oldest resident group of priests, the Franciscans. One of the

most revered Christian sites is the place of Jesus's baptism on the Jordan River. For a long time neglected, the site has been newly marked and is now commemorated in word and deed by more and more devotees.

Interfaith, the dialogue of hope: The existence of modern Israel has brought together Christian, Muslim and Jew in a once-in-a-thousand-years opportunity for inter-faith dialogue. When they do occur, such encounters provide a means of transcending the most intransigent problems with new understanding. As Dr Abu Ghosh of Israel's Sharya Muslim Court says: "Islam is extraneous to the present political strife. Islam, Christianity and Judaism can live peacefully side by

side, as is the case in Israel." Mary Carse, a Carmelite from Vermont, winters every year in Israel where she studies "at the feet of the rabbis." In Israel, she found that "everything began to fall into place." French Dominican priest Marcel Dubois also believes that "we are witnessing a Christian rediscovery of the continuity in the design of God." Sent to East Jerusalem in 1962, he became an Israeli citizen on Christmas Day, 1974. Appointed head of Hebrew University's Philosophy Department, he is fully aware of the tensions that exist around him, but speaks of more than just himself when he observes that "Jerusalem is the capital of contradictions."

Left, an Egyptian Coptic priest. **Right,** conducting a bat mitzvah at the Western Wall.

One of the most remarkable facets of the rebirth of the Hebrew nation was the revival of the Hebrew language. Not that the language had been forgotten, but through the 2,000 years of dispersion it had become almost solely a language of worship and expression of the yearnings for Zion.

Some small communities of Sephardic Jews in Jerusalem used Hebrew for everyday speech but the lingua franca of the Jews in exile had become either the language of the country in which they found refuge, or special Jewish dialects that developed as an amalgam of the local language with an admixture of Hebrew. In such a way there evolved Yiddish as a combination of Hebrew with medieval German, Ladino – Hebrew with Spanish, Mughrabi – a North African blend of Hebrew, Arabic and French, and others. The first pioneers who arrived in 19th-century Palestine brought with them their own languages, usually Yiddish or Russian, but they insisted on using Hebrew in conversation in the early agricultural communities and the recreation of Hebrew became a cornerstone of Zionist ideology.

In fact, the rebirth of Hebrew was virtually the work of one man, the Zionist thinker and leader, Eliezer Ben-Yehuda. Born in Lithuania in 1858, he immigrated to Palestine in 1881. He saw the revival of the language as an indispensable aspect of the political and cultural rebirth of the Jewish people and with single-minded, almost fanatic, determination embarked upon a lone campaign to restore the Hebrew tongue as a vibrant, living vehicle for everyday expression, not just in the synagogue but in the street, in the market-place and in the home. When he and his new wife Dvora arrived in Jaffa he informed her that henceforth they would converse only in Hebrew and their son Itamar became the first modern child with Hebrew as his mother tongue. His efforts horrified the Orthodox population of Jerusalem who, when they realised that Ben-Yehuda proposed using the Holy Tongue to further secular, nationalist and political causes, pronounced a *herem* (religious excommunication) against him. To this day, the Ashkenazi ultra-Orthodox Jewish community condemns

the secular use of Hebrew and the defilement of the "holy" language, and confine themselves to Yiddish for everyday speech.

Yet the introduction of Hebrew for secular communication was not greeted with universal acclamation even by the non-Orthodox, or the supporting Zionist bodies and organisations abroad. Bitter battles were fought over the language of instruction to be used at, for example, the Bezalel School of Art in Jerusalem (founded in 1906), and the Technion (founded in 1913). The latter was

opened with German as its official language and it took a strike by both faculty and students to compel the supporting institution, the *Hilfsverein*, to give way on the issue. Only a few years after that, the language of teaching in all Jewish schools in the country (except for those of the ultra-Orthodox, of course) was established as Hebrew.

The crowning achievement of Ben-Yehuda's life was the publication of his *Dictionary of Ancient and Modern Hebrew*, which was completed after his death by his son Ehud and his second wife, Hemda (Dvora's younger sister). This dictionary, and the Academy of the Hebrew Language, which Ben-Yehuda established in 1890, were the main vehicles through which a new and modern vocabulary was disseminated. He wrote in the introduction to his dictionary: "In those days it was as if the heavens had suddenly opened, and a clear, incandescent light flashed before my eyes, and a mighty inner voice sounded in my ears: the renascence of Israel on its ancestral soil." Through his dictionary, the Academy, and several periodicals that he founded and edited, Ben-Yehuda coined literally thousands of new

makushit ("something that is tapped upon") take the place of "piano".

No one has yet successfully coined Hebrew words to replace the ubiquitous "automati", "mekhani", "democratia," etc., although the existence of such words in the language seriously disturbs Hebrew purists, just as *le weekend, le piquenique* and *le football* disturb Francophone purists. Some post-Ben-Yehuda slang neologisms would undoubtedly make him turn in his grave as they have become soundly embedded in the

words and terms relating to every field of life and every discipline.

Not all of Ben-Yehuda's neologisms took root. Modern Hebrew, which is today the all-purpose language of the country from mathematics, physics, medicine, agriculture to the most arcane fields of scientific learning, still borrows a great number of words from other languages which sound familiar to the non-Hebrew-speaking ear. Ben-Yehuda's *sah rahok* ("long-distance speech"), for instance, never displaced "telephone", nor did

Left, a Torah scribe preserves the sacred script. **Above**, the real thing, in secular script.

language. "Tremp" (clearly from "to tramp") is the Hebrew for "hitchhiking", a sweatshirt is a "svetcher", over which you might pull a "sveder" if it gets cold. When your "breks" fail, the garage might find something wrong with your "beck-ex," or even, God forbid, with your "front-beck-ex". Most of these words do have Hebrew equivalents, but they have often been pushed aside in common usage.

Despite these contemporary dilutions, there's no denying that Hebrew is once more a thriving, and still-evolving, vehicle of daily discourse employed in great works of literature and the backs of postcards alike.

Jerusalem is an excavation-mad town. "Archaeology in Israel," writes Amos Elon, in his brilliant book *The Israelis*, "is almost a national sport. Not a passive spectator sport but the thrilling, active pastime of many thousands of people, as perhaps fishing in the Canadian lake country or hunting in the French Massif Central."

The first to systemically excavate Jerusalem was a stern, adventurous British man named Charles Warren, who was sponsored by the Palestine Exploration Fund in London in the 19th century. The British have proceeded with some important excavations ever since, most recently under the leadership of Dame Kathleen Kenyon in the 1960s. When the city was "reunified" in 1967, the Israeli archaeology establishment, saddened at the way the Jordanians carelessly let the Old City go to waste, had the whole area made a protected antiquities landmark.

A detailed study of the Old City was prepared in 1968, and 300 separate sites of historical, religious, or architectural significance were identified. The law in the Old City of Jerusalem now is that before you're allowed to build up, you must first dig down. As a result, many development projects have been stalled for years, if not indefinitely, while archaeologists sift through countless layers of time lying beneath the city. Walk through the Jewish Quarters today and you can see new pieces of the historical jigsaw puzzle fit together before your eyes.

The most prominent find in the Old City was the Cardo, the ancient Roman/Byzantine commercial thoroughfare that crossed Jerusalem, and which stands out on the 6th-century Madaba Map. A huge section of the street has been restored – remains of the actual stone road as well as a row of ancient columns. In 1985, the City of David, which is perched on a ridge below the southeast corner of the Old City, was opened to the public. It highlights a structure from the 10th

Left, excavations and reconstruction at the Cardo in the Jewish Quarter of the Old City.

century BCE, perhaps built by King David himself. During the excavation in the late 1970s, a small group of ultra-Orthodox Jews attempted to halt the dig, arguing that sacred and ancient graves were being desecrated. Although the archaeologists won that particular fight, demonstrating that this was not a grave site, in many other cases in Israel religious protesters have prevailed.

For religious Jews, the Torah provides a sufficient sense of history and ties to Jerusalem and Israel. But for the young and secular state, archaeology is the means by which a history justifies Jewish claims to the land and a mythology weaves a national story well beyond the current politics.

As Amos Elon writes: "There are undoubtedly deep psychological reasons that lend Israeli archaeology its distinctive political, even chauvinistic air... It is possible to observe in the pursuit of patriotic archaeology, as of faith or Freudian analysis, the achievement of a kind of cure; men overcome their doubts and fears and feel rejuvenated though the exposure of real, or assumed, but always hidden origins."

Some of the most spectacular archaeological digs have taken place at Masada and the Qumram caves, the latter of which is where the Dead Sea Scrolls were found. In all this work, Israel has produced some of the world's greatest archaeologists – Eliezer Sukenik and his son Yigael Yadin, for example. At the same time, young Jews and archaeology buffs from around the world have come to Jerusalem and Israel to volunteer their services for these landmark digs. These digs seem to have aroused passion in Jewish youth that even Judaism itself has not always been able to inspire.

As Elon points out in his book, Israelis customarily describe the national attitude toward archaeology as a *bulmus*, which is actually an ancient Talmudic phrase. "It denotes a ravenous hunger," says Elon, "a faintness resulting from prolonged fasting, an exaggerated eagerness, a fit, a rage, a mania."

With religion playing the central role in the historical development of the Holy City, it is no surprise that the city has a rich heritage of synagogues, mosques and churches. But visitors expecting inspiring works of religious art in Jerusalem are likely to be disappointed. Both orthodox Jews and Muslims follow the biblical prohibition of "graven images" making only abstract art acceptable. And though the concept of Jerusalem was always central to Christianity, European leaders sent small

In fact, Jerusalem possesses few ancient buildings which are truly works of art. The one glorious exception is the Dome of the Rock, the world's oldest Muslim monument, built on the Temple Mount in 691 by Caliph Abd El Malik. The striking exterior with its tile ornamentation, geometrical and floral themes and exquisite calligraphy shows how Islam has developed abstract art forms in accordance with the need to avoid graven images. The exterior is actually from the

change for the construction of churches, keeping the major funds for cathedrals at home in Rome and Constantinople, London and Paris.

Sadly, the Romans did an effective job of razing the city to the ground in AD136 so besides an abundance of archaeological remains, no Jewish architectural riches remain from the biblical period. The Byzantines built modest chapels on the sacred sites but most were destroyed by Persians in the 7th century or by the 11th-century Muslim Caliph Al-Hakim. The Crusaders built the existing Church of the Holy Sepulchre, an unexceptional hotch potch of icons and frescoes.

16th century. In contrast, the El Aqsa Mosque is a far more austere building, though the dozens of Persian rugs which carpet the floor lend a sense of lavishness.

The Mamelukes introduced a distinctive use of coloured stones, as seen in buildings in the Mameluke Quarter, the part of the Muslim quarter closest to the Western Wall. The Ottomans, too, neglected the city, with the exception of Suleiman the Magnificent who built the Old City Walls and some attractive late 19th-century residential houses. The 19th-century German architect Conrad Schick adapted the Turkish style to build some attractive homes around Hanevi'im Street and he also designed Me'a She'arim.

But while it is over 3,000 years since King David made Jerusalem his capital, not much remains from before the mid-19th century when the great European powers began building religious institutions as a form of imperialist expression, while the advent of Zionism saw the Jews embark on major projects.

Despite the fact that each nation built in its own national style, the use of Jerusalem Jewish purists. Inside are three tapestries and a mosaic by the Russian-born Jewish artist Marc Chagall depicting Jewish history.

Elsewhere the Supreme Court, looking unexceptionally solid from the outside, has a complex interior which uses light and geometric shapes in a thought provoking way. The Israel Museum is designed like an Arab village with a series of pavilions on the hillside, while the Hebrew University on Mount Scopus is meant to mirror the Old

stone on the facade of all buildings lends the city a harmonious architectural heritage. The British mandatory authority insisted all buildings be faced with Jerusalem stone and the Israelis extended the edict, save for a period after 1948 when the need for cheap building seemed more urgent than aesthetics.

Modern Israeli architecture has tried to consolidate the city's position as Israel's capital. The Knesset, its parliament, is built in neo-classical style, much to the chagrin of

Left, ornate detail, Dome of the Rock. **Above**, the modern Supreme Court building.

City walls but looks more like a fortress. The nearby Mormon University blends delightfully into the hillside and is one of the city's more successful modern structures.

The newly built Jewish Quarter in the Old City has effectively recreated the modest narrow alleyways of the destroyed neighbourhood, but the Great Synagogue has been criticised by many Jews because of its cathedral-like – rather than traditional synagogue – proportions. Occasional ugly errors aside, Jerusalem's stone faced buildings, in hues of pink, beige and cream, are an integral part of the charm of this most enchanting of cities.

Israel

50 miles / 80 km

Beirut

LEBANON

Damascus

Tyre

Metulla
Kiryat Shmona

SYRIA

GOLAN
HEIGHTS

Nahariya

Safed

Acco

Tiberias

Sea of Galilee

Haifa

Nazareth

Mediterranean Sea

Zikhron Yaakov

Afula

Binyamina

Jenin

Hadera

Netanya

Nablus

Herzliya
Ramat Gan
Tel Aviv-Jaffa

WEST
BANK

Bat Yam
Rishon Le Zion

Lod

Ramallah

Amman

Rehovot

Ramla

Jericho

Ashdod

Jerusalem

Ashkelon

Bet Shemesh

Bethlehem

Dead

Kiryat Gat

Gaza

Hebron

Sea

GAZA STRIP

Khān Yunis

Arad

Port Said

Rafah

Beersheba

Dimona

Sodom

Yeroham

Neot Hakikar

Sde Boker

Avdat

Hazeva

Ramon Crater

Mitzpeh
Ramon

NEGEV

Paran

Suez

EGYPT

Paran
Valley

Gulf
of
Suez

Yotvata

Timna

S   I   N   A   I

Eilat

Gulf of
Aqaba

SAUDI ARABIA

Jordan

A   M   M   A   N

D   E   A   D

R

O

Jerusalem rests at the edge of the Judean desert, and is roiling hot during the summer days. At this time of year, it's best to do your touring in the morning and evening. The nights, even in the summer, are always crisp and pleasant. That's because the city is in the mountains and is itself surrounded by mountains. As a result, the winters are cold and wet, while spring and autumn are the most pleasant times to visit.

Outlined on the following pages are suggested tour routes which include all of the traditional tourist attractions and some additional nooks and crannies which might otherwise be overlooked. However, Jerusalem is not a linear place and visitors are best advised to wander by instinct, to be willing to get lost. Given a short visit it's best to check out the historical sites in the Old City by day and hit the restaurants and cafés of the New City at night.

The first suggested route starts at the Jaffa Gate in the Old City and winds through the four quarters: Armenian, Jewish, Muslim, and Christian. After which, it doubles back across the Kidron Valley to Palestinian East Jerusalem, before visiting the New City.

Before the city was reunified in 1967, the Israelis controlled only West Jerusalem, which today is considered the New City. The tour of the New City begins with its oldest neighbourhoods, those established in the 19th century. Next, the route zigzags about the downtown area from Zion Square across the café-dotted Ben Yehudah Mall, where the nightlife really gets cracking. It continues down some of the major thoroughfares, Jaffa Road and King George Street, with the latter leading towards the tree-lined streets of Rehavia and the German Colony.

Crossing the city, the tour resumes at Zahal Square in the downtown area. From here, it leads through the Russian Compound, around the Street of the Prophets, and into two intriguing neighbourhoods: ultra-Orthodox Mea She'arim and the century-old Bukharin Quarter.

After surveying the northern rim of the city, the route moves west into the Valley of the Cross, where the national parliament and the Israel Museum are located. Finally it ascends two more peaks that overlook the city – the Hill of Evil Council to the southeast and Mount Scopus to the northeast.

Many people who come to Israel for a short visit spend most of their time in Jerusalem and give a day or two to Tel Aviv and the rest of the country. The Day Trips chapter concludes the itinerary with some of the most popular excursions from Jerusalem, such as Bethlehem, the Dead Sea, Herodian, and Masada. None of these places is more than an hour and a half away.

Preceding pages: Jerusalem as seen from the Mount of Olives; the Golden Gate, or Gate of Mercy, which both Christians and Jews believe the Messiah will open when he comes to Jerusalem; Damascus Gate at festival time.

Northern and Central Israel

20 miles / 32 km

Mediterranean Sea

LEBANON

SYRIA

GOLAN HEIGHTS

GALILEE

JEZREEL VALLEY

SAMARIA

WEST BANK

JUDEA

JUDEAN DESERT

GAZA STRIP

NEGEV

Dead Sea

Sea of Galilee

Jordan

Tyre
Metulla
Tel Dan
Kiryat Shmona
Merom Golan
Kuneitra
Rosh Hanikra
Achziv
Hula Valley
Nahariya
Mt. Meron
Safed
Katzrin
Gamla
Acco
Capernaum
Haifa
Kiryat Ata
Tiberias
En Gev
Atlit
Nazareth
Mt. Tabor
Hammat Gader
MT. CARMEL
Nasholim Beach
'Afula
Belvoir
Tel Dor
Megiddo
Zikhron Yaakow
Bet Shean
Caesarea
Binyamina
Mt. Gilboa
Hadera
Jenin
Mikhmoret Beach
Yamma
Zababida
Mehola
Netanya
Tulkarm
Sebastia
Mt. Ebal
Herzliya
Nablus
Kfar Sava
Mt. Gerezim
Mekhora
Bnei Brak
Azzun
Tel Aviv-Jaffa
Petach Tikva
Sawiya
Ramat Gan
Shiloh
Bat Yam
Gilgal
Rishon Le Zion
Lod
Jericho
Ammān
Palmachim Beach
Ramla
Jericho
Yavne
Rehovot
Modiim
Ramallah
Ashdod
Bet Shemesh
Jerusalem
Nizzanim Beach
Qumran
Ashkelon
Bethlehem
Mar Saba
Kiryat Gat
Beit Guvrin
Kfar Etzian
Gaza
Lachish
Hebron
Bet Qama
Ein Gedi
Khān Yūnis
Massada
Rafah
Beersheba
Nevatim
Tel Arad
Arad
Shibbolim
Bureji
Neve Zohar
Dimona
Sodom
Dead Sea Works
Sde Boker

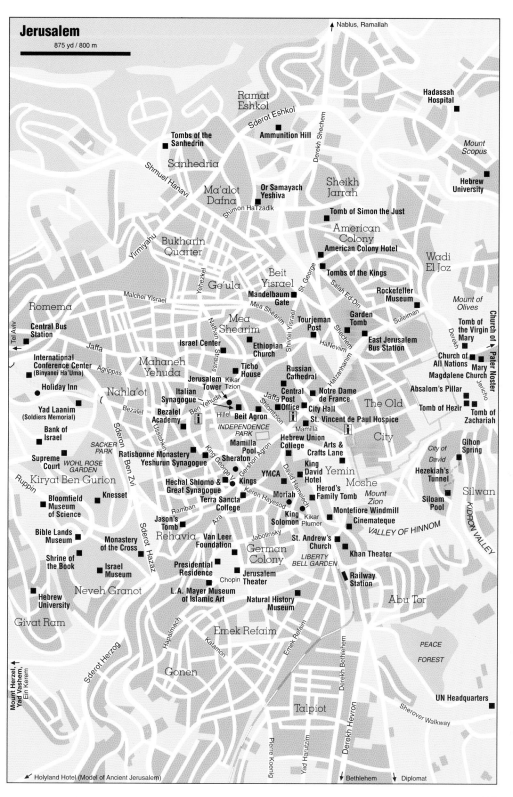

Jerusalem

875 yd / 800 m

↑ Nablus, Ramallah

Ramat
Eshkol

Sderot Eshkol

Ammunition Hill

Derekh Shechem

Hadassah
Hospital ■

Tombs of the
Sanhedrin ■

Sanhedria

Mount
Scopus

Shmuel Hanavi

Ma'alot
Dafna

Or Samayach
Yeshiva ■

Shimon HaTzadik

Sheikh
Jarrah

Hebrew
University ■

Tomb of Simon the Just ■

Yirmiyahu

Bukharin
Quarter

American
Colony

American Colony Hotel ■

Wadi
El Joz

Ge'ula

Beit
Yisrael

St. George

Tombs of the Kings ■

Rockefeller
Museum ■

Mount of
Olives

Romema

Malchei Yisrael

Mandelbaum
Gate ■

Salah Ed-Din

Mea Shearim

Central Bus
Station ■

Tel Aviv

Jaffa

Israel Center ■

Nathan Strauss

Mea
Shearim

Ethiopian
Church ■

Shivtei Yisrael

Tourjeman
Post ■

Shechem

HaNeviim

Garden
Tomb ■

Suleiman

Church of
Derekh

Tomb of
the Virgin
Mary ■

East Jerusalem
Bus Station ■

International
Conference Center
(Binyanei Ha'Uma) ■

Agrippas

Mahaneh
Yehuda

Ticho
House ■

Russian
Cathedral ■

HaTzanhanim

Church of
All Nations ■

Mary
Magdalene Church

Holiday Inn ●

Nahla'ot

Jerusalem
Tower ■

Kikar
Tzion

Jaffa Post
Office

Central
Post

Notre Dame
de France ■

Absalom's Pillar ■

Pater Noster
Church of

Yad Laanim
(Soldiers Memorial) ■

Bezalel

Italian
Synagogue ■

Ben Yehuda

Shlomzion

City Hall

Tomb of Hezir ■

Tomb of
Zachariah ■

Bank of
Israel ■

Bezalel
Academy ■

Hillel

Beit Agron ■

St. Vincent de Paul Hospice ■

The Old

Supreme
Court ■

SACKER
PARK

Ussishkin

INDEPENDENCE
PARK

Mamilla

Hebrew Union
College ■

S. Andrew's

City

Gihon
Spring ■

City of
David

WOHL ROSE
GARDEN

Ratisbonne Monastery ■

King George V

Mamilla
Pool ■

Gershon Agron

Arts &
Crafts Lane ■

Hezekiah's
Tunnel ■

Kiryat Ben Gurion

Ruppin

Yeshurun Synagogue ■

Sheraton ■

YMCA ■

David Hamelech

King
David
Hotel ■

Yemin

Moshe

Silwan

Sderon Ben Zvi

Hechal Shlomo &
Great Synagogue ■

Kings

Moriah ■

Herod's
Family Tomb ■

Mount
Zion

Siloam
Pool ■

Bloomfield
Museum
of Science ■

Knesset ■

Ramban

Terra Sancta
College ■

Keren Hayesod

King
Solomon ■

Kikar
Plumer

Montefiore Windmill ■

Cinemateque ■

KIDRON VALLEY

Bible Lands
Museum ■

Jason's
Tomb ■

Aza

Jabotinsky

VALLEY OF HINNOM

Shrine of
the Book ■

Sderot Hazaz

Monastery
of the Cross ■

Rehavia

Van Leer
Foundation ■

German
Colony

St. Andrew's
Church ■

LIBERTY
BELL GARDEN

Khan Theater ■

Israel
Museum ■

Presidential
Residence ■

Chopin

Jerusalem
Theater ■

Railway
Station

Abu Tor

Hebrew
University ■

Neveh Granot

L.A. Mayer Museum
of Islamic Art ■

Natural History
Museum ■

Givat Ram

Emek Refaim

PEACE
FOREST

Hapalmach

Katamon

Emek Refaim

Mount Herzel,
Yad Vashem,
Ein Kerem

Sderot Herzog

Gonen

Talpiot

Derekh Bethlehem

UN Headquarters ■

Pierre Koenig

Yad Harutzim

Derekh Hevron

Sherover Walkway

↙ Holyland Hotel (Model of Ancient Jerusalem)

↓ Bethlehem   ↓ Diplomat

103

OLD CITY SITES

Imagine the absurdity: in 1987, Kyoto hosted a "World Conference of Historical Cities" in Japan and, although relatively prepubescent towns like Boston, Kiev, and Montreal attended, Jerusalem, the most wizened and immortal city of them all, was conspicuously uninvited. They might as well have gathered the planets in the solar system and told Earth it didn't belong.

For, as you stand here in the Old City of Jerusalem you realize almost immediately that nowhere could exude a more potent historical feeling than this. If anything, the place suffers from being *too* historical. In the babble of tour guides ticking off dates and names, first-time visitors often contract epochal vertigo. Tarry here long enough and you'll likely to imagine Mohammed, Jesus and Abraham engaged in a constant theological brawl over Turkish coffee at the corner falafel stand.

The history doesn't come in a nice, neat package and, if you expect to retain any of it, don't try to absorb too much at once – especially during a short visit.

The Israeli capital could not be included in the historical cities conference, the organizers said, because it was "the subject of political controversies". This is an understatement. It means quite simply that, unlike other so-called "historical" cities, Jerusalem's history is not finished, written or fossilized. You are not about to enter a mausoleum, but a *living* museum. Precisely because of these political controversies (and philosophical, archaeological and military ones), a historical drama is being played out every day. Adding to the amusement, the characters themselves look and act as if they'd just stepped out of the previous millennium or two.

Before entering this maze, you can

Preceding pages: Dome of the Rock. **Right,** aerial view of the Jewish Quarter.

orient yourself by climbing the stairs at any one of the main gates and follow a **Ramparts Walk** (open Sun–Thurs 9am–5pm, Fri 9am–3pm) around the Old City walls. These were built by the Ottoman Emperor Suleiman from 1537–41 and are 2½ miles (4 km) all the way around.

You can "walk entirely around the city in an hour," Mark Twain once said. "I do not know how else to make one understand how small it is." It is hard to believe that such a small place has come to be the most contested thatch of land since the beginning of time.

Entering the Old City: The **Jaffa Gate** marks the end of the road from the ancient port of Jaffa to Jerusalem, and like the hard-core pilgrims from centuries before them, most Western travellers today still step into the spiritual labyrinth of the Old City through this very entrance.

To the right of the gate, the only real break in the city walls is visible, a paved 39 ft (12 metres) opening. The rampart here was destroyed and the moat filled in

1898 to prepare for the ostentatious entrance of German Kaiser Wilhelm II – an important political guest of the Turkish Sultan – who didn't care to dismount his white horse on cruising into town.

Inside the gate to the left is the **Municipal Tourist Office**, which is a decent repository of maps and information, as is the **Christian Information Centre**, which is located on the first right just before the start of the boisterous Arab market.

Next door, in the **Anglican Compound**, is the **Christ Church**, the first such Protestant edifice in all of Palestine. Built by stone masons brought in specially from Malta in the 1840s, the church became the locus of a budding Protestant Quarter, serving missionaries and British explorers.

Opposite the church is the famed **Citadel**, strategic high ground that has been controlled and fortified by virtually all of Jerusalem's conquerors. The **Tower of David**, despite its name, has nothing to do with King David, but is believed to

Citadel of David.

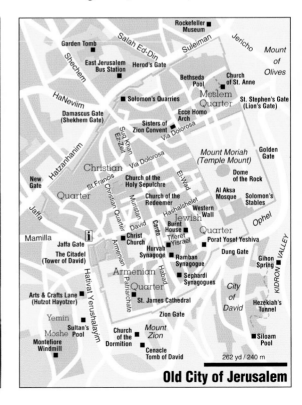

Old City of Jerusalem

be a remnant of King Herod's palace, placed on this site 2,000 years ago.

A case study in paranoia, Herod probably set up his home here on the edge of town because he felt more vulnerable to attack by his fellow Jews inside the city than by the Romans outside.

In 1967, the Israelis turned the Citadel area into the **Tower of David (History of Jerusalem) Museum** (open Sun–Thurs 10am–4pm, Fri/Sat 10am–2pm), and from the ruins inside you begin to get a sense of the layers of time here: a **Herodian mikvah** (ritual bath), for instance, served later as a Roman king's pool and then a Byzantine quarry. It's also worth checking out the **Model of Jerusalem**, another useful tool for getting your bearings. In addition, there's a regular slide presentation and in the evenings a schmaltzy sound and light show is offered in different languages.

Armenian Quarter: As you leave the Citadel, on the right is the Israeli Police Station, which served as the Jordanian Police Headquarters before 1967. Just

beyond it on the left you will enter the **Armenian Quarter**. Home to 2,000 Armenians and representing about one-sixth of the area of the Old City, it is certainly the most tranquil quarter inside its walls.

Although the quarter may seem an inhospitable place for curious travellers, spend some time here and discover a proud and friendly people more than willing to show visitors around and tell a story of their nation.

Armenia, an independent republic that used to be part of the former USSR, boasts that it was the first nation to convert to Christianity – about 300 years after the birth of Christ. Well before the Emperor Constantine's conversion and Queen Helena's discovery of the "holy places," Armenian pilgrims were already flocking to Jerusalem.

Armenians have traditionally stayed as apolitical as possible here – and that, perhaps, accounts for their relative success in making their way among much larger and more powerful factions. For

Armenian Easter celebration.

just six weeks, in 1300, when the king of Armenia conquered Jerusalem, did the Armenians wield any degree of effective power.

Between 1915 and 1918, when the Turks exterminated one and a half million Armenians, as many as 10,000 sought temporary refuge here, and the quarter was bursting at its seams. Today, the Armenians run a large monastery. Behind the monastery, the southwestern corner of the city is a giant garbage dump, one of the few patches of completely undeveloped land within city walls.

Across from the monastery is a simple portal leading to the **St James Cathedral**, one of the most important and beautiful Christian sites in the Old City. This is believed to be the place where, in 44CE, Mary was sitting when she was brought the head of the martyred apostle St James. This cranium is supposed to be buried inside the Cathedral.

Through the iron gate is a courtyard, inside of which you see two wooden clappers, reminders of the Turkish rule when bells were forbidden. In the Cathedral itself is the **Throne of St James the Lesser**, upon which the Armenian Patriarch sits once a year – on the Feast of St James.

Behind the Cathedral is a very private courtyard, not normally open to tourists, except on request. Here is a fine Armenian school and the **Gulbenkian Public Library**, which was established in 1929 and houses a number of rare books and manuscripts.

There is access to the **Armenian Museum** either through this courtyard or by the main road. The museum displays archaeological findings from the quarter, Armenian art and books, and an exhibit on the genocide.

The Armenian Patriarchate Road leads toward the Zion Gate and Mount Zion, but we'll come to that later. In the meantime, backtrack 50 yards (45 metres) and turn down St. James Road. Tucked away on your right is an Armenian pizza place that's only open Wednesday night

St James Cathedral in the Armenian Quarter.

and Saturday afternoon; it's an unusual place to grab a meal.

Jewish Quarter: If you continue along this alleyway, the name changes to Or Hayim Street and you enter the **Jewish Quarter** – without question, the most affluent one in the Old City. After the Six Day War, when the Israelis assumed control of the Old City, Jews returned to this quarter and they've been building it up ever since. Although they've tried to preserve the sense of architectural tradition, space is so tight that they've raised the skyline, putting a third floor on many previously two-storey flats.

Despite the physical and political tensions, apartments in the area have remained in tremendous demand – and very expensive. Security in the Old City is fierce to protect these burgeoning economic interests.

To the left of what is now Or Hayim Street, is the **Old Yishuv Court Museum** (open Sun–Thurs 9am–4pm), which preserves relics of life in far less bourgeois times. The *Old Yishuv* refers to the Jewish settlement in Palestine before statehood, when the Jewish Quarter was a dirty, disease-ridden ghetto.

In the museum, you can compare the essential stylistic and aesthetic differences between the *Sephardic* (Spanish and Eastern) and *Ashkenazi* (Eastern European) Jewish settlers.

The museum has also refurbished two simple but elegant synagogues. **Ha-Ari** ("The Lion") is a Sephardic synagogue named after the great 16th-century mystic Isaac Luria, who, according to tradition, was born on this spot. Luria devoted his entire life to the study of *Kabbalah*, a Jewish mystical tradition passed down orally to a select few from Mount Sinai. An ascetic and visionary who believed that he was in constant contact with the prophet Elijah, Luria founded a Kabbalistic school in the Holy City of Safed.

The **Or Hayim Synagogue** was founded by a Moroccan rabbi, but later became one of the central synagogues for the Ashkenazim in the old *yishuv*.

Shopping along the Cardo.

If you continue on this street you'll come to Habad Road and the **Habad House**, underneath which begins the Champs Elysées of Roman and Byzantine Jerusalem, the **Cardo**. When the Romans rebuilt Jerusalem as Aelia Capitolina, they laid it out like a traditional Roman city and it is this character that shapes the city today.

For the Crusaders, the Cardo was their main market thoroughfare but after they were expelled the road was eventually buried underneath 13 ft (4 metres) of rubble. Historians guessed such a street existed from the famous map, but only in digging up the Jewish Quarter during the early 1980s did archaeologists come upon this magnificent discovery.

It's been beautifully preserved – you can see how wide the street must have been and the pillars that ran along it – but the commercial row these days, including a ridiculous fur shop, raises the tacky quotient one notch too high.

Continuing down Habad Street, you'll reach **Archaeological Seminars**, which organizes the best and most comprehensive tours of Jerusalem at very reasonable prices. Even further still is a set of metal stairs that take you up on the rooftops for a view of the city.

Above the Cardo is the Jewish Quarter Road, where you'll find the **Jewish Quarter Museum**, which gives the history of the area since 1948. A multimedia show here emphasizes the loss of the quarter to the Arab Legion and its recapture by Israeli forces in 1967. Across the way is a **War of Independence Memorial** that highlights on an electronic map the house-by-house battles that took place in 1948.

Just above the memorial is the **Hurvah Synagogue**, a piling on of ruins. In 1701 a one-time believer in the famed false messiah Sabbatai Tsvi, Judah the Hassid came to Jerusalem from Poland with 500 followers, one of the largest single immigrations before modern Zionism. He died five days after he arrived, but his disciples continued to build the syna-

Left, soldier patrols the Old City Wall. **Below**, Hassids in the Jewish Quarter.

gogue here, borrowing the funds from local Muslims. When they couldn't meet their debts, the synagogue was burned down by their creditors in 1720, reduced to a ruin (*hurvah*).

In 1856 it was rebuilt, and became the centrepiece of the growing Jewish community in the Old City, but in 1948 it was blown up by the Arab Legion, left in a ruin once again.

The arch you see today has been reconstructed in a manner which gives you an idea of its once grand scale. Much talk is spent on how the Hurvah Synagogue should be rebuilt, but not surprisingly the different Jewish theopolitical factions in Jerusalem can't seem to reach an agreement.

And below the Hurvah is the **Ramban Synagogue**, the oldest in Jerusalem. The Ramba (Rabbi Moses ben Nachman or Nachmanides), a famed Talmudic exegete essentially exiled from his native Spain after successfully disputing the king, founded the first Jewish settlement in Jerusalem since the Second Temple was destroyed. At first he wanted to establish a synagogue near the Tomb of David on Mount Zion, but it's said he was scared off by the Bedouins. Instead, he put his house of worship here on ancient ruins. There has been a continued Jewish presence in this city ever since. The Ramban Synagogue has been refurbished and is in full use today.

Legend has it that the **mosque** preserved above the synagogue was built by a disaffected Jew from the Ramban congregation who converted to Islam.

In the courtyard adjacent to the Ramban Synagogue, are several Jewish educational institutions, including the **Jewish Heritage Information Centre** and the **Aish HaTorah Yeshiva**. Many offer free tours of the quarter, places to sleep, Shabbat meals, and Talmud classes.

It begins this way: A young Diaspora Jew on a two-week tour of Israel visits the Western Wall. In short order he is asked by a Hassidic man, "Do you want to put on *tefillin?*" Or perhaps another

Remains of the Hurvah Synagogue.

Orthodox Jew offers to set him up for a Shabbat meal or to give him a free place to sleep as long as he's in the Old City. There follows a series of provocative discussions about the nature of Judaism, and how assimilated Jews of America and elsewhere have lost touch with their roots. Would the young man be interested in pursuing the issues farther? And so it goes on until he is fully ensconced in one of Jerusalem's many **ba'al teshuvah yeshivot**.

Ba'al teshuvah means "master of return," and in the past 25 years a large number (some rabbis put the figure at 20,000) of the assimilated Jews – both male and female – have returned to the religious observance of their ancestors, through the yeshiva experience. The yeshiva is an age-old Jewish school, where students (*buchers*) pore over the Talmudic laws. The Talmud is comprised of commentaries in Hebrew and Aramaic on the oral law that God gave the Jews along with the written Torah at Mount Sinai. The yeshiva is based on the idea that the best way to learn these oral laws is by engaging in a constant, hands-on-text discussion of these commentaries.

In the courtyard next to the Ramban and Hurvah Synagogues are several Jewish educational centres, including **Aish HaTorah Yeshiva**. (Another big *ba'al teshuvah yeshiva* is **Or Samayach** outside the Old City.) The **Heritage House** will put you up for a few nights as you begin to enter the yeshiva world. If you partake, be prepared to face considerable (if gradual) pressure to conform to various religious observances.

The *shuls*: Following Hakehuna Street to the right to complex of **Four Sephardi Synagogues**: the **Elijah**, the **Yohanan Ben-Zakkai**, the **Stambouli** and the **Middle**, as they are called. Originally built by Jews expelled from Spain, they served for several centuries as the chief places of worship for Jerusalem's Sephardic community. Note the underground entrance and Islamic architecture, which was perhaps intended to

A social encounter at the Western Wall.

mask the religious significance of the complex to hostile strangers. The *shuls* which were bombed in the 1948 war and used as stables during Jordanian rule have been beautifully restored.

In the opposite direction from the Ramban Synagogue courtyard, down Tiferet Yisrael, you'll find an 8-metre wide collection of stones known as the **Broad Wall**. Discovered only in recent times, it has supplied important archaeological evidence of a major chapter of Jewish history.

King Hezekiah mobilized the entire population to build – in just three months – an enormously thick wall around the city to protect it against the invading armies of Assyrian King Sennacherib in 701BCE. The Bible says this wall was put up so quickly that it had to run through entire homes, one of which seems to be visible on the present archaeological site.

Head back north up Tiferet Yisrael to the **Burnt House** (open Sun–Thurs 9am–5pm, Fri 9am–1pm). An eerie and exciting place, it is literally a frozen moment of history – a time capsule of Jerusalem during the Second Temple period. It is believed to have been burnt when Titus razed Jerusalem in AD70. A regular slide show here helps makes sense of the collected artifacts.

The holiest shrine: Past the Burnt House, down a set of stairs, and through the requisite Israeli security check, you enter a bustling plaza at the end of which is the holiest shrine in all of Jewish civilization, the **Western Wall**.

When the Romans burned and destroyed the great Temple in AD70, all that was left was a heap of rubble. All, that is, except for one remaining wall, which was built – by the poorest of Jews, it is said – to support the western portion of the Herodian Temple Mount. According to traditional Judaism, the Temple cannot be rebuilt until the Messiah comes, and the Diaspora Jews regard The Wall (or *HaKotel*) as their most sacred shrine.

To pray here has been the abiding

Worshipping at the Wall.

dream of observant Jews ever since the beginning of their exile 1,900 years ago. The wall, which is as smooth as the endless stream of tears spilled mourning the destruction of the Temple, has come to be known as the Wailing Wall.

The Wall itself is 50 ft (15 metres) tall, and most of the stones were carved and stacked here during Herod's time, but those at and near the top were put there during restoration by the Mamelukes and Turks. When the Jordanian Legion captured the Old City in 1948, Jews were forbidden – as they had been many times throughout history – to worship at the Wall. So it was with special meaning on 7 June 1967, that Jews everywhere watched TV footage of the Israeli Army retaking the Old City, and the young soldiers praying and weeping at the Wall.

Immediately following the Six Day War, the Arab shanties in the large area in front of the Wall were cleared, and the plaza was made into a place of worship. Traditionally, observant Jews gather here on holidays and days of mourning – especially on Tisha ba'Av, the anniversary of the Temple's destruction. In recent years, extensive tunned chambers beneath the walls have been opened to the public.

Anyone may approach the Wall and lodge paper prayers in its cracks (*see photograph on page 220*). You will note that women ("modestly dressed") enter on the left, men (heads covered) on the right. Remember, too, that photos are forbidden on Shabbat.

To the left of the prayer area and leaning on the Wall itself is **Wilson's Arch**, discerned by the 19th-century British surveyor Charles Wilson to be part of the bridge over which ran a road from the Upper City to the Temple Mount. To the right of the prayer area by the southwestern corner of the Temple Mount is **Robinson's Arch** (named for a 19th-century American scholar/adven-

Right, Jews gather on Sukkot at the Western Wall plaza.

turer), which was presumably part of a similar bridge.

In front of the Wall is the entrance to the controversial **Hasmonean Tunnel.** Here archaeologists have dug out a 2,000-year-old street leading along the rim of the Temple Mount, several hundred metres northwards to the Via Dolorosa as it passes beneath the Muslim Quarter. The Arabs have always maintained that the tunnelling was a Zionist plot to enter under the Temple Mount and blow up the mosques, even though the excavations are not under the Haram El Sharif at all. In fact, the tunnel has been open to visitors as a cul-de-sac since 1987, but the opening of the northern entrance in 1996 sparked serious Palestinian rioting.

At the other end of the Wall, below Robinson's Arch and along the southern wall, are the **southern excavations**. The slope just outside the city wall below the southeast corner of the Temple Mount is called the **Ophel**, and has been the site of extensive archaeological excavations since 1968. Three tour routes are marked off for your convenience. One of the most impressive finds are remains of the ancient staircase and the Hulda Gate through which pilgrims climbed the Temple compound. Note the stairs are of uneven size, designed so that pilgrims would not casually bound up to the Temple Mount to worship, but would concentrate upon the meaning of their ascent.

Beneath the Ophel are the **City of David** excavations, where it is believed King David laid the foundations for the city of Jerusalem around 1000BCE. The digs here, which began in 1978, have produced ruins related to the Canaanite settlement of Jerusalem even before King David in the third and second millennia BCE.

If you make the detour this way, follow the hill down to the water source that probably attracted King David to this site, the **Spring of Gihon**. Because the spring was located outside the city walls, in a cave at the bottom of the Kidron Valley, Jerusalem was in danger of having its water supply cut off by Assyrian invaders in 701BCE. Therefore, the shrewd King Hezekiah had a tunnel built to connect the Gihon spring to the **Siloam pool** inside the city. If you wish to explore Hezekiah's Tunnel, bring a candle or flashlight, and prepare to roll up your pants or get wet. An early explorer of this tunnel was the 19th-century British archaeologist Charles Warren. He also discovered an underground well, **Warren's Shaft**, where Jerusalemites could fetch their water in ancient times.

It is worth strolling along the new **promenade** running east from the Dung Gate which overlooks the Kidron Valley, dominated beneath in this section by Absalom's Tomb. Beyond the valley this walkway also offers an excellent view of the Mount of Olives and its vast Jewish cemetery and attractive churches.

The Temple Mount: Now climb back up to the Old City through the **Dung Gate**, so called for the heaps of rubbish that

"Pinnacle" of the Temple Mount.

were left here during Roman and Byzantine times. As you face the Temple Mount, remember that this is reputed to be the place where Abraham prepared to sacrifice Isaac, and where in ancient times a Temple twice the size of the Dome of the Rock stood in its place. The southeastern corner of the Temple Mount is sometimes called the "pinnacle" since legend has it that Satan brought Jesus to this spot from the place of the Temptation.

When Israel conquered the Old City in the 1967 War, the Israeli government decided to put the Temple Mount under the jurisdiction of the Wakf – the Muslim Religious Trust. Though the Arabs control it today, there have been stirrings in some very right-wing religious circles to retake the mount and rebuild the Jewish Temple. There have been protests and increasing violence on the Temple Mount since the Palestinian strike and uprising of late 1987.

Below, praying at the Al Aksa Mosque. Right, inside the Dome of the Rock.

But to the solitary searcher of spiritual light, the Temple Mount still holds itself like the name the Arabs call it,

Haram esh-Sharif, or "Noble Sanctuary". And the **Dome of the Rock** is perched like Jerusalem's crown.

Centre of the earth: Muslims (and many Jews) believe that the Dome of the Rock (or *Haram esh-Sharif*) was placed on the precise spot where the great Temple once stood, and that the rock itself rests on location of the "Holy of Holies," where the Jewish high priest communed with God once a year. The rock was widely believed to be the Stone of Foundation, the very centre of the earth.

The Dome is the oldest, one of the most important and probably the most beautiful monument in all of Islam. It was put up by Caliph Abd al-Malik, the ninth successor of the prophet Mohammed, in AD691. Influenced by the Christian edifice industry of his time, the Caliph commissioned Byzantine architects to do the job, and they constructed it on the exact scale of the Church of the Holy Sepulchre.

Caliph Abd al-Malik had his name and the year inscribed inside the dome,

but two centuries later the Caliph al-Mamoon replaced his predecessor's name with his own. In one of the better bloopers in history, however, he forgot to change the date and his fraudulence is here for all to see to this very day. The structure has been renovated throughout history, most notably during the reign of Suleiman the Magnificent, whose mosaic tile work gives the Dome its ornate and rich Eastern flavour.

Inside of the Dome, you can see the holy rock (called, in Arabic, *Kubbet es-Sakhra*) upon which it is believed Abraham prepared to sacrifice Isaac and from which Mohammed rose to heaven. Next to the rock there is a box that is said to contain a few hairs from the Islamic prophet's beard. In the underground cave referred to as the **Well of Souls**, the dead, according to tradition, congregate for their prayer meetings.

There are 10 portals leading to the Temple Mount. At the kiosk inside the southeastern **Mughrabi Gate**, so named for the Moroccan and Algierian Islamic pilgrims who settled here, you can buy a ticket that permits multiple entrance to the Dome of the Rock, the Al-Aksa Mosque, and the Islamic Museum.

Muslim holy place: The silver-domed edifice on the Temple Mount is called the **Al-Aksa Mosque**. Some say it was originally built in the 6th century as a church honouring the Virgin Mary, and that it was converted into an Islamic place of worship, but Muslims scoff at this notion. According to their tradition, the Umayyad caliph had it built in the early 8th century. It has been destroyed and renovated many times since.

Unlike the Dome of the Rock, Al-Aksa is a mosque, and as such, is the most important Muslim place of worship in Jerusalem, one of the most famous in the Islamic world. Non-Muslims are not permitted to enter the mosque during prayer. When you do go in (remember to take your shoes off, according to custom), you have the feel-

Right, Ramadan at the Dome of the Rock.

120

ing as though you are walking into an elaborate carpet warehouse. It's actually quite beautiful in its simplicity, and innovative for its use of six rows of columns set perpendicular to the wall which it is customary to face when one prays. Where Jews the world over face Jerusalem when they pray, Muslims face Mecca; in this case, that's toward the southern or back wall.

It was in front of Al-Aksa in 1951 that a fanatic Muslim murdered Jordanian King Abdullah in front of his grandson, the current King Hussein. In 1969, an Australian set the mosque aflame, provoking calls for jihad against Israel. When Anwar Sadat visited in 1977, he came to pray at Al-Aksa. There are still demonstrations there today, either by Palestinians trying to raise the national flag or by Israeli right-wingers.

When the Crusaders conquered Jerusalem, they transformed Al-Aksa into a royal palace before finally setting up the headquarters of the Order of the Knights of the Temple here – the Templars. Below the mosque, along the southeast corner of the Temple Mount are **Solomon's Stables**, where the Crusaders kept their chariots and horses; the building has been converted into a mosque, with no access for non-Muslims. The **Islamic Museum** across from Al-Aksa is worth a short visit, especially for its large collection of beautifully calligraphied copies of the Koran.

Exactly in the middle of Al-Aksa and the Dome of the Rock is the 14th-century **Fountain of Al Kas** (or "the Cup"), which once hooked up with an extensive subterranean system of cisterns from Temple times. The Dome of the Rock sits on the Upper Platform of the Temple Mount. The eight staircases leading up topped by stone arcades are the **Mawazzin**. It is said that on Judgment Day only the virtuous souls may continue through the Mawazzin. Behind the Dome of the Rock is the **Dome of the Chain**, one third its height, though built in a similar form.

If you leave the "Noble Sanctuary"

by way of the **Iron Gate**, turn right through a small alley to the **Small Wall**, which is actually another section of the sacred Western Wall of the Temple Mount. Some religious anti-Zionists prefer to pray here rather than at what they feel is the circus-like atmosphere at the Wailing Wall.

If you leave the Temple Mount by the **Gate of the Chain**, you may wonder how this gate got its name. In Temple times when a Jewish court met here, the accused were asked to hold a certain chain. Anyone who could hold the chain was considered innocent; if someone grasp at the chain and it disappeared, they were found guilty.

Mameluk architecture: The Street of the Chain leads to the Muslim Quarter markets, but along the way it has a few examples of Mameluke architecture worth mentioning. *Mamluke* means "owned" in Arabic and in 13th-century Egypt, the Mamelukes were high-class slaves of Turkish origin who overthrew their masters, thereby gaining control of

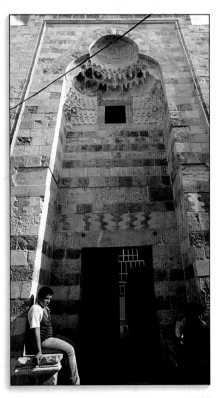

Left, Arab shopkeeper. **Right**, the Mameluke architectural style.

Jerusalem, among other places. In this city, they are remembered best for the ornate, stylish buildings – a kind of early precursor to Art Deco.

The first building on the left of the gate, with the black and white interlacing stone facade, is the **Madrassa Tankiziyya**. *Madrassas,* of which the Memelukes built many, were Muslim theological seminaries. Further down along the Street of the Chain are some other Mameluke gems, including the tomb of a princess (at number 149) and another *madrassa* (number 106).

Stepping back in time: The Muslim Quarter is the largest, most crowded, and most confusing quarter in the Old City. You don't sightsee here, you wander. And if you get lost in the labyrinthine alleyways, that's the point. The Muslim Quarter gives one the sense of how Jerusalem looked, smelled and sounded up until the 20th century.

Many visitors start their adventure just inside either the Damascus or Jaffa Gates, people-watching over Turkish

coffee before wading through the souk. Here you'll find for sale endless rows of mummy bead jewellery, fake antiques, olive wood, Roman glass, Turkish coins, Bedouin carpets, and *keffiyahs* (the popular Arab headcoverings).

Haggling is the native sport, and one must not be put off by the overbearing, hard-sell approach; most shopkeepers speak many languages and have interesting stories to tell if you take the time to chat with them over tea.

The Muslim Quarter isn't a place where you go to have a sit-down meal, but rather to sample the local cuisine. As you walk along, try picking up *houmous* at **Abu-Shukri's** at **El-Wad Street** along the Via Dolorosa. Although it's reputedly the best houmous in Israel, save some room for the goodies on the silver trays at the pastry shops along **Suq Khan**: *baklava, kanaffi,* and other honey-and-nut combinations. If a kid approaches you with a huge brass, samovar-like vat, don't be afraid; he's probably trying to sell you a serving of *sachleb,* a sweet, hot, milky, wintertime drink topped with dried fruit, cinnamon, raisins and nuts. Since West Jerusalem is closed on a Friday night, many gather at the *schleb* stands at the **Damascus Gate** on this night.

Money-changers abound and will offer far better exchange rates than the banks, though official Israeli guides will discourage you with anti-Palestinian propaganda. All Jewish money-changers and official Israeli guides complain about them as well. ("They're undermining the value of the shekel!")

The Damascus Gate, which is the fulcrum of Arab life in the Old City, was built in the 16th century by Suleiman the Magnificent. Underneath it, archaeological excavations have revealed an earlier portal from the Roman period, suggesting that it was the major entryway for Emperor Hadrian's Aelia Capitolina. From here, you can wind your way through the Old City or walk along the outside of the walls to the Lion's Gate for a tour of the Via Dolorosa.

Left, the **Damascus Gate**. **Right**, the **labyrinthine Muslim Quarter**.

VIA DOLOROSA

Putting aside the crass commercialism of the local merchants hawking Jesus paraphernalia, an excursion down the **Via Dolorosa** (or Way of Sorrows) is one of the most culturally resonant routes in the Western World. This is the fabled path that Jesus was said to have taken to meet his fate of crucifixion.

The Fourteen Stations of the Cross leading to the Calvary in the Church of the Holy Sepulchre (nine were described in the Gospels and five by tradition) were fixed during the time of the Ottoman rule.

Most historians and archaeologists today debunk the authenticity of these particular sites, but suggest that Jesus may have followed a path very similar to it. The controversy doesn't discourage pilgrims from all over the world every year at Easter to gather here to follow Jesus's footsteps, many of them

dressing and acting the part of the ancients with considerable flourish.

It's best to start down the Via Dolorosa from the **Lions' Gate**, where a pair of lions (some say panthers) flank both sides of the entrance. According to legend, Suleiman the Magnificent dreamed one night that four lions were ripping him to shreds. The interpretation of the local sages was that the Lion of Judah was enraged because the Holy City was in shambles as no wall had been built around it.

Upon hearing this, Suleiman immediately erected walls – the very ones you see today – and had the four lions carved to commemorate his dream. When the Israeli Army penetrated the Old City during the 1967 War, they entered through the Lions' Gate.

To the Christians, however, it is known as **St Stephen's Gate** because Stephen the Martyr is said to have been stoned to death at this very site. Just inside the gate is the **Church of St Anne**, which was built by Crusaders on the remains

The "Way of Sorrows" in Hebrew, Arabic and Latin.

of a Byzantine church to commemorate the traditional place where Anne lived when she gave birth to Mary. **Mary's Birthplace** is specifically marked by the crypt underneath the church. The **Bethesda Pool**, where Jesus miraculously gave the water curative power, is in the courtyard.

Turn right as you leave the church, and you will come to the **First Station of the Cross**, where Jesus was sentenced to crucifixion by the Roman Procurator Pontius Pilate. Today this is a Umariayah school for Islamic boys, built during the Ottoman Empire on the site of the **Antonia Fortress**, the Roman administrative headquarters in the time of Jesus.

From the courtyard is a splendid view of the Temple Mount. Also, this is the point from which the Franciscans lead a procession down the entire Via Dolorosa every Friday afternoon. Good Friday proves to be a veritable mob scene every year.

Continuing along, on your right you will come to the **Second Station**, where Jesus was brutalized by the Romans, a crown of thorns put on his head. The spot is marked on the street, just in front of the **Chapels of the Condemnation and the Flagellation**.

Overhead as you continue is the **Ecce Homo Arch**, named for Pilate's words of scorn: "Behold the man!" But the name is somewhat misleading: after considerable archaeological excavations conducted by the Sisters of Zion, it was determined that the arch did not even exist in Jesus's time.

In the process, this intriguing religious order became expert in the field, and the entire **Convent of the Sisters of Zion**, on your right, is an archaeological museum all its own.

Past the convent, a century-old **Austrian Hospice**, on the right, has recently reopened as a delightful guesthouse. Then you must follow Jesus's path to the left, a short walk along El Wad Street. Here on the left side of the street is a pillar in the wall which marks the

Retracing Christ's steps along Via Dolorosa.

Third Station, where Jesus first fell under weight of the cross. Immediately after it, you see the **Fourth Station**, where Jesus is said to have met Mary. A 6th-century mosaic in the crypt of the **Armenian Catholic Church of Our Lady of the Spasm** here depicts the outline of sandals where Mary is reckoned to have stood when Jesus passed by the spot.

Before turning right down a bustling Old City thoroughfare grab a snack at the hummus stand of **Abu-Shukri**, one of the tastier (if not more expensive) tourist haunts along the way.

After turning right, you come to the **Fifth Station**, where the Roman soldiers commanded Simon the Cyrenian, a Jew from North Africa, to carry the cross the rest of the way.

The **Sixth Station** is a short way down on the left. It is also called the **House of Veronica** because this is where St Veronica dabbed Jesus's brow with her veil and then miraculously watched his image appear upon it.

At the corner of Via Dolorosa and Suq Kahn Ez Zeit Street is the **Seventh Station**, where Jesus fell once again. Also called the **Gate of Judgement**, it is believed this was the site of the gate leading outside the city in Jesus's time. Historically this makes sense to the extent that Jewish law says one cannot be buried inside city walls.

The **Eighth Station**, just outside the Greek Orthodox **Chapel of St Chralampos** and the **German Lutheran Hospice of St John**, is where Jesus is said to have addressed the women: "Do not weep for me, weep for Jerusalem." The Via Dolorosa as a street ends here.

To reach the **Ninth Station**, retrace your steps and climb the flight of stairs to the **Ethiopian Coptic Church**. There's a pillar inside the entrance that marks where Jesus fell the third time.

Past that pillar, you will come onto one of the most serendipitious sites in Jerusalem. Here is a generous courtyard on the top of the Church of the Holy

Pilgrims pass the "Holy Fire" at Easter.

128

Sepulchre: the dome you see in the middle of the terrace is actually the roof of the **Chapel of St Helena**, where it's believed the cross was found. The **Ethiopian Village** up here is literally out of this world – an African village transported to the midst of a bustling metropolis.

The last five stations are inside the **Church of the Holy Sepulchre** itself. As you enter the Church follow the stairs to the right to the rocky hill lock over which this edifice was erected. It is called **Calvary** in the Latin tradition, **Golgotha** in Greek tradition. Golgotha is actually the Hebrew world for skull and this place was so named because of the Christian belief that Adam was buried here and that a drop of Jesus's blood fell upon Adam's skull.

Up here are four stations: in the Catholic room on the right is the **Tenth Station**, a floor mosaic that marks where Jesus was forced to strip off his clothes; behind the altar you will find the **11th Station**, a mosaic that indicates the spot where Jesus was nailed to the cross; in the Greek Orthodox room on the left is the **12th Station**, where the cross was fixed and Jesus died; outside of the room, a statue of Mary wearing a diamond and gold crown represents the **13th Station**, where she took Jesus into her arms.

Down the stairs is the **14th Station**, the **Holy Sepulchre** itself, where Jesus was laid to rest. Inside the rotunda it is the miracle rock that was said to have rolled away from the entrance to the tomb. The holes you see in the tomb itself is where the Greek Orthodox Bishop receives the "Holy Fire" from God on Easter every year.

Also underneath the rotunda is the **Angel's Chapel**, so called because when Mary Magdalene came to visit Jesus's grave on Sunday after the crucifixion, she saw no trace of his body, but rather an angel perched on a stone altar.

At the rear of the sepulchre, there is a small, but important chapel that belongs to the Copts, their only "possession" in

Olivewood images of Jesus and Mary.

the Church. On the other side of the sepulchre is a bulky Greek Orthodox cathedral called the **Cathlicon**. The Greeks believe that the chalice on the floor is the centre of the world.

As you follow the stairs down to the lower part of the church, you will see a vast number of crosses etched into the walls. At the bottom is the Armenian's **Chapel of St Helena**, whose dome we noted from above on the terrace of the Ethiopian compound. The contemporary floor mosaic is an Armenian Genocide memorial.

Farther down, there is the **Chapel of the Finding of the Cross**, where Queen Helena discovered the True Cross. Remember that she actually found three crosses – one that had been used to crucify Jesus, the other two used for a couple of thieves.

How did she know which was which? According to one tradition, at least, it is said that the queen touched a dead baby with each cross, and it was the True Cross that restored the child to life.

Be sure to look at the stones which are in the cave. Archaeologists now believe that the stones from this very quarry were the ones that were wheeled into the Old City and used to build the Temple Mount and perhaps to build Herod's Temple.

Just south of the church is the **Mosque of Omar**, where the Caliph came to pray when his armies conquered Jerusalem. It is said that the Byzantine patriarch at the time invited him to pray at the Church of the Holy Sepulchre, but the Caliph did not want to dignify it or Christianity and so chose this spot. The minaret went up in 1417.

Leaving the Church of the Holy Sepulchre plaza, to the southeast you will see a sleek and elegant tower that makes up part of the **Church of the Redeemer**.

Built on the ruins of a Crusader Church, this German Lutheran building was dedicated on the occasion of Kaiser Wilhelm II's visit to Jerusalem. The view from the belfry is about the best you'll get in the Old City and the occasional concert here is another draw.

Opposite the church is what is known as the **Muristan Quarter**. The name is Persian for hospital and this is where the hospitals and hospices were in Crusader and, some say, Byzantine times. During Roman rule it was the site of a forum; today it is a rather unremarkable little bazaar.

The **Eastern Orthodox Church of St James** is northwest of the Church of the Holy Sepulchre. The nearby **Greek Orthodox Patriarchate**, on the road by that name, is an entire complex that includes, most notably, a library with fragments of the Dead Sea Scrolls, and a **museum** that displays several archaeological finds from the Old City.

Technically, the **Christian Quarter**, as this entire area is called, starts at the **New Gate**, which is new by Jerusalem standards, having been opened in 1887.

Should you overdose on churches, as any tourist is inclined to do in this particular city, you might well note that it is the quickest point of egress too.

Left, a 3rd-century pilgrims's drawing. **Right**, the 14th Station of the Cross – Jesus's tomb.

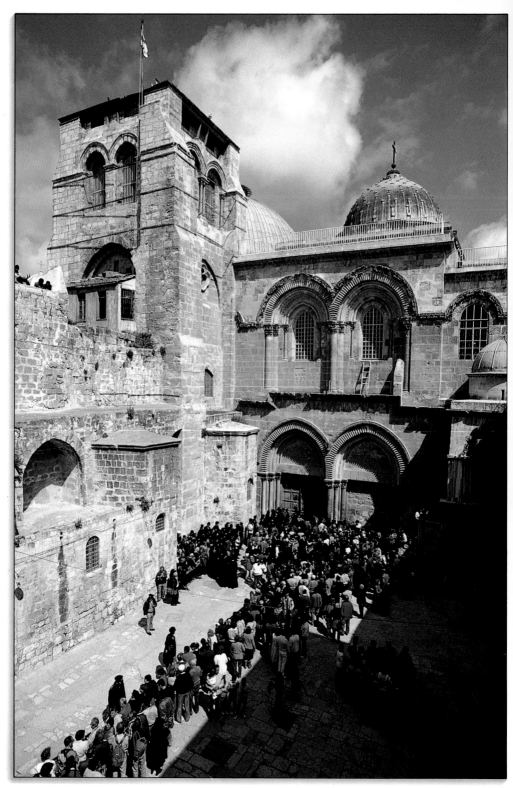

CHURCH OF THE HOLY SEPULCHRE

When in AD326 Constantine's mother Queen Helena started exploring Jerusalem assisted by a bishop (so she said) as her guardian angel, she came upon a Temple of Venus, which was built by Hadrian. The Roman Emperor, she surmised, must have put his pagan edifice on top of a holy one, and when she discovered a crypt and three crosses, she was sure it was where Jesus had been crucified.

The original Church built by her son, Emperor Constantine, must have been truly magnificent for it was twice the size of the church we see today. It was destroyed by the Persians three centuries later. Its replacement was the victim of an earthquake one century later in AD746. The fiercest of about 50 earthquakes that have rocked the place during its history. The church we see today is a Crusader church built in its place, and it is one of the oldest standing buildings in Jerusalem.

For the Western Christian pilgrim coming upon it for the first time, the church has a very definite Eastern, exotic aura, which reflects how little the place has changed in the past 800 years. Such may well have been what made the English General Gordon so uncomfortable during his visit here in the 1840s. General Gordon rejected the church as Jesus's burial place and established the Protestant site as the Garden Tomb near what is today the East Jerusalem bus station.

An amateur historian and archaeologist, General Gordon said that Jewish cemeteries were always outside city walls and this Holy Sepulchre was not. What he did not realize is that in Jesus's time, it may well have been outside the city walls, since the current wall outline was established after the crucifixion.

Of course, when General Gordon made his visit, the Protestants had no "possessions" inside the church, those having been apportioned to the various Christian sects before the Reformation. The church is divided between six such sects, and each believes it should rightfully control the entire complex. This has been the source of an ongoing acrimonious struggle between them, which until a recent rapprochment has caused the church to fall into a terrible disrepair. Who shall dust this archway, who shall fix these steps?

The most fascinating time to visit the Church is during the Greek festival of Easter week. The festival culminates in an extraordinary event. On Easter Eve, the "Holy Fire" descends from heaven in the Chapel of the Sepulchre. Thousands of pilgrims from all over the world gather to light their candles at the flame as it shoots forth from the grave of Jesus Christ.

The fire itself is not considered dangerous; the faithful are convinced that it will do them no harm. However, many pilgrims have lost their lives in their struggle to fulfil their faith.

Left, outside the church. Right, where Christ lay in the Holy Sepulchre.

MOUNT ZION

Nobody knows exactly where the real Mount Zion is. What is today called Mount Zion was in Temple times simply the Upper City of Jerusalem, where the affluent families in town lived. This particular hill probably got its name when it was left outside the walls of the Roman city of Aelia Capitolina. Legend has it that Suleiman the Magnificent had his architects beheaded for following the Roman example in excluding this place from the confines of the Turkish city walls.

Whatever its history, Mount Zion acquired a certain symbolic significance as the heart of the Jewish homeland and gave its name to the political movement that eventually recaptured Jerusalem and all of Israel.

The place to start is **Zion Gate** at the end of the Armenian Quarter. Structurally, the gate was built at a right angle so the onrushing invader would be vulnerable at the turn. Also you will note the slats above the gate, from which hot oil can be poured on the enemy. The entire portal is pock-marked with bullet holes made by the Israeli forces during an unsuccessful attempt to penetrate it in the 1948 War of Independence.

Head straight from the gate to the second path, and turn right. Just up ahead is the **Diaspora Yeshivah**, a very weird place where Jewish Orthodoxy meets 1960s hippies and which gets savagely satirized in the Phillip Roth novel *The Counterlife*. Just adjacent to it is **King David's Tomb**, though many believe he was actually buried in the City of David. Nevertheless, an enormous number of Jewish pilgrims come here to pray. The tomb served much the way the Western Wall does today during Jordanian rule when the Old City was off limits.

In the back is **Chamber of the Holocaust**, a memorial to the Jews killed in Europe. Desecrated Torah scrolls and yellow stars of shame are on display.

Upstairs from David's Tomb is the **Cenaculum**, a sparse room with vaulting arches where Jesus presumably ate the Passover seder better known as the Last Supper. This is where Jesus also instructed his disciples on the basic points of Christianity and where the apostles – in that Pentecostalist miracle – began speaking in tongues.

Turn right as you leave the Hall of the Last Supper, then proceed along to the left and you will find the **Church of the Dormition**, completed by the German Benedictines in 1910. Recognized on the Jerusalem skyline for its black cone roof, this is where Mary fell into an eternal sleep (or dormition) after the crucifixion. The acoustics in the basilica are splendid for the many classical music concerts presented here.

Nearby in the **Old Protestant Cemetery** lie many British archaeologists, diplomats and missionaries who shaped Jerusalem during the British Mandate and the end of Turkish rule.

Left, the Dormition Abbey on Mount Zion. Right, blowing the shofar at the Tomb of King David.

THE MOUNT OF OLIVES

Once the Mount of Olives was covered with olive trees, but the Romans chopped them down to assemble the war machines they used to destroy Jerusalem in AD70. In ancient times, Jewish pilgrims brought red heifers here for purification on their way to making sacrifices at the Temple. Today, the Mount of Olives is revered by all: Muslims live up here, Jews are buried here, and the story of Jesus is told in the shrines which draw the tourists to this hill daily.

The popular starting point for any tour is at the top, just beneath the **Seven Arches Hotel** – a place that outrages Jews because it was built on the holy Jewish grave sites during Jordanian rule. This is where you can get the obligatory camel shot and a view that is without parallel in the city especially at dawn and dusk.

Even though Jesus walked up this mountain the evening of the Last Supper, it is customary and physically less demanding for visitors to follow another route in the opposite direction.

Take the road to your right to the Carmelite Sisters' cloister, the **Church of the Pater Noster**. Here is where the Lord's Prayer is handsomely calligraphied in 63 different languages on the courtyard walls.

Also on the property are the ruins of the Byzantine **Eleona Church** that marks the secret cave where Queen Helena said Jesus taught his controversial doctrine at a safe distance from both the Romans and Jews.

Outside the Pater Noster on the right is the **Chapel of Ascension,** the traditional site where Jesus rose to heaven 40 days after his resurrection. On this, the highest point on the mountain, the Crusaders rebuilt an earlier Byzantine edifice and for a time the Muslims converted it into a mosque. Inside, the supposed footprint of Jesus is preserved. On the Christian Feast of the Ascension,

Preceding pages: ancient olive trees in the Garden of Gethsemane. Left, Jewish cemetery, Mount of Olives. Below, domes of the Russian Orthodox Church.

138

most sects gather here. The Russian Orthodox Church, however, believes Jesus rose from the place marked by their steepled **Church of the Ascension** and **Russian Monastery** very close by.

Now backtrack to the hotel and take the path leading down the mountain along the famous **Jewish cemetery** where one can still be buried at the cost of as much as $50,000 a plot. The price is expensive because Jewish tradition says that when the Messiah comes to Jerusalem, he will sweep across the Mount of Olives, gather the dead here and enter the Old City through the **Gate of Mercy.**

Actually the Jews and Christians agree the Messiah will appear through these **Golden Gates,** as they're also known. You can see the gates just across the Kidron Valley. You might also notice in the valley the Muslim cemetery strategically positioned in front of the gates just in case the Messiah comes and resurrects the dead. On your left as you descend the hill, are the **Tombs of the Prophets**, caves where Haggai and Malachi rest.

Nearby is an orange sign that calls your attention to a **Mass Grave,** where the heroic last defenders of the Jewish Quarter in 1948 were moved after Israel regained the city and the Mount of Olives in 1967. Many of the other graves you see were desecrated during Jordanian rule; tombstones were carted away and used to build everything from homes to latrines.

Ancient burial grounds: Was this ground used for burial in the time of Solomon, perhaps even Abraham? Take the path to your right, you will discover an ancient **Jewish Necropolis** that has led some archaeologists to this conclusion.

In ancient times, the dead were wrapped in shrouds and then placed in small niches for 11 months, after which time their bones were put in boxes called ossuaries which were as wide as a skull bone and as long as the thigh bone.

Continue along this side path to the

Easter procession starts on the Mount of Olives.

Franciscan **Basilica of Dominus Flevit**, an architectural gem designed by the Italian architect Antonio Barluzzi in 1956 and built on the ruins of a Crusader church.

The chapel is supposed to be shaped like a tear because it marks the place where Jesus cried over the future destruction of Jerusalem. One can almost imagine Jesus gazing on the Temple as he wept. You shouldn't miss the view of the Mount from inside the chapel as it is one of the best in the city.

Further down the mountain is the Russian **Church of Mary Magdalene**, which distinguishes the Jerusalem skyline with its golden onion-shaped domes. The church was built by the czar in grand Russian style in the late 19th century. It is said that the crypt inside contains some of the hearts of the royal Romanov family which was brutally murdered in the Russian Bolshevik Revolution.

Route of Jesus: Next you come to **Gethsemane**, the garden where Jesus prayed after the Last Supper before being betrayed by Judas Iscariot. The original Hebrew name, *Gat Shemanim*, means "olive tree press" and, for whatever it's worth, the olive trees themselves have been carbon-dated, revealing themselves to be as old as the saviour. Unfortunately, because so many pilgrims have ripped off whole tree branches to bring back home with them, the garden itself has been roped off.

If you follow the path through, you arrive at the **Church of All Nations** (also known as Basilica of the Agony), a Catholic institution which was also designed by Barluzzi, in 1926, and built on the ruins of a Crusader Church.

The Crusader Church was itself built on the ruins of a Byzantine one. Barluzzi used stained glass and purple alabaster and put stars on the ceiling to simulate the night-time (because it was said to be evening here when Jesus arrived to ask God why he had to suffer and die). The front of the church is beautiful, aside from those weird creatures on the roof.

Camels are a common sight.

Did Barluzzi really think that reindeer lived in Jerusalem?

Below the garden, at the bottom of the mountain, you finally come to **Mary's Tomb,** a candle-lit cave controlled by the Greek Orthodox and Armenian churches. It was preserved during Muslim times as a mosque because the Islamic tradition also venerates Mary. Notice once again the way to the tomb was hacked away by greedy little pilgrims over the centuries. Is there not a town in Europe that doesn't claim to have a piece of the cave at its municipal museum? Some say that Mary's parents are buried on the right of the cave's entrance, Joseph on the left.

The bridge leading back up to the Old City is known as the **Bridge of Blood** because it was here that Israeli soldiers lost their way one night in the Six Day War and were sitting ducks before the Jordanian army.

Kidron Valley: Before going this direction, you may want to follow the upper portion of the Kidron Valley, also known as the Valley of Jehosaphat, to three more intriguing grave sites. Shaped like a stocking cap is **Absalom's Pillar,** which probably marks the grave of someone very rich and important, but who lived at least 1,000 years after the time of David's rebellious son.

Someone in the Middle Ages had found an important grave, saw that it was near the City of David, and pointed to Absalom's name in the Bible. This is how arbitrarily many places were so dedicated in Jerusalem.

Next to the pillar are the **Tomb of Zachariah** and the **Tomb of Hezir**, part of the same 1st-century cemetery. According to Jewish law they needed to be placed outside the walls of the city.

The Kidron Valley here is now a garbage dump. However, above you on the left is the boisterous Arab town called **Silwan**. Solomon, it is said, gave the town to his wife, Pharaoh's daughter, by political treaty as a wedding present so that she could worship idols upon it.

Tomb of Zachariah in the Kidron Valley.

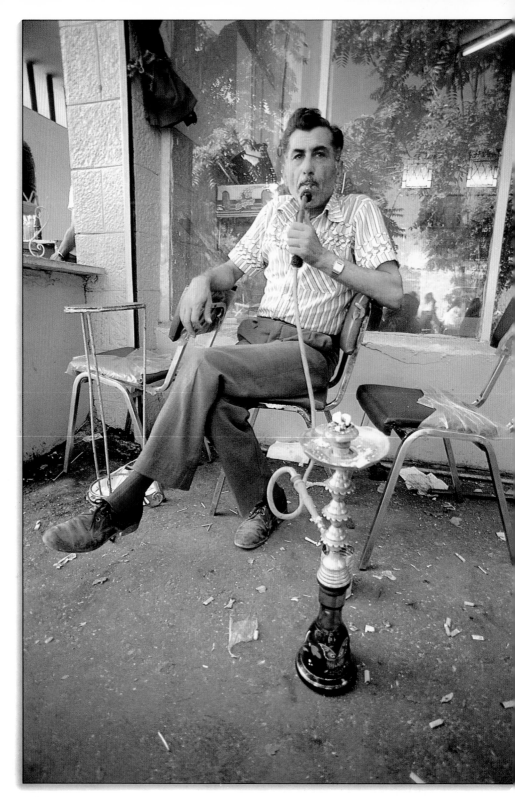

EAST JERUSALEM

The Israelis may believe they "reunified" Jerusalem in 1967, but in truth the city remains bitterly divided. Arab East Jerusalem has its own food, music, and pace of life; its own banks, buses, utility companies, and newspapers. It is largely made up of middle-class Christian Arabs, many of whom understandably complain about the sky-high municipal taxes they must pay, given that Israeli Jerusalem provides them with few services. Although Arabs go daily into West Jerusalem – to work, to shop, to travel – Jews scarcely ever venture into East Jerusalem.

For the traveller, however, East Jerusalem should not be missed. One can hardly understand the nature of the current controversies without a visit. The best time to visit is on Saturday, when West Jerusalem closes down. (The Muslim day of rest is Friday.)

For sightseeing, remember, if the Via Dolorosa is an endless row of churches, East Jerusalem is Sarcophagus City. Just north of the city walls, it must have been one of the most popular places in ancient times to bury important and influential people.

The road from Damascus to Jerusalem ends at the **Damascus Gate,** far and away the most impressive port of entry to the Old City. It serves as the hub of Jerusalem's Arab community, leading toward the Muslim Quarter in the Old City and facing Palestinian East Jerusalem outside it. The area in front of the gate is a favourite meeting place. It contains a refiguration of an ancient Muslim drinking fountain, what is known as a **sabil.** Underneath the gate is the **Roman Square Museum,** which highlights the city in Roman times.

Across the way is the **East Jerusalem Bus Station,** where you can catch a bus to Arab towns on the West Bank. Above the bus station is the **Garden Tomb** (open Mon–Sat 8am–1pm and 3.30pm–5pm), which the Protestants believe to be the true place where Jesus was laid to rest. In 1867, when Britain's General Gordon visited Jerusalem, he concluded that Jesus couldn't have been entombed in the traditionally accepted site, the Church of the Holy Sepulchure. Number one, the place didn't feel right to him. Number two, he knew that according to Jewish custom, Jesus's grave had to be outside the city walls, and – at least at the time of Gordon's visit – the Holy Sepulchre was inside the Old City. During his trip, Gordon lodged in East Jerusalem, and one morning, looking out of his hotel window, he spied a piece of land that looked like a skull, which is how **Golgotha** is described in the gospels. To him, it was a revelation. When a grotto was indeed found on this spot, the Protestants were certain they'd located the real Calvary.

Next to the bus station is **Jeremiah's Grotto,** supposedly the spot where this prophet composed his Lamentations on the fall of Jerusalem. Back across **Suleiman Street** is the **Cave of Zedekiah,**

where mean, foolish King Zedekiah fled from the Babylonian invaders, all the way to Jericho. (Whereupon his pursuers caught him, forced him to watch his family murdered, and then made him poke his own eyes out.)

Follow Suleiman Street west to the **Rockefeller Museum** (open Sun–Thurs 10am–5pm, Fri/Sat 10am–2pm), a white building with the commanding octagonal tower. It's perched on the hill the Crusaders used as a launch point for their invasion of Jerusalem in 1099.

In 1967, the Israeli Defence Forces made similar use of it to retake the Old City. The museum itself was financed by archaeology enthusiasts in the Rockefeller family and was built during the British Mandate.

Heading back toward the bus station, turn right at **Salah ed-Din,** and follow it past the **Albright Institute** and the Anglican **St George's Cathedral** (modelled on Oxford colleges) to the major intersection with **Shechem.** Here you may enter the **Tomb of the Kings.** This

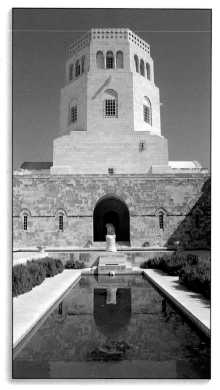

is the burial place of Queen Helena of Adiabene (in Mesopotamia) who, along with her children, converted to Judaism and travelled to Jerusalem in 45. She became a heroine when, during a famine, she procured necessary foodstuffs from foreign lands.

Continue down Shechem to the **American Colony Hotel,** a grand Muslim mansion with a peaceful courtyard that has been a haven for foreign dignitaries for more than a century. The American Colony was founded here in 1881 by the Spaffords of Chicago. After their four daughters drowned in a tragic boating accident, they moved here and dedicated their lives to helping the poor. Several tours of East Jerusalem start from here and the hotel nightclub bar offers entertainment from jazz musicians to belly dancers.

The best restaurants in the area to try are **Philadelphia, Dallas,** and **Sea Dolphin,** the last of which is an especially popular place jointly owned by an Arab and a Jew.

If you continue north, before you come to the Arab neighbourhood of **Sheik Jarrah,** you may follow a narrow road (Othman Ben-Afan) to the right to the **Tomb of Simon the Just,** which marks the burial place of the venerable High Priest of the Jews at the time of Alexander the Great.

Alexander stormed through Asia and Persia, and was on the verge of reducing Jerusalem to rubble, when – according to one esoteric legend – he was appeased by this Simon. Alexander was plagued by dreams of a wise old man with a long grey beard, and when he beheld Simon the Just coming toward him, he was awestruck – for this was the very man.

Alexander agreed to spare Jerusalem, on condition that a statue of himself be erected in front of the Temple. Since statues were proscribed by Jewish law as forms of idol-worship, Simon came up with another idea. His diplomatic suggestion for a more fitting tribute was that each male child born that year be named after him: Alexander.

Left, the Rockfeller Museum. **Right,** Palestinian potter.

THE NEW CITY

For several millennia, Jerusalem consisted of merely a few acres, and even those must have seemed very small, surrounded as they were by a fortress-like wall. Today the city sprawls over an eclectic collection of neighbourhoods covering some 40 miles (64 km). Together they comprise the "New City", and by Jerusalem standards they are very new indeed, having sprung up just since the mid-19th century.

At that time, the Jews – many of them recent *Ashkenazi* immigrants from the Pale of Settlement – made up nearly half of Jerusalem's population of 15,000. And yet they were all crammed into the then filthy, disease-ridden Jewish Quarter, which made up only one-tenth of the area of the Old City.

Still, the idea of moving outside the Old City was unthinkable. There was a pervasive fear of the Bedouin and outlaw tribes lurking in what is today the New City of Jerusalem, but was then considered "wilderness". Nobody wanted to be caught outside the Old City when its gates were locked at the end of the day.

So, in the 1860s when Moses Montefiore, a secular, aristocratic Jew from England, and Yosef Rivlin, a religious Jerusalem-born Jew, began building neighbourhoods beyond the gates, they met considerable resistance. Many thought them crazy. It is said that when Rivlin began sleeping outside the Old City, his friends and relatives would dash over to his place each morning expecting to find him dead and his home pillaged.

His "survival" day by day allayed his community's fears. Anxiety or no, Jerusalem simply had to expand – there was no longer enough space in the old Jew-

Preceding pages: a neighbourhood playground; view of the New City. **Right**, Hebrew University campus.

ish Quarter to accommodate all the new immigrants. By the end of World War I and the start of the British Mandate, Jerusalem's population was 55,000, and by the end of World War II, it was more that 140,000.

Still, when Jerusalem was "reunified" in June, 1967, after the Six Day War, it didn't radiate any air of significance. Its most glorious neighbourhoods were abandoned and disfigured for having been caught on the border and its growth was stunted by its isolation from the rest of Israel.

When the Israelis resumed control of all of Jerusalem, they began a veritable building boom, putting up whole neighbourhoods especially to accommodate the vast numbers of North African and Middle Eastern Jews who'd arrived in Israel since 1948.

Given Jerusalem's grand architectural traditions, most of the recent housing structures are miserable failures. It has been said they resemble military garrets more than residences, but perhaps this expresses – even more than editorials in right-wing newspapers – how Jerusalemites feel about their condition here.

The saving grace of the architectural landscape is a 1918 decree made by the British High Commissioner. He said that, henceforth, no new building could go up in Jerusalem that wasn't made from its indigenous golden white Jerusalem stone. Even where old meets new, therefore, the city bears a striking consistency in tone and texture.

There are several places in the New City to capture a broad view of Jerusalem: the YMCA tower, the City Tower, the Hill of Evil Council, and Mount Scopus – all described later. As you scan the Jerusalem skyline, you will note that most of the skyscrapers – such as the City Tower, the Sheraton Hotel, the King Solomon Hotel and the Holiday Inn – are in strict violation of the city's building codes against such heights.

For a time in the tourist industry boom following 1967, the municipal govern-

ment was handing out exemptions like they were going out of style – all in the name of helping the economy. Citizen outrage prevailed for a while, but in the early 1990s construction of high-rise buildings began again.

A useful introduction to Jerusalem – a way to gain your bearings – is a special city bus (number 99) called the **Circle Line**, so named because it takes you on a circle of the city. The bus leaves from the Jaffa Gate every hour on the hour, and makes 34 stops at some of the major sites throughout the town.

The other municipal buses, while not catering exclusively to tourists, go everywhere and are cheap if weekly or monthly multi-ride tickets are purchased. The **Central Bus Station** is on Jaffa Road on the Western rim of city. Remember: taxi drivers may well rip you off unless you demand they turn on the meter when you get in.

Getting around: Walking around Jerusalem is no easy trick, though the downtown area of West Jerusalem is fairly

compact. The heart of it is formed by a triangle between **King George Street** (Hamelekia George) **Jaffa Road** (Yafo) and the **Ben Yehuda Mall**. This area is offered up in stark contrast to the solemnity of the Old City.

If the latter has captured the foreign traveller's imagination for centuries, the former is capable of showing you a hardy, living city that's grown, quite spectacularly, out of a dying one.

Modern Moses, new neighbourhood: An appropriate place to start your tour of the "New City" is at its oldest and most famous landmark, the **Montefiore Windmill,** that conical, four-blade structure that wouldn't know how to turn if a tornado hit it. Built in 1858, it was meant to provide a source of employment for the city's burgeoning Jewish community.

It was never of much use until the 1948 war, when it served as an observation post. The top of the windmill was blown up by the British in what the Jews facetiously described as "Operation Don Quixote". Today the windmill houses a small museum dedicated to the life of its builder, Sir Moses Montefiore, a visionary Jewish philanthropist from England, and to the neighbourhood that sprang up here.

When Montefiore visited Jerusalem in the middle of the 19th century, he was appalled at the deplorable living conditions of Jews in the Old City. At first he wanted to build a hospital here, but then, with the encouragement of wealthy benefactors and the permission of the Turkish Sultan, he set about building the first Jewish Quarter outside the city walls. When it was finished in 1860, he called it **Mishkenot Sha'ananim,** which literally means "Dwellings of Tranquillity". It looked like a long, squat rampart, and indeed it was well-sealed to protect its inhabitants. Even so, the Jews were so fearful of the "wilderness" (as this area was regarded) in those days, that it took a solid decade before anyone decided to live there.

Today the Jerusalem Foundation op-

Shops and galleries of Hutzot Hayotzer.

erates Mishkenot Sha'ananim as an artists' colony, a subsidized guest house which has been used by such celebrities as Saul Bellow, Joan Didion, Arthur Rubinstein, and Isaac Stern.

Below the windmill, is the **Jerusalem Music Centre** – a respected recording studio – and the **Mishkenot Sha'ananim Restaurant,** which offers a kosherized version of the French high-cuisine and a splendid view.

In 1892, Montefiore expanded the quarter on the adjacent plot of land, **Yemin Moshe,** which you can see as you follow the European-styled red terracotta roofs north. Like Mishkenot Sha'ananim, during the partition period Yemin Moshe fell on the Jordanian-Israeli armistice line, or "green line" as it was called, and as a consequence it also fell into terrible disrepair. After "reunification", the indigent Jewish tenants who braved the no-man's land conditions were bought off by the city government and the entire quarter was gentrified. In moved the chic artists and affluent families, as the neighbourhood quickly became the most prestigious address in the city.

At the end of Yemin Moshe, follow stairs down to **Hutzot Hayotzer,** or the Arts and Crafts Lane. Here several Jerusalem artisans sell directly from their studios – jewelers, silversmiths, sculptors, and potters. At the end of the lane is a mediocre, but conveniently located Chinese restaurant. Also nearby is the **Mitchell Garden,** a quiet, sunny spot.

Next to it, and directly below Yemin Moshe, is the **Sultan's Pool,** which now serves as a concert park. It was originally designed as a reservoir to store rainwater, stopping the flow down the valley to the Dead Sea. Sultan Suleiman the Magnificent renovated it, and thus it took his name. Today, the Sultan's Pool is where stars such as Bob Dylan appear on stage, coming to light up and rock Jerusalem.

Sinner's valley: Curving south and west from Sultan's Pool is the **Valley of Hinnom.** A valley that cuts a wide

Concert at the Sultan's Pool.

swathe between the New City and the Old City, it has long been recognized as the physical location of hell itself. *Gai Hinnon* (Hebrew) is where the false-god Moloch stood, arms outstretched, demanding child sacrifices. It is said that fire rose from Moloch's belly, which perhaps explains what the Torah means when it says that the foul King Menasseh made his own children pass through fire here. It is from this, finally, that the valley became known as the place where sinners burn – *gehenom,* or simply hell.

As the Valley of Hinnom has become a centre for Jerusalem secular culture, Orthodox Jews today might still regard it (albeit with a sardonic smile) as a place where sinners go. There is, of course, the Sultan's Pool, but the real cultural nerve centre is the small building just above it, the **Cinemateque.** In this film-crazy town, movies are prized on both an aesthetic level and as a means of escape, and people flock here – sometimes, despite Orthodox Jewish protests on Shabbat – from all over.

Upstairs, the Cinemateque Cafe is where the chic Yerushalmi sip oversweet coffee and eat rich pastries while discussing Fellini and Clint Eastwood. Sit on the patio overlooking the Old City long enough, and you may be deceived into thinking that Jerusalem is really a peaceful place, that it can be just like any other city.

Below the Cinemateque, on the bridge that leads you across the Valley of Hinnom, you can see yet another **sabil,** a Turkish water fountain built by Suleiman. Above the Cinemateque, **Derekh Hevron** is the road that takes you to that embattled city. Just on your left is a row of overpriced restaurants that sell the view more than the food.

Across the street is a unique institution called the **House of Quality.** The government awards various artists with a seal of approval and studio space in this charming old converted eye clinic.

If you're in the shopping mood, the gallery downstairs sells their crafts but more worthwhile is a tour around the

Reflections of the New City – banks and beggars.

building – take time to talk to the artists or watch them at work.

The stone structure on the hill behind the House of Quality with a white dome and a blue-and-white Scottish flag on the top is the **St Andrew's Church,** built after World War I to commemorate the Scottish soldiers who died in combat. It was named for the Galilean fisherman who became the patron saint of Scotland. Here you will also find a memorial to King Robert Bruce, whose final request – that his heart be transported to Jerusalem – was not ultimately honoured, the organ having been buried in Spain when the courier was killed by Moors en route.

On the other side of the church is the **Railway Station,** which has been in operation since 1892, when the Turks laid tracks between Jaffa and Jerusalem, the first train route in Palestine. Today, however, the bus is far and away the preferred means of transportation in Israel. The late 19th-century *khan* down the block once served as a storehouse for cargo coming in by train. It has since been converted into the **Khan Theatre,** a respected cultural centre that serves as home to the Jerusalem Repertory Company.

King David Street: On your right, as you leave the Khan, you will pass the **British Consulate** before you come to **King David Street (Hamelech David).** Across the way is the **Liberty Bell Garden,** which offers a range of free athletic and cultural activities throughout the summer – especially notable is the annual book fair. The **Train Theatre** here puts on puppet shows.

As you continue along King David, on your left is the headquarters for the **Jerusalem Foundation.** This is a private institution which has poured $200 million into various urban renewal projects. One such effort is the **Bloomfield Garden** on your right. If you duck into this pleasant park at Abba Sikra, you will come to **Herod's Family Tomb.** You will recall that the paranoid-schizophrenic king was from an

Getting immunized at a local hospital.

ancestral line of Edomites, who'd been forcibly circumcised and made to worship the Jewish God.

Herod's wife Miriamne, however, was of the Hasmonean family, descended from Judah the Maccabee. When Herod became afraid – however irrational it was – that the Jewish people might rally around his young sons or some future offspring his wife might bear him, he slaughtered all three of them, and perhaps, feeling some compunction, had them buried in this very cave.

Further down on King David Street is the grand **King David Hotel**, the most prestigious hotel in the Middle East, where Jimmy Carter, Anwar Sadat, and Henry Kissinger stayed when they came to Jerusalem. The long odds on prospects for permanent peace in the region can be surmised by walking into the lobby. Here you will often find a host of world leaders and would-be diplomats clucking about and popping aspirin: their "missions" in Jerusalem test the limits of diplomacy to destruction.

Built in 1931, the hotel served for a time as a British base of command. It was during this period, in 1946, that the Irgun guerrillas, led by Menachem Begin, set off a bomb that killed 91 and destroyed the southwest part of the building, evidence of which you can still see today. The guerrillas blamed the British for disregarding their warnings and failing to evacuate the building in time. The top two floors are the most recent additions to the hotel. It has style, an old-world ambience, and beautiful gardens overlooking the city.

The tower across the street is part of the **YMCA**, built in the early 1930s by the power-tower architecture firm of Shreve, Lamb & Harmon, the same people who wrought the Empire State Building. From the top, it presents a spectacular view of Jerusalem.

The YMCA is a moderately-priced and an exceedingly convenient place to set up your lodgings. The cafeteria is a favorite meeting spot and the **YMCA Auditorium** is the home of the Israel

The King David Hotel dominates the hill.

Chamber Orchestra. And weekly choral and chamber music concerts are scheduled here.

All along King David Street are car rental places. During the off-peak season, you can usually do pretty well bargaining, but generally expect these agencies to pass along to you the high rates they have to pay insurance companies. For obvious reasons, Israel is not considered a low risk country.

On the right side of King David Street is the **Hebrew Union College**, an outpost of the American-based Reform Judaism movement. In recent years, the college has been sponsoring more activities for visitors, desperately trying to compete with their Orthodox counterparts for the souls and minds of wandering young Jews. But the truth is, the Reform movement is not too strong in Israel.

Mamilla: At the intersection of King David and **Mamilla Road** is a paean to those dreaded taxes, the **Taxation Museum**. (Only in Jerusalem!) You can head straight toward the downtown area, or follow Mamilla to the right. This was once one of Jerusalem's biggest commercial centres.

The massive structure on your left is the **St Vincent de Paul Hospice**, and on your right is the **Stern House**. A plaque here marks the spot where the young Viennese journalist and crusading Zionist Theodore Herzl, author of the visionary *Alteneuland* ("Old-New Land"), stayed during his brief pilgrimage to Jerusalem in 1898. *(For more on Herzl, see page 158.)*

Like Montefiore before him, Herzl was not favorably impressed with Jerusalem. "The musty deposits of 2,000 years of inhumanity, intolerance, and foulness lie in your [Jerusalem's] reeking alleys," he wrote. "If Jerusalem is ever ours I would begin by cleaning it up."

If the Mamilla neighbourhood underwent improvements after Herzl's visit, it fell completely apart during the partition period (1948–67), a border area

A Shabbat stroll in Independence Park.

cum war zone abandoned by all the old merchants. The neighbourhood has now been revitalised and includes a new Hilton, luxury apartments and underground parking for the Old City

To The "Estate of Seven": Mamilla Road takes you down to the Jaffa Gate and the Old City. If you head back from where you came, King David Street branches off to the left to **Hillel Street**. On your left is a **Muslim Cemetery**, and within it the **Mamilla Pool**, an ancient rainwater cistern. Some speculate that the name derives from the Arabic *mayah min Allah,* meaning "water from God".

As you continue, the cemetery turns into the **Independence Park**, where families take afternoon strolls on Shabbat and where young couples issue their mating calls every other day of the week. This is Jerusalem's largest park.

A legend began here in the Middle Ages about a friendly lion, whose cave was shown to pilgrims of various religions. In this cave the lion gathered and protected the bodies of religious martyrs so that they would not be destroyed or abused by animals or vandals. At a northwest entry to the park are three undulating columns by the renowned Dadaist sculptor Jean Arp.

On the right side of Hillel Street is the **Italian Synagogue,** an elaborate building built in 1719 and moved here from a small town near Venice in 1952. But before you come to the synagogue, there is an ugly and unremarkable building, the **Beit Agron**, which houses the government press office.

Behind Beit Agron is **Rivlin Street**, named for the great 19th-century neighbourhood-builder Rabbi Yossef Rivlin. Like his secular counterpart Moses Montefiore, Rivlin was sickened by the yishuv ghetto conditions in the Old City, and he too set about starting a settlement outside it.

By the late 1860s, he was one of seven ambitious young Eastern European Jews who collectively bought a small piece of land here specifically for the purpose of moving out of the city walls and

Famous Café Atara on the Midrahov.

building a new neighbourhood. They called it, straightforwardly enough, **Nahalat Shiva**, or The Estate of Seven. Houses were built first, then synagogues and workshops.

Little is left of the neighbourhood today, though one can gather from the narrow old alleyways, such as Rivlin and Salomon Streets, some idea of how it was set up. The arrival of a pedestrian mall in 1990 began the area's modern renaissance and today, tucked away in the recently renovated car-free neighbourhood, are several nightclubs and some of the most extraordinary restaurants in Jerusalem. It's a district well worth exploring.

Zion Square: Follow Salomon Street up to **Zion Square** (**Kikar Tzion**), where all things and all people meet in downtown Jerusalem. The square earned its name from either the Zion Cinema, which was razed here some time ago, or from the fact that zealous young Zionists would gather here for political rallies before statehood. That seven-storey

Café scene on Ben Yehudah Mall.

cement and glass monstrosity you see here today is called **Beit Yoel**, and represents one of the few subjects upon which everyone in Jerusalem can agree upon: *Never again!*

Zion Square leads into the **Ben Yehudah Pedestrian Mall**, the lifeline of secular Jewish Jerusalem, where the café scene gets into full swing, and where the young especially come to see and to be seen. On Saturday nights, after Shabbat, the place is packed wall to wall with people.

For a pleasant detour away from the mall madness, go back to Zion Square and head up Jaffa Road one block to HaRav Kook Street, and turn left. Tucked away at the end of the block is the **Ticho House**, which operates a couple of small museums and a peaceful café overlooking a soothing public garden. The building itself is the recently restored turn-of-the-century home of Abraham Ticho, Jerusalem's first eye doctor, and (in later years) Anna Ticho, the artist.

Next door is the **Rav Kook House**, the modest dwelling of the first chief Ashkenazi Rabbi of Palestine. At a time when the conventional wisdom among Orthodox Jews was to reject Zionism outright, Kook was a bridge between the two camps.

Even though Zionism was strictly a secular political movement, Kook believed that it was a healthy impulse. He thought that the cultural or national identification of assimilated Jews might later be transformed into a more profound religious observance.

Back on Jaffa Road, on the left side, just before King George Street, is a beloved Jerusalem institution called **Fefferberg's**, which serves the Yiddish-mama's cooking from the old country. The intersection of Jaffa and King George is the busiest in the city. Jaffa Road itself was paved for Kaiser Wilhelm's trip toward the Jaffa Gate in 1898, and it leads north to the glorious **Mahaneh Yehuda**, the finest outdoor food market in the city. The best time to visit is on Friday morning, when families are buying food for the Shabbat dinner. There are several unassuming, traditional restaurants in the neighbourhood – cheaper, too, for being off the beaten tourist track.

South of Mahaneh Yehuda, in the quaint hillside neighbourhood of **Nahla'ot**, is **Pargod**, a veritable jazz cave, where you'll find the widest spectrum of musicians jamming this side of the Mediterranean.

If, at the Jaffa/King George intersection, you turn right, you'll be heading toward Mea She'arim, which we'll describe in more detail later. Here, you can continue your tour of the downtown area by turning right.

King George V Street: A few paces up, there is another entrance to the Ben Yehudah Mall. Before it are pizza parlours, where young Orthodox Jews hang out, and after it, the **King George Youth Hostel**, which is a sort of hippie central for the foreign traveller.

Still further on your left, where King

Jerusalem by bus.

George meets Hahistadrut, is **Fink's**, an unassuming joint that's reputedly the best bar in Jerusalem. Celebrities from all over the world discreetly make reservations here months in advance, as word of its goulash soup has reached many a far-flung land.

Across the street, go to the top of the **City Tower** for the panoramic view. In front of the City Tower is an Ottoman entranceway and clock that have been preserved long after the building on this spot was destroyed. It's a common meeting place and archaeologists of the future will certainly have a lot to ponder.

A computer terminal outside of the **Ministry of Tourism** is a useful source of information. Directly behind the tourist office is the **Bezalel Academy of Art and Design**, established in 1906, with its popular **Artists' House Café**.

Continuing on King George, just across from the garden, Jerusalem's largest *shul*, the **Yeshurun Synagogue**. Yeshurun was the name by which Moses addressed the 12 tribes of Israel in verse. Behind it is the **Ratisbonne Monastery**, established in 1874 by Alfonso Ratisbone, the founder of the Sisters of Zion.

Further down, the **Hechal Shlomo** is where the powerful Chief Rabbinate of Israel meets. Inside the building, the **Wolfson Museum** presents a collection of Jewish ceremonial objects. Next door, in the **Great Synagogue**, note the 18th-century ark covering the Torah scrolls, which has been transported here from Padau, Italy.

Several free tours of the city's neighbourhoods originate from the Plaza-Sheraton Hotel across the street. At the corner, the **Terra Sancta College** belongs to the Franciscan order, and was borrowed by Hebrew University when Mount Scopus was first made inaccessible in 1948. Diagonally opposite is the Conservative Jewish movement's outpost in Jerusalem, and next to it, on Gershon Agron Street, is the **Alliance Française**, a French cultural centre with a hip café.

Clock tower in downtown Jerusalem.

Rehavia: In the opposite direction, Ramban Street takes you into the heart of **Rehavia** – "God's expanse". Founded along with other secular neighbourhoods during the early days of the British Mandate, it became a magnet for German Jews and some of the great Zionist leaders and intellectuals, who wanted none of the restrictions of the religious enclaves. At 30 Ramban, the Ottoman-style **Ruppin House** was the first home built exclusively by Jewish workers, whom the owner paid in cows.

By the mid-1930s, however, Jewish architects escaping from Nazi Germany began experimenting with more modern styles. Among them, the most talented was Erich Mendelsohn, who designed the bold, minimalist **Schoken Library** at 6 Balfour Street.

The pervasive influence of Mendelsohn's style can be seen as well at the **Prime Minister's House** at 9 Somolenskin, designed by Richard Kauffmann. Among the well-known who set up their homes in Rehavia were Golda Meir, Levi Eshkol and Menachem Ussishkin.

Peculiarly in the midst of all the residential dwellings, there's a large Roman-era crypt on Alfasi Street. Called **Jason's Tomb**, it was discovered quite accidentally during recent building construction.

German Colony: South of Rehavia is the **German Colony**, founded in 1873 by the German Templars, most of whom left during World War II. Today the neighbourhood is one of the city's most diverse and fashionable. Its tree-lined streets do not feel like Jerusalem at all. To the west of the German Colony, you'll find the **Van Leer Foundation**, the **Israeli Academy of Arts and Sciences**, the **Presidential Residence**. Behind them is the **Jerusalem Centre For the Performing Arts**, which serves as an unofficial culture centre. The **Henry Crown Symphony Hall** is the home of the Jerusalem Symphony Orchestra, and the Jerusalem Theatre hosts a wide range of experimental plays and films.

Children dress up for Purim.

Close by is the **L.A. Mayer Museum of Islamic Art** and the **Natural History Museum**.

Zahal Square: Make your way back to just outside the southwestern corner of the Old City, where Jaffa Road meets Shlomo Hamelech Street. Before 1948 it was named Allenby Square, for the British general, and since it's been called **Zahal Square** (**Kikar Tzahal**) to honour the Israeli Defence Forces.

As you head back up Jaffa toward Zion Square, you'll pass **Gan Auster**, a charming little garden. Behind it are located two French hospices, **St Louis** and **Notre Dame de France** and the relatively new **City Hall** building.

Further up on the block, the **Bank Leumi**, was originally built to house the Anglo-Palestine Bank, designed by the renowned modernist architect Erich Mendelsohn, as were several other neighbourhood buildings. Next door is the city's **Central Post Office**. From here you can veer right into an area known as Little Russia.

The Russian Compound.

The Russian Compound: In the 11th century, a determined and devout Russian abbot personally walked from Kiev to Jerusalem, carrying a silver lamp to the Church of the Holy Sepulchre, and his countrymen have been making regular pilgrimages to the Holy City ever since.

By the middle of the 19th century, an increasing number of Russian peasants, especially women, set about this journey. Like the immigrant Jews of their time, however, they quickly learned upon arrival that Jerusalem could be a most uncomfortable and unsafe place to transplant their roots.

Seeking to protect his population here and perhaps to exert more influence in the Holy Land, Czar Alexander II put together a deal in 1860. He bought some land outside the Christian Quarter of the Old City, and the Turkish sultan tossed in a part of it for free.

The Russians initially called these 32 acres "New Jerusalem", however the neighbouring Arabs dubbed it "el-

Moscoobiya". Eventually over time it became known simply as the **Russian Compound**.

When construction began in the 1860s, it represented no less radical a project than the neighbourhoods of Montefiore or Rivlin, though certainly better funded and more grandiose. The new set-up had the effect of encouraging even more pilgrimages than before, so that by the start of World War I, more than 10,000 were making the trip annually, including the Czar's evil adviser Rasputin.

In Russia, Rasputin gave Christianity a bad name, and after the Bolshevik Revolution in 1917, religion itself was scorned as "the opium of the masses". No longer would Russians be permitted to make the Jerusalem pilgrimage, and the priests and nuns already there were effectively cut off from their country. So their joined a kind of Russian Orthodox Church-in-exile, or the "White Russian Church", as it's commonly called.

Occupying the highest ground on the compound is the sculptural green-domed Russian Cathedral, the **Church of the Holy Trinity**. This is said to be where the Assyrians bivouacked during their unsuccessful attack on the Old City in 701BCE, and where Titus's legion did the same before its successful raid 770 years later. Not long after the walled-in Russian Compound was completed did rumours arise in certain anxiety-ridden Ottoman circles that the Russians were planning to use it as a base for an invasion of the Old City.

Today, the cathedral is controlled by the "Red Russian Church", though most of the rest of the compound is owned by the Israelis. The White Russians, however, still maintain jurisdiction over churches on the Mount of Olives and in the Old City.

Opposite the cathedral, notice the massive pillar resting horizontally. It has earned the nickname **Finger of Og**, for the giant ruler of Bashan, whom the Jews killed in ancient times. On a less folkloric level, many believe there was a quarry here 2,000 years ago and that

Street musician in the Russian Compound.

this particular pillar had been prepared for Herod's Temple. It must have broken in the process and left here, only to be found during construction of the Russian Compound.

The two buildings next to the pillar were originally used as pilgrims' hostels, but today serve as the city police station and **Court Building**.

Behind the cathedral, at the back of the complex is another pilgrims' hostel. Today it is called the **Hall of Heroism**, which in a way tells the curious history of the compound in the aftermath of 1917. Throughout the Mandate period, the British occupied the Russian Compound, making it their administrative headquarters. At the end of their rule, it was heavily secured behind barbed wire, earning it the facetious sobriquet "Bevingrad" (after the British Foreign Minister Ernest Bevin). This particular building was converted into a prison where members of the Jewish underground were held. After the British evacuation and Israeli independence, it

Jerusalemites are rarely people of few words.

was further converted into a Hall of Heroism, a museum commemorating the very Jewish underground that was jailed here.

Beyond the Russian Compound on Heleni Hamalka Street is a bulky structure with the stylish turret, which was where the rich Russian pilgrims lodged. It was named the **Sergei Building** for the Czar's son, Prince Sergei Romanov. In the courtyard next to the turret, the Ministry of Agriculture operates a low-key **Farm Tool Museum**.

Here also are the headquarters of the **Israel Nature Preservation Society**, where you can sign up for some superb tours of the nearby desert and mountains. For lunch or dinner, check out the nearby **Pie House**. At night, Monbaz and Heleni Hamalkaia streets in the Russian Compound are the heart of a very lively pub scene from midnight onwards.

Street of the Prophets: Walk north a few blocks to the Street of the Prophets, or **Rehov HaNevi'im**, as it's called in

Hebrew. At the intersection with **Strauss** is the **Israel Centre**, which hosts daily lectures and classes on the Torah and Judaica for English-speaking visitors. (Check the calendar here for other events as well.)

Before reaching the Israel Centre you will come to the **Thabor House**, where the eminent 19th-century German archaeologist-architect Conrad Schick once lived. Some say Schick, a Protestant missionary, was largely responsible for drawing the broad outlines of the Orthodox Jewish Mea She'arim.

Today Schick's residence is the home of the **Swedish Theological Seminary**.

Curling off HaNevi'im is **Ethiopia Street**, so named for its **Ethiopian Church**. As you enter the gates leading to the church courtyard, you will see the Lions of Judah. The Ethiopians believe that King Solomon himself presented this symbol to his lover the Queen of Sheba, a native of that African country.

Opposite the church and monastery is the **Ben Yehudah House**. Eliezer Ben Yehudah was an early Zionist leader and the father of modern Hebrew. He transformed a biblical, mainly written language into a modern, everyday, spoken tongue, and invested in the project a wellspring of nationalist aspirations and political imperatives.

When he moved his family from Lithuania to Palestine, he refused to speak to his own wife in their native Yiddish or Russian, and would respond to her only when spoken to in Hebrew. To understand the radical nature of Ben Yehudah's work, remember that the Orthodox Jewish establishment considered the use of the Holy tongue for secular purposes a sacrilege and branded this man who promoted such a thing a heretic.

Heading east along HaNevi'im, you will pass another curious architectural specimen, the 19th-century **German Probst Building**, which now serves as an ORT Vocational School. If you were to continue along for half a mile, you'd end up in East Jerusalem. The only

The Tourjeman-Post between East and West Jerusalem.

170

passageway linking Jordanian East Jerusalem and Israeli West Jerusalem during the 1948–67 partition period was the **Mandelbaum Gate** near the intersection with Hel Hahandasa. The portal itself having been removed, the site is marked today by a plaque.

The Israeli border during the partition period was fortified here at the **Tourjeman-Post**. A battle-worn, bullet-riddled old building, it has recently been restored and transformed into a multimedia museum dedicated to describing the division of the city. The roof top offers a fine vantage point for viewing both sides of the green line, and the multi-media displays make some sense of the confusing military history of the country.

The old world of Mea She'arim: Shortly before reaching the Tourjeman-Post, you will see the street Shivtei Yisrael on your left. At the corner is the **Ministry of Education and Culture**. As the road branches off into **Mea She'arim Street** you pass the **Jerusalem Gate** entering

the heart of the **Mea She'arim Quarter**. This is the famed ultra-Orthodox Jewish neighbourhood, where modesty in dress is not simply requested, but demanded. Mind the signs: you do not want to roam here in tank-top shirts and bikini bottoms.

Ultra-Orthodox Jews here are called *haredim*, which literally means "the God-fearing". The fur hats, long coats, and earlocks (*peyot*) are carried over from the Eastern European traditions. Women must cover their heads (with scarves and wigs) in strict observance of Jewish law.

The strange language that you hear is Yiddish, an expressive melange of German, Russian, Polish, and Hebrew. These are the people who never accepted Ben Yehudah's proposition that Hebrew should become an everyday spoken language, and so they use it only in their prayers. This seems to be another place in time.

The story of Mea She'arim starts in Lithuania in the later part of the 18th

Aerial view of Mea She'arim.

century. There, in a town called Vilna, a rabbi called the Vilna Gaon (widely regarded as one of the greatest Talmudic sages in Jewish history) told his followers that it was not sufficient merely to wait for the coming of the Messiah. He believed that the Messiah would come only after the Jews had physically returned to Jerusalem and resurrected the Holy City once again from its ashes.

It was this very idea that led an increasing number of Eastern European Jewish families to move to Jerusalem over the next century.

One family's descendant, Rabbi Yosef Rivlin, was largely responsible for building the first religious neighbourhood outside the Old City, Nahalat Shiva. His work understandably sparked a profound dispute among those who still followed the teachings of the Vilna Gaon. They came to Jerusalem to rebuild the city but was the land beyond the walls even considered Jerusalem? If not, wasn't it better to dwell in squalor within the city than live comfortably outside it?

Furthermore, pious Jews feared that the desire for brand-new homes represented an urge toward material comfort, which would (inevitably) trigger a downward spiral of spirituality. This very fear was a tender point in the 1870s, when the tendency toward assimilation among world Jewry was very powerful.

Perhaps it was to protect themselves against the encroaching *haskala*, as these secularizing, modernizing, and assimilationist tendencies were called, that the zealous Jews of Jerusalem finally built their own neighbourhood. They constructed Mea She'arim to resemble a walled-in fortress, one that effectively isolated them from the outside world and the temptations of their time, but also kept them close to their places of worship.

Established in 1874, Mea She'arim could only be entered through various gates, traditionally said to be 100 in number. Thus the name Mea She'arim, which literally means 100 Gates. So fearful were these Jews of the modern **The *haredim* of Mea She'arim.**

world that they banned Yosef Rivlin from sermonizing in the very neighbourhood he built.

The best way to tour Mea She'arim is simply to roam around it, to peek in the numerous synagogues and yeshivot, to stop in the kosher bakeries and to wander about the markets.

Continuing along Mea She'arim Street, you will come to the **Northern Gate**, also known as Mohammed's Gate for a Muslim who once guarded it.

On your right, in the beautiful, peaceful courtyard below, are the "Hungarian Homes" of the **Beit Ungarin Quarter**, which was established in the 1880s by Hungarian Jews.

Now Mea She'arim Street stretches up to Yehezkel Street. The intersection here has been dubbed **Shabbat Square**, for the massive protests waged by the ultra-Orthodox Jews of Mea She'arim against the municipal government until the latter agreed to stop traffic here on Shabbat.

Assuming you don't drive, Shabbat is

the best time to visit Mea She'arim. A peaceful atmosphere prevails as you watch huge family clans strolling joyously down the centre of the street. And you may leave with a more sympathetic picture of the *haredim* than perhaps the dim, dark one which you may have arrived with.

Bukharin Quarter: North of Mea She'arim on Yehezkel you enter the Bukharin Quarter, first established in the late 19th century by affluent Jews from Bukhara, an Asian province in what is today part of the Commonwealth of Independent States. These Jews – who wore long, silk khaftans and colourful hats – flourished here for many years. Today, there are scarcely any Bukharin families living in the quarter.

Turning left on HaBucharim Street there is a large crafts store called **Kuzari**, which itself occupies an impressive Bukharin building. In addition to working with the local women to preserve artistic traditions, the store sometimes offers historical tours of the neigh-

bourhood and is a good place to start your visit.

Migration began in the 1870s when a wealthy owner of a Bukharin tea company named Shlomo Mussaieff became a religious Zionist before the practice was common (especially among the rich) and thereupon moved his family to Jerusalem. The trip, by camel caravan, took nine months. Upon his arrival, it is said, Mussaieff immediately decided his father must come here to die and so turned around to fetch him.

The story of Mussaieff and others spread in Bukhara, and with the advent of rail transportation in the 1880s, a wave of immigration began. The Old City was too much a series of ghettoes to suit these bourgeoisie Jews, and so they set about building their own quarter. Mussaieff himself travelled to Vienna, Paris, and Rome to study urban planning and the quarter bears a distinct European influence as a result.

Unlike the rest of Jerusalem, you will note the streets here are straight and wide. Above all, the Bukharin Jews didn't want communal courtyards on the order of Mea She'arim. Instead they insisted on private aristocratic estates. This community in essence became the first Jerusalem suburb.

To reach the **Mussaieff House**, continue on HaBucharim Street to David HeHazan. Although it has fallen into considerable disrepair, one can imagine its former splendour from the elegant exterior designs. Peek in at the expansive courtyard, upon which the Bukharin Jews obviously placed such a high premium.

A few blocks away on Ezra Street, there is another idiosyncratically designed mansion called **The Palace**. It was built for the Chafetz family at the turn of the century in some sort of Italian revival style. Because there was no real Jewish architecture in the Diaspora when Jerusalem was resettled in the 19th and 20th centuries, those who could afford to do so contracted foreign architects. This resulted in *ongepotchket* – a Yid-

Newspaper stall on Ben Yehuda Street.

dish expression for slapped together without form or sense.

By 1914, there were as many as 1,500 Bukharin Jews living in the quarter, but during and after the Russian Revolution, their money was cut off. The once magnificent summer homes were parcelled into multi-family apartments. During the 1920s, many of the early Zionists gathered here before finally settling Rehavia, and after 1948, a large number of North African Jews were billeted here.

Northern neighbourhoods: East and north of the quarter, Yehezkel turns into Shimon HaTzadik (Simon the Just) Street. This takes you into **Ma'alot Dafna**, which, in its simplicity, is typical of the post-1967 Jewish neighbourhoods. Here is **Or Samayach Yeshiva**, the largest and most controversial educational institution for assimilated young Jewish boys thinking of returning to their forefathers' religious observance.

North of Ma'alot Dafna along the street **Shmuel HaNavi** (Samuel the Prophet) in **Sanhedria** are the **Tombs of the Sanhedrin**. In Temple times, the Sanhedrin was the high court of 71 sages who issued *halachic* (Jewish law) decisions, and tradition claims they were buried here.

Despite the secular State of Israel and the increasingly powerful Chief Rabbinate, most believe that any type of Sanhedrin cannot reconvene until the Messiah comes. In the interim, *halachic* questions are normally put to the leading rabbis around the world.

East of Sanhedria is **Ramat Eshkol**, the first post-1967 neighbourhood, and **Ammunition Hill**. At the latter, trenches and bunkers have been starkly preserved to give some idea of what it was like during perhaps the most decisive battle of the Six Day War.

This was the main Jordanian outpost on the Jerusalem front, and when the Israeli Defence Forces captured it the stage was set for the conquest of the Old City. At the top of the hill, a memorial museum commemorates the Israeli dead.

Below, the Sanhedrin Tombs. Right, Gilo.

Maps and models tell the story of the battle, as does a weekly film shown here.

The road Shmuel HaNavi leads north of the city limits to the suburban neighbourhood of **Ramot**, which sprang up in the early 1970s. Check out the experimental housing tract known as **B'nai Beitcha**, which literally means "Build Your Own Home".

The tract has been divided into one-eighth acre plots for single-family dwellings. A mile and a half from Ramot is the Arab village of **Nebi Samuel**. Here a mosque marks the place where it is incorrectly believed Samuel was entombed. Even though there's fairly solid evidence that he was buried east of here in **Ramah**, both Jews and Muslims consider this a sacred site, and the location affords a superb view of the surrounding mountains and Jerusalem.

To The Capital: West of the central part of Jerusalem is a huge valley where Israel's most important cultural and political sites lie. It's sometimes called the **Valley of the Cross** for the unusual, hulking, fortress-like structure, the **Monastery of the Cross**. Tradition holds that the wood for Jesus's cross was taken from here. Originally built in the 7th century as a Georgian monastery, today it serves as a Greek Orthodox Church.

The squat, wide, modern building you see on the nearby hill is the **Knesset**, the seat of the Israeli government. When the capital was moved from Tel Aviv to Jerusalem, in an act of defiance against the United Nations (which wanted to make the city an international zone), the national parliament first met in what is today's Government Tourist Office. Meanwhile the Rothschild family sponsored construction of the new building, which was finished in 1966 but whose neoclassical monumentalism did not meet with universal acclaim. The legislative body of the Knesset consists of 120 elected officials, and the coalition that makes a majority then selects a cabinet and Prime Minister.

You can watch the Knesset in action,

Monastery at the Valley of the Cross.

as long as you remember your passport for the visit. Note the mosaic in the lobby by Marc Chagall. The **Menorah** (candelabra) in front of the Knesset, a gift from the British Parliament, is by Benno Elkan and displays various scenes in Jewish history.

Nearby is the verdant **Wohl Rose Garden**, containing 450 species. It is a choice spot for diplomatic receptions. Within it is a Byzantine-era mosaic moved here from the north.

Across the way is the **Israel Museum** (open Sun, Wed, Thurs 10am–5pm, Tues 4pm–10pm, Fri 10am–2pm, Sat 10am–4pm). In very short order (it only opened in 1965) the museum has become one of the world's great archaeological and historical museums. The futuristic, domed **Shrine of the Book** houses the decidedly ancient Dead Sea Scrolls, and is the gem among gems in the museum complex. As you enter, you will see 15 letters written by brilliant Jewish General Simmon bar-Kochba, who led the revolt against Rome in 132.

The **Dead Sea Scrolls** themselves, which represent the huge collection of 1st-century Hebrew documents discovered at the caves of Qumran in 1947, are on display in the main hall. Among them is a copy of the **Book of Isaiah**, the oldest known complete biblical document in existence today.

On your right as you leave the shrine for the main part of the museum is the **Billy Rose Art Garden**, designed by Isamu Noguchi. Displayed here are sculptural works by Rodin, Picasso, Henry Moore and several prominent Israeli artists.

The Israel Museum is known best for its archaeology section, which displays mainly artifacts that have been unearthed in Israel, and is organized chronologically. The highlight of the Jewish art and ethnography section is a group of Torah scrolls that have been gathered from all over the Diaspora. There's also a section devoted to Muslim art, and a 19th and 20th-century art wing, which is especially strong on the French, with

Inside the Shrine of the Book, where the Dead Sea Scrolls are kept.

works by Monet, Cezanne, Renoir, Van Gogh, and Klee.

Opposite the Israel Museum are two recently opened attractions: the **Bible Lands Museum** (Sun–Thurs 9.30am–5.30pm, Fri 9.30am–2pm) displays artifacts from throughout the Middle East in biblical times, while the **Bloomfield Science Museum** (Mon, Wed, Thurs 10am–6pm, Tues 10am–8pm, Fri. 10am–1pm, Sat 10am–3pm) demonstrates how to make the subject of science fun for children with the help of hands-on exhibits.

The **Hebrew University** campus at **Givat Ram** was built with considerable haste in 1948 when the Mount Scopus campus was cut off from the rest of the city. Today the campus is mostly used for its departments in the natural sciences. It also includes a memorial to Israel's war dead and the **National University Library**, said to be the largest in the Middle East.

Beneath Givat Ram is Jerusalem's **Botanical Garden**, which has a pleasant lakeside café and Italian restaurant, and next to the university is the government complex, including the **Bank of Israel** and **Supreme Court Building**. The court building, opened in 1992, uses light and shade to great effect, with many glass walls offering the visitor striking perspectives, including a panorama of the city.

North of the University, next to the **Holiday Inn Hotel** and across from the **Central Bus Station**, is the **Jerusalem International Conference Centre**. This is also where the dramatic and drawn-out 1987 trial of the alleged Nazi war criminal John Demjanjuk was held; he was eventually acquitted.

A visit to Herod's Temple: If you're interested in gaining some perspective on what Jerusalem may have looked like in ancient times, be certain to stop at the **Holyland Hotel**, just south of the Orthodox enclave of **Bayit Vegan**. (The Circle Line drops you off right in front.) Ever since the Second Temple was destroyed, Jews have struggled to recon-

Hebrew letters at the Billy Rose Sculpture Garden spell "love".

struct it in their collective imagination. Maimonides himself made a series of drawings based on Talmudic sources.

What makes the late Avi Yonah's huge and detailed model of the Second Temple so miraculous is that when he finished it in 1969 it was just as the Israeli government was beginning to unleash archaeologists to sort through the rubble of the reunified Jerusalem. What they found during the next two decades largely confirms the accuracy of Yonah's vision.

The model, while large, is built on a scale of 1:50. To imagine how large the Temple was, consider that it was twice the size of the Dome of the Rock that now sits in its place.

The walls around the Old City represented here were about 70 percent greater in circumference than the ones you see today. You can see that the City of David and Mount Zion were within these walls. At the location of today's Jaffa Gate, is where Herod originally built his palace. A reconstructed model is on

view close to the three larger towers.

The Temple itself sits opposite and you can see the heavily gold-coated panels. It is said that at sunrise the Temple would shine as though it were on fire and anyone who gazed at it directly risked becoming blind. The gold spikes were purposely placed there to stop birds from sitting on and befouling the sacred shrine.

The greenish gate is known as Nikanor's Gate because (so the Talmud tells us) Nikanor, a fabulously rich merchant from Alexandria, donated them. They were originally wrought out of copper in Egypt, and covered with gold, silver, and jewels. While the gates were being shipped across the Mediterranean, one of the gates fell overboard during a storm. When Nikanor reached Palestine, he bewailed this loss until the gate miraculously appeared on shore. Unfortunately, the gate appeared without its lavish adornments.

Finally, Herzl's home: West of Bayit Vegan, at the intersection of Sderot Herzl

Model of ancient Jerusalem at the Holyland Hotel.

and Hazikaron, is a huge red installation, a "Homage to Jerusalem" by Alexander Calder, inventor of the mobile; he referred to this work as a "stabile". There's a road here that takes you several miles to Ein Kerem and one that stretches back a few hundred yards to the Holocaust Memorial, Yad Vashem (*see facing page*).

The entire hill is called Mount Herzl, or **Har Herzl** as it's known in Hebrew. The **Herzl Museum** across from the Calder work commemorates the Viennese journalist who was the founder of modern Zionism. It traces his careers in law and journalism through photographs and his papers. His comfortable Vienna office is also preserved.

Herzl was an entirely assimilated Jew, whose vestigial tribal instincts were finally aroused during his reporting on the Dreyfus Trial in Paris in 1891. It was here that he realized a modern social anti-Semitism was gaining, and would never be eliminated. His interest was not in perpetuating the Jewish culture or faith, but rather in developing a strategy whereby the Jewish people might simply survive.

And so it was that he began crusading for a Jewish state. He met with the Turkish Sultan, Kaiser Wilhelm, and other world leaders; he published in 1896 the first Zionist manifestos, *The Jewish State* and *Altneuland*. Although he ideally saw the Jews resettling Palestine, he considered for a time purchasing land for a Jewish home in Uganda and South America.

Herzl died in 1904 at the age of 44, a broken-hearted man, his dream some decades away from being realized. His last wishes were that his body be interred in the Jewish homeland, wherever that land might be. In 1949, after Israel was established, his remains were brought "home", and a simple grave here marks his name in the cemetery behind the museum. Other Israeli leaders, including the assassinated prime minister Yitzhak Rabin and the late President Chaim Herzog, are also buried here. **New apartments.**

Near the museum is the **Tomb of Vladimir Jabotinsky**, a controversial and brilliant Russian Jew who broke ranks with the Zionists' establishment by demanding, well before 1948, the immediate creation of a Jewish state and separate armed forces.

Those who died during the War of Independence in and near Jerusalem are buried in the adjacent **Military Cemetery**. Close to the entrance is a pool commemorating those who drowned in the Mediterranean. Around the corner the home of the former Prime Minister Menachem Begin.

A fitting memorial: To the west of Mount Herzel is **Yad Vashem**, a remembrance of the Holocaust which takes its name, meaning "an everlasting memorial", from the Book of Isaiah. At its entrance, the narrow path leading toward the museum is called **The Avenue of the Righteous Among the Nations**. Each of the 6,000 trees planted here honours a Gentile who risked his or her life for Jews during the Nazi purges.

At the end of the path you reach the museum with a celebrated sculpture by Naftali Bezem, the *Wall of Holocaust and Heroism*, at the entrance. The first panel depicts the Holocaust; the second, Jewish resistance; the third, the return to the land of Israel; and the fourth, rebirth as a nation.

The museum itself takes you step-by-step through the story of the Holocaust through photographs, documents and various artifacts.

Adjacent to the museum is the **Hall of Names**, which preserves the names of those known to have perished in the Holocaust. The list is very far from complete because whole communities were wiped out, leaving no way of tracing many individuals.

The two sculptures outside this building were created by Nathan Rapaport, a Holocaust survivor. In addition, there's an **Art Museum**, which houses many works of art created by the Jews during the Holocaust. These works, completed under extreme duress and prohibited by

Below, soccer at Givat Ram. Right, a statue expresses grief at Yad Vashem.

Below, soccer at Givat Ram. Right, a statue expresses grief at Yad Vashem.

the Nazis, are evidence of the unshakeable spirit of those who knew they would die to leave some expression of their experience for future generations.

The **Hall of Remembrance** is the long tent-shaped building with walls made of large stones. Inside, the mosaic floor is inscribed with the names of the 22 largest Nazi concentration and death camps. The ashes of martyrs have been gathered together and brought to Israel from these camps. They have been placed in the vault you see in front of the Eternal Light. The names of more than 2 million Jews exterminated by the Nazis are recorded in the Room of Names.

The surrounding area here is called the **Janusz Korczak Park** for the Polish teacher who refused to abandon his students and thus was gassed in a concentration camp with them. The 65-ft (20-metre) tall edifice here is called the Pillar of Heroism.

Nearby you can enter the **Children's Memorial**, which opened in 1987. It is perhaps the most haunting memorial of all: here you walk through dark corridors of mirrors and candles and hear an endless list of names of some of the 1½ million children who perished in the Holocaust.

The **Central Archives for Holocaust Studies** houses the most comprehensive collection of Holocaust research in the world, containing more than 50 million documents and including some 30,000 eyewitness testimonies of survivors, photographs, films and other artifacts. The library contains more than 75,000 books in 50 languages. Research here has served as the basis for evidence against Nazi war criminals such as Adolf Eichmann.

Beneath the Yad Vashem complex is the **Valley of the Lost Communities**. There, the names of 5,000 villages and Jewish ghettoes destroyed by the Nazis are etched on stones.

New amenities: While the past must not be forgotten, the present is very much concerned with building a future for Israel's growing population. One

Modern factories have been expanding.

good example is **Malkah**, a delightful village to the southwest of the city centre which has become swallowed up by Jerusalem's greedy urban sprawl. The valley beneath Malkah was transformed in the early 1990s into a leisure and commercial centre.

Amenities include the **Teddy Kollek Soccer Stadium**. This compact, attractive looking 12,000-seat stadium is the home of Betar Jerusalem, one of Israel's leading teams. To the fans, the stadium is a more important shrine than any of the religious sites in the city. This is the only public facility that the former mayor Teddy Kollek allowed to be named for him because of the satisfaction he received on its completion, overcoming 20 years of fierce opposition from the city's ultra-orthodox residents.

Adjacent to the stadium is the **Malkah Shopping Mall**. Except for the Jerusalem stone facade, this could be any modern shopping centre in Europe or America. But the airconditioning and/or heating makes this a comfortable venue for shopping. There is also a wide choice of restaurants and an eight-cinema entertainment complex inside.

Nearby (but not within walking distance) is the new **Biblical Zoo**, a beautifully landscaped zoo featuring the animals mentioned in the Bible. Also worth visiting, further into the valley, is the **Ein Yael Living Museum**, which offers a "hands-on" biblical experience. Visitors can create their own mosaics, harvest crops as if they were farmers living 2,000 years ago, practise ancient crafts such as weaving, basketmaking and pottery, and participate in archaeological excavations.

Embracing Mountains: If Jerusalem is strategically well-positioned, this is due in no small part to the mountains which surround it on all sides. The Hill of Evil Council is where Jesus said he believed he was the son of God, and his elders ripped his robe and called him blasphemous. Christians also regard this as the spot where Judas Iscariot got his 30 pieces of silver. The Jews called the

The Malkah Shopping Mall.

place **Givat Haananiah** because a high priest by this name was buried here during the time of the Second Temple.

The view from the **Haas Promenade** and **Sherover Walkway** towards the Temple Mount is nearly perfect.

The white building with the blue flag is the **United Nations Headquarters**. It formerly served as the residence for the "High Commissioner" during the British Mandate. In 1967, the Jordanians crossed the armistice line into this neutral UN zone and occupied the building. It was understood they had joined Egypt in the war against Israel.

South of the Haas Promenade is **Kibbutz Ramat Rahel**, which marked the southernmost point of Jerusalem before construction recently began on the controversial Har Homa neighbourhood to the south. To the north is the beautiful, if wistfully named **Peace Forest**, and the industrial neighbourhood of **Talpiot**. A burgeoning artists' colony is developing loft space here as well.

Further north still is the Arab neighbourhood of **Abu Tor**, a name that was actually given long ago to the entire hill. It means "father of the bull" because the hill was the prize for a brave Muslim bull rider who helped defeat the Crusaders in battle in 1187. Abu Tor, the neighbourhood, had the misfortune of being "partitioned" between Israel and Jordan from 1948 to 1967. As such, it was virtually a continual battle zone, as you can see from the bullet holes in house after house.

Jerusalem has always been most vulnerable to invasion from the northeast over Mount Scopus. When the Roman Titus scooped out the holy city from this very spot in AD70, he must have licked his pagan chops and prepared his Roman troops to storm the Temple. Surely the Crusaders felt the same sort of exhilaration here in 1099.

After the dust settled in the 1948 war, Israel maintained control of Mount Scopus itself, even though it was virtually an island in Jordanian territory, cut off from the rest of Jewish Jerusalem.

Haas Promenade on the Hill of Evil Council.

Following an armistice agreement an Israeli convoy, under United Nations protection, was allowed to shuttle up the mountain, a barely tenable arrangement that continued until Jerusalem was reunited in 1967.

Today, Mount Scopus is known primarily as the site of the country's greatest school, **Hebrew University**. Dedicated in 1925, under the guidance of future Israeli President Chaim Weizmann, Jewish scholars gathered from all over the Diaspora to teach here and at the time, it represented one of the single greatest achievements of Zionism.

Since 1967, there have been massive renovations on campus, and the school is bursting with foreign students. Check the calendar for various lectures and concerts, or come up to enjoy yet another splendid view of Jerusalem.

The University amphitheatre, at the rear of the campus, with its breathtaking view of the barren **Judean Hills**, reminds you that you are on the fulcrum of two worlds. The renowned **Hadassah Hospital** here was built in 1939. After the Arab Legion massacred a group of scientists and staffers in 1948, however, a new facility was built post haste at Ein Kerem.

The road from Mount Scopus heads south along the ridge to the **Augusta Victoria**, a large structure built by the Germans as a hospice, now used as a hospital.

A bit further down on your right is the new **Brigham Young University** campus. Its construction was bitterly opposed, primarily by Orthodox Jews, who feared that Mormonism was a proselytizing religion. The administration of Mayor Teddy Kollek permitted it anyway in accordance with the principle of cultural and religious tolerance. It is worth taking one of the hourly guided tours of this attractive campus.

Finally, the road leads to an Arab village called **E-Tur**, which contains the Russian Church of the Ascension, and eventually connects up with the Mount of Olives.

Hadassah Hospital.

EIN KEREM

Ein Kerem is calm, lush, rural and not too touristy, a welcome reprieve from pressure-packed Jerusalem central. Follow the road from Mount Herzl a couple of miles into the valley, full of olive trees and rich in vineyards. The valley was populated mostly by Arabs until 1948, but now, aside from the Christian clergymen, it's a predominantly affluent Jewish settlement. This is prime real estate space for local artists and one can well understand the source of their inspiration here.

Ein Kerem is a good place to stroll for an afternoon or hear some music at night. If you feel like staying longer, there are a few hotels, and the **Youth Hostel** on top of the ridge is one of the best kept secrets in Jerusalem. The restaurants are delightful, especially the **Goulash Inn**, a little bit of Hungary in the middle of the Judean hills.

The most important site in Ein Kerem is the **Church of St John the Baptist**, a Franciscan edifice (1674) on top of ruins from Crusader and Byzantine times. Tradition has it that John was born in the **grotto** down the stairs in the back of the church.

If you walk back to the centre of town, you will pass a pleasant café on your left before coming to the **Spring of the Vineyard** (or Spring of the Virgin), from which the small town gets its name and from where it is said that Mary once drank. Follow the road to the right up to the impressive **Church of the Visitation**, built in 1956 by the Italian architect Antonio Barluzzi (who also designed two other churches on the Mount of Olives).

According to Christian tradition, John the Baptist's parents, Zacharias and Elizabeth, had their home here. It was during a visit to Elizabeth that the Virgin Mary received from the Angel Gabriel the Annunciation of the future birth of Jesus.

Continue up the hill to the **Russian Church**, with the resonant red turret. Note another church here was never finished, a casualty of the Russian Revolution. Nearby you can see the **Sisters of Zion Convent**.

On the hill above Ein Kerem, and just a short drive or bus ride away, is the **Hadassah Hospital**, a remarkable medical facility, but even better known for the **Chagall Windows**. The first Hadassah Hospital on Mount Scopus could no longer function after the 1948 War, and not long thereafter construction began here. In the small synagogue to the left of the main entrance are the stained-glass windows made by the Russian Jewish artist Marc Chagall. Each of the 12 represents one of the 12 tribes of Israel, the symbols in various ways corresponding to the blessings Jacob gave his sons.

Note the bullet holes made by Arab shelling during the Six Day War. About 2 miles from the Hadassah Hospital is the **John F. Kennedy Memorial.**

Preceding pages: Ammunition Hill, scene of fighting in the Six Day War. Left, lush Ein Kerem. Right, the Church of the Visitation.

TEL AVIV–JAFFA

The road leading from Tel Aviv to Jerusalem was literally the latter's lifeline during the 1948 War of Independence. It was by this route that the Israeli Haganah hauled supplies and ammunition to the border, and to make this trip in those days was to become a sitting duck for the Arab snipers in the hills. Today, the trip down from the Jerusalem mountains to the coastal town of Tel Aviv is an easy 43-mile (69-km) drive. But to many, it is a journey across the world: from sacred religious centre to secular mecca, from politically unstable border town to fun, sun-baked Mediterranean metropolis.

In recent years, thousands of Jerusalem families have dug up their roots and made this trip a permanent one. To be sure, they have been lured by better jobs and less expensive housing. But, which is even more striking, they have been attracted by the drastically different lifestyle. Whereas Jerusalem is built on stone, upon which every footstep is scrutinized for its political or religious signification, Tel Aviv is built on sand, and you can continually remake of it whatever you wish.

At the moment, with more than 2 million people living in the Tel Aviv metropolitan area (85 percent of them secular), representing more than a third of the population of Israel, this is clearly the country's economic nerve centre. It is also its reluctant diplomatic capital since most foreign countries refuse to locate their embassies in Jerusalem.

As hot and arid as the climate may be, it is a place that breathes relief from all the battles everywhere else in the land. The sparkling beachfront crouching behind all those deluxe hotels is a national playground; by night, the party shifts to the pubs, clubs, and cinemas

Preceding pages: a "Fun Day" in Tel Aviv; coastal hotels. **Right,** Jaffa's ancient port.

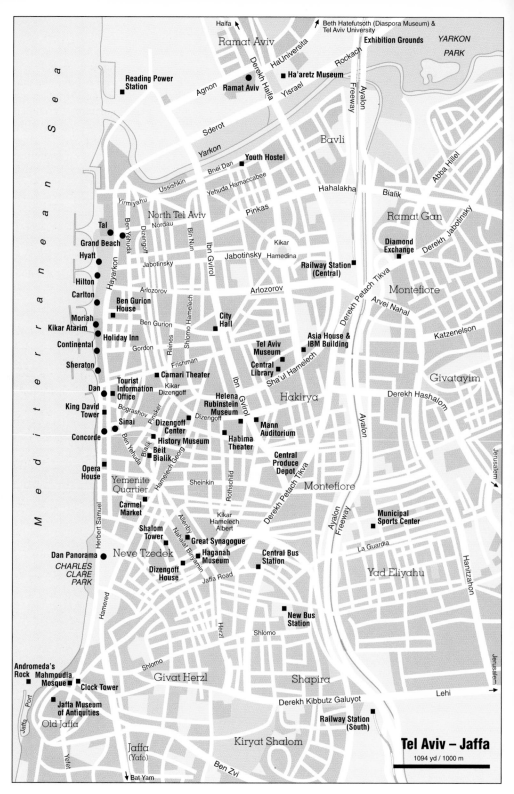

Haifa

Beth Hatefutsoth (Diaspora Museum) &
Tel Aviv University

Exhibition Grounds

YARKON PARK

Ramat Aviv

HaUniversita

Derekh Haifa

Rockach

Ayalon Freeway

Agnon

Ramat Aviv

Ha'aretz Museum

Yisrael

Reading Power Station

Sderot

Yarkon

Bavli

Bnei Dan

Youth Hostel

Ussishkin

Yehuda Hamaccabee

Hahalakha

Abba Hillel

Yirmiyahu

Yehuda Hamaccabee

Bialik

Ramat Gan

North Tel Aviv

Nordau

Pinkas

Derekh Jabotinsky

Tal

Ben Yehuda

Dizengoff

Bin Nun

Ibn Gvirol

Kikar

Diamond Exchange

Grand Beach

Jabotinsky

Jabotinsky

Hamedina

Montefiore

Hyatt

Arlozorov

Railway Station (Central)

Arvei Nahal

Hilton

Arlozorov

Derekh Petach Tikva

Katzenelson

Carlton

Shlomo Hamelech

Moriah

Ben Gurion House

City Hall

Givatayim

Kikar Atarim

Ben Gurion

Asia House & IBM Building

Derekh Hashalom

Continental

Holiday Inn

Reines

Tel Aviv Museum

Gordon

Central Library

Sha'ul Hamelech

Sheraton

Frishman

Hakirya

Dan

Camari Theater

Ayalon

Tourist Information Office

Kikar Dizengoff

Helena Rubinstein Museum

King David Tower

Bograshov

Pinsker

Dizengoff Center

Dizengoff

Mann Auditorium

Concorde

Ben Yehuda

Bialik

Hamelech Georg

History Museum

Habima Theater

Sinai

Beit Bialik

Central Produce Depot

Opera House

Yemenite Quartier

Sheinkin

Rothschild

Derekh Petach Tikva

Montefiore

Herbert Samuel

Carmel Market

Allenby

Kikar Hamelech Albert

Municipal Sports Center

Dan Panorama

CHARLES CLARE PARK

Shalom Tower

Nahalat Binyamin

Great Synagogue

Haganah Museum

Central Bus Station

La Guardia

Yad Eliyahu

Hanizahon

Neve Tzedek

Dizengoff House

Jaffa Road

Hamered

Herzl

Shlomo

New Bus Station

Ayalon Freeway

Andromeda's Rock

Mahmoudia Mosque

Clock Tower

Givat Herzl

Shlomo

Shapira

Lehi

Jaffa Port

Jaffa Museum of Antiquities

Derekh Kibbutz Galuyot

Old Jaffa

Railway Station (South)

Jaffa (Yafo)

Kiryat Shalom

Yefet

Ben Zvi

Jerusalem

Jerusalem

↓ Bat Yam

Tel Aviv – Jaffa

1094 yd / 1000 m

Mediterranean Sea

that line Dizengoff, or more trendy Sheinkin or Florentine. They stay open well into the early hours of the morning, *especially* on Shabbat. Compared to most cities its size, Tel Aviv is a relatively safe, clean place, but some regard it as a modern-day Sodom.

The truth is that, while scarcely religious, Tel Aviv is nevertheless somewhat miraculous. It sprang up from of the earth outside of the ancient port of **Jaffa** (whose sites we'll discuss at the end of this chapter), the first strictly Hebrew city in the world.

In 1887, about 20 affluent Jewish families, searching for calm outside the clamorous, Arab-dominated Jaffa, founded a suburb of sorts just north of there. They called it **Neve Zedek**, and it was an early stomping ground of the Nobel Prize-winning Hebrew writer S.Y. Agnon. A century later, it has become a artsy, chic, gentrified enclave, which includes the **Neve Tzedek Theatre**, home of the Inbal and Batsheva dance companies. As you head uptown from here, at Lilenbulum and Pines Streets is the **Eden Cinema**, Israel's first movie theatre, built in 1914.

About that skyscraper: In 1907, fed up with the deplorable living conditions in Jaffa and anxious to build a strictly Jewish/Hebrew city, 60 families gathered on the beach and raffled off a nice swathe of land north of Neve Zedek. They named the place "Tel Aviv", chosen for its Zionist resonance. The name also is the Hebrew translation of the title of Theodore Herzl's utopian book *Altneuland* (Old-New-Land).

The first main thoroughfare was named for Herzl – **Herzl Street** – and the first high school at the top of this street. **Herzlia Gymnasium** was built in grand fashion, and when finished, it was the first school where all subjects were taught in Hebrew.

Sadly, however, this architectural and historical landmark was razed in 1959 to make room for that hideous monstrosity that dwarfs the Tel Aviv skyline, the **Shalom Tower**. At 35 stories

Watching the world go by.

high, it had, when it was built, the dubious reputation for being the tallest skyscraper in all of the Middle East. Still, the view from the **observatory** here is extraordinary: on a clear day, you can see Jerusalem. Also you'll find here a four-floor shopping centre, a cramped amusement park, and a **Wax Museum**, which houses the modern-day Golems. Near the Shalom Tower is the **Yemenite Quarter**, featuring interesting **Arab Stone Houses** and a **Yemenite Market**.

Rothschild Boulevard: Just a block from the Shalom Tower on Herzl Street starts the grand **Rothschild Boulevard**, named for the famous family of Jewish financiers who poured a chunk of their vast wealth into the early settlement of Israel, and it takes you into the heart of the modern city.

In the mid-1930s, refugees from the Bauhaus School in Germany came to make Tel Aviv the first *wholly* modern city, a place that would revolutionize the face of the urban centre. These "International Style" architects began build-

ing like crazy, one white box after another – so much so that Tel Aviv earned the sobriquet, "The White City". The buildings have not aged well and many have fallen into disrepair, and to live up to its nickname,parts of the town desperately need a fresh coat of paint.

On the southern part of Rothschild is the **Haganah Museum**, which displays weapons used by the Haganah, Israel's underground defence force, during the War of Independence. It is in the home of Eliahu Golomb, one of the head commanders. At **Allenby Road**, turn west toward the sea. You will pass the **Great Synagogue** and through **Magen David Circle** until you come to the bustling **Carmel Market**, a great place to shop for fruits and vegetables or soak up the local scene.

Still further on Allenby is **Bialik Street**, named for Israel's first "national" poet Chaim Nachman Bialik; his home, **Beit Bialik**, at the end of the block. It was to this neighbourhood that the vast influx of Russian immigrants (turned

away from America) came in the mid-1920s. Also on this block is the **Rubin Museum** which houses a collection of paintings and drawings by Israeli artist Reuven Rubin. Finally, you come to the **Museum for the Tel Aviv–Jaffa History Museum**, a building that served as the City Hall until 1968. Next to the museum is a staircase that leads to **Gan Meir**, a charming garden on one of the more charming streets.

If you make your way back to Rothschild and start north you will arrive at Habima Kikar. The delightful circular building is the home of the renowned **Habima Theatre**, founded at the dawn of nationalism by a group of Jewish actors who fled Russia after the revolution. Many productions offer simultaneous translations so that tourists can follow the Hebrew. Next to the theatre is the **Mann Auditorium**, where you can see another national jewel, the **Israel Philharmonic Orchestra** (long conducted by Zubin Mehta). Get your tickets early, as tickets fetch a mighty

The curvaceous Asia House and the IBM Building.

price on the scalper's market. Behind these buildings is the **Helena Rubinstein Museum for Modern Art**, and aesthetes gather at the **Apropos Cafe** in the little park across the way to discuss the latest exhibitions.

From here head north up **Ibn Gvirol Boulevard** and west across **King Saul Street** (Sha'ul Hamelech) to the **Tel Aviv Museum** (open Sun–Thurs 10am–9.30pm, Fri 10am–2pm). The museum has several galleries, most notable for their collection of Israeli artists, though with modest holdings from the Impressionist and post-Impressionist periods. The museum attracts large crowds when it hosts cinematic retrospectives and other cultural events in its auditorium.

Next door is the recently opened **Tel Aviv Centre for the Performing Arts**, home to the Israel Opera Company and Rishon Le Zion Symphony Orchestra.

Further down on King Saul Street are among the city's more recent architectural success stories. The **Asia House**, designed by Mordecai Ben-Horin, is an undulating, sensual edifice that does far more than the Bauhaus buildings in creating a distinct Tel Aviv feeling. That cyclindrical object next door is **IBM Building**. Across the way is the **German Templar Colony**, founded in 1870 and abandoned in 1939 at the height of Hitler's war against the Jews.

In the 1960s Tel Aviv reached so far north that it crossed **Yarkon River**. The Yarkon flows west from the mountains until it spills into the sea, and served as the geographical boundary between the tribes of Ephriam and Dan. Across the river is the **Diaspora Museum** (open Sun–Thurs 10am–5pm, Wed until 7pm), one of the most interesting of its kind in Israel and indeed the world. The museum is on the campus of **Tel Aviv University** (*see pages 182–183*).

Another worthwhile place to visit north of the river is **Tel Kasila**, a rich archaeological site that is now part of the **Eretz Israel Museum** (open Sun–Fri 9am–1pm, Sat 10am–1pm), which is actually a whole complex of muse-

Dizengoff Circle.

ums which include folklore, glass, ceramic, copper, and neumismatic; there is a planetarium as well.

Night life: In the evening, the centre of Tel Aviv and its most frequented meeting place is **Dizengoff Square**, site of the unusual water fountain/sculpture by the Israeli artist Agam. Here you'll find the multiplex cinemas that lure the secular Jews from Jerusalem, the best falafel stands in the city. Two blocks away is the **Dizengoff Centre**, the modern mall, which came to Israel in the early 1980s to the great fascination and pleasure of the shopping-crazy, film-buff, food-mad Tel Avivis.

Dizengoff Street is one long see-and-be-seen party strip. But younger visitors may prefer the chic cafés of Sheinkin Street and the more rugged bohemian atmosphere of Florentine.

If you turn west on Ben Gurion Street, you will come to **David Ben Gurion's House**. This was his permanent residence until the latter part of his life when he settled on the Kibbutz Sde Boker. Despite the 20,000-volume library, it's a modest dwelling in the heart of a city that the first Prime Minister never really cared for all that much.

If you head further west, you'll get to the beachfront, studded with hotels, but delightful nonetheless for the **Tel Aviv Promenade**. Several embassies are also located down here, including the notably ugly American consulate.

Most of the big hotels on the beachfront are overpriced, but the smaller ones, mainly for young travellers, are dirt-cheap. While the presence of prostitutes down by the beach has led some religious Jews to complain, generally the waterfront is sparkling clean.

Old Jaffa: If you were to walk south on the beach, you would come to the source of Tel Aviv, the ancient port of Jaffa. And if you stand on the port and gaze out at the Mediterranean, you can see a group of rocks, the most prominent of which is very important in Greek legend. It is known as **Andromeda's Rock** because it is reputed to be the place

Jaffa: where Jonah departed, Zionists arrived.

where that mythic lady was once manacled by Poseidon. She was awaiting sacrifice when her beloved Perseus, wearing the winged sandals of Hermes, swooped down, slew the Sea Monster, and saved her. If there were ever any opportunity to verify deatils of this account, however, they may well have been destroyed during a recent renovation of the pier.

This very port also figures prominently in the story of Jonah, the reluctant prophet. Imagining that he could escape God's orders, Jonah hopped a ship from Jaffa to the land of Tarshish, got caught in a storm, and was swallowed whole by a whale. In addition, this was the port where the cedars of Lebanon arrived on floats before being sent to Jerusalem for the building of the temples. It is said the Hasmonean King Jonathan reconquered Jaffa in the 2nd century BCE, before it came successively under the rule of the Greeks, Romans, Crusaders, Saracens and Turks.

In the late 19th century, near the end of Turkish rule and before Tel Aviv sprouted up, Jaffa assumed far more significance than it does today. With 8,000 Arabs and 2,000 Jews, it was the largest city along the Mediterannean coast betweeen Port Said in the south and Beirut in the north. It was the primary seaport and trade centre for all of Palestine during that time.

Still, it was a dingy town when many of the earliest Zionists washed up on its shores from Eastern Europe. The new immigrants were thoroughly disappointed, even shocked. When David Ben-Gurion, Israel's first Prime Minister, then 20, left his home in Czarist-ruled Poland for Palestine, he was repulsed by Jaffa. This was not the Zionist dream that had possessed him. Even though he was exhausted after an arduous, three-week trip, he refused to spend the night there and set off by foot to Petach Tikvah.

Jaffa today: If you are coming to Jaffa from downtown Tel Aviv (walking along the beach is impractical) ask the bus

St Peter's Monastery: Napoleon slept here.

driver to drop you off at the **Clock Tower** on Yefet Street and start your tour here. Each of the stained-glass windows on the tower recalls a particular part of Jaffa's history.

The **Armenian Hostel** across the way practically served as a check-off point for Zionists on their way from the Diaspora to start settlements in the new old land. The **Mahmoudia Mosque** just ahead was built in 1812.

The nearby **Jaffa Flea Market** is more low-key and authentic than anything in Jerusalem. It's a fine place to browse for ancient relics and modern trash. The restored section of Jaffa is the other way. The **Jaffa Museum** offers a solid collection of archaeological exhibits, but not nearly so interesting to look at as the building in which they are housed: the headquarters of some former 18th-century Ottoman governor.

The **Franciscan Monastery of St Peter** is the large maze edifice at the top of the hill that defines the Jaffa skyline. And St Peter himself casts a long shadow over Jaffa lore. When the disciple Tabitha fell ill and died, St Peter proclaimed, "Tabitha arise!", and she did. Thereafter, St Peter spent much time in Jaffa, lodging at the **House of Simon the Tanner**. Tradition places this site where a tiny mosque now stands near the monastery. In the courtyard is the **St Louis Monastery**, so named for the French king who led a Crusade here in 1147. Another Gallic ruler, Napoleon, is said to have rested his imperialistic bones here after conquering Jaffa some 750 years later.

The minaret is part of the **Jama El-Baher Mosque**. Next door is Jaffa's first Jewish house, built in 1820. Nearby, behind the museum, is a Turkish mansion *cum* bath house *cum* nightclub and restaurant called **El-Hamam**. Atop the hill, past the park, follow the narrow alleyways through a maze of artists' studios, galleries and shops. The art isn't cheap but the browsing is fine. On Pasteur Street, that huge, anachronistically ugly building is a modern mall.-

Back at the centre of the town square, called **Kikar Kedumin**, a number of Jaffa excavations are on display. Across the way, are some of the town's most hoppin' night haunts. Peaceful by day, Jaffa absorbs much of Tel Aviv's bustle and commotion in the evening.

The suburbs: Ringed around Tel Aviv/Jaffa like ripples from the sea are the city's bedroom suburbs. Among the noteworthy are **Beni Brak** and **Petach Tikva**. The former was established by *frum* (pious) Jews from Poland in 1924, and is the best known *Haredi* enclave outside of Jerusalem. The latter was founded by secular Jews in 1878, and is considered the first Zionist settlement. Today it is a modern industrial city, but at the turn of the century it was known for its beautiful orange groves. Ben Gurion walked there the first night after landing at Jaffa. He wrote: "My heart overflowed with happiness as I had entered the realm of joy... I am in a Hebrew village in the Land of Israel, in a Hebrew village called Petach Tikva."

Left, nightlife in the town square. **Right**, artists abound in Jaffa.

202

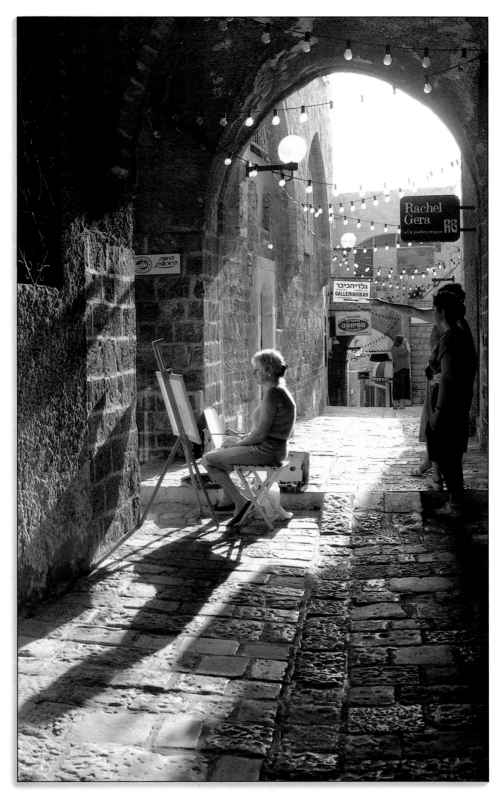

THE DIASPORA MUSEUM

Modern sceptics of organised Judaism are liable to argue that, if the religion were true, we should be able to witness God's hand in today's affairs the way ancient Jews supposedly experienced it in their times. Why, these sceptics ask, do we no longer see burning bushes, or parting seas or credible prophets?

To this, one may occasionally hear the response: "The story of the Jewish Diaspora, the very survival of the Jewish people for several millennia of wandering in many a far-flung land, is perhaps the most miraculous of all." Now the sceptic comes back: "It all depends on how you define a miracle."

To which the religious Jew finally says: "When Moses saw a bush that was on fire but would not consume itself, the miracle wasn't only the bush, but the fact that Moses *noticed* it."

Understood this way, it would appear that the aim of the Diaspora Museum in Tel Aviv is to spark the flame of awareness in visitors to noticing the miracle of the survival of the Jewish people in their exile.

Founded in 1979, the Diaspora Museum (or Beth Hatefutsoth, as it is called in Hebrew) is sited on the campus of Tel Aviv University and is designed unlike any other museum. It doesn't display valuable objects or art, but uses a multimedia presentation to tell the story of the Jewish people. The main exhibit is organised around several themes of Jewish life in the Diaspora: Family Life, Community Life, Religious Life, Culture, Relations with Non-Jews and the Return To Zion.

The word "Diaspora" comes from the Greek for dispersion or scattering. The Hebrew word for it is *Galut*. The first scattering of the Jews occurred in the 8th century BCE, when the Assyrians wiped out Samaria and 10 of the 12 tribes of the Israelite people.

Nobody knows what happened to the

Family traces its lineage at the computer study centre.

"Ten Lost Tribes", as they are called, though some speculate that the Jews of Ethiopia or India or China represent one such lost tribe. In 586 BCE, the Babylonians killed many Jews who belonged to the remaining two tribes and sent the rest to exile in Babylon (modern-day Iraq). Others fled to Egypt and established a huge and prosperous community in the port city of Alexandria.

Jews continued to settle in the Mediterranean and Northern Africa. With the rise of Islam, many were massacred, but as time went on Judaism was generally tolerated under Muslim rule.

After the Christians vanquished the Muslims from Spain, the government demanded that Jews convert to Christianity or die. Those who paid lip service to conversion, while maintaining Jewish customs in private, were called *Marranos* (literally "pigs"); those who were found out in the Spanish Inquisition were burned at the stake. The Jews who could, fled from the Iberian peninsula to Northern Europe Protestant nations, such as Holland, England, and Germany. Others set out for America; some even speculate that Christopher Columbus himself was a *Marrano.*

The French Revolution and the Enlightenment gave Jews political rights in Western Europe. No longer facing massacres, many of these Jews began to lose their Judaism through assimilation. This was especially true of the German Jews and the Russians Jews who emigrated to America.

By the dawn of the 20th century, it was apparent to many that "emancipation" had been a failure and some Diaspora Jews began to hook up again with their tradition by returning to the Land of Israel.

The miracle of the Diaspora Jewry wasn't merely surviving the tortures and massacres mentioned above, but the fact that it preserved the heritage and tradition of the Israelite people who have been wandering since the time they received the Torah in the desert at Mount Sinai.

Diaspora Museum, story of a miracle.

DAY TRIPS

Located just 10km (6 miles) south of Jerusalem, **Bethlehem** is one of the most sacred places in Christendom. Revered as the birthplace of Christ, the town has many Old Testament associations. Rachel, the second wife of Jacob is buried near the northern entrance to the town, while Ruth the Moabite was courted by Boaz in fields nearby, and last but by no means least King David was born here. Nevertheless, the city is not considered to have any sacred status by Jews.

Since 1995, Bethlehem has been part of the Palestinian Autonomous region, though crossing the army checkpoint between Jerusalem and Bethlehem is usually routine. After all tourism is the economic life blood of Bethlehem and even during the most violent days of the intifada incidents were rare in the town. It is no coincidence that Bethlehem's veteran mayor Elias Freij serves as Minister of Tourism in the Palestinian Authority. However, before visiting other towns and attractions in the region, in particular Hebron, you are advised to take advice on the prevailing security situation.

Derekh Hevron leads south through the suburbs of Jerusalem. The kibbutz of Ramat Rachel marked the border between Israel and Jordan before 1967, while today the new neighbourhood of Gilo overlooks Bethlehem, virtually forming a conurbation between Jerusalem and the Palestinian town. To the east of the highway is a splendid view of the Judean Desert.

Less than a kilometre past the entrance to Gilo is the checkpoint between Israel and the Palestinian autonomous zone. Several hundred metres further south on the right is **Rachel's Tomb**,

Preceding pages: the impressive mount of Masada. **Right**, view from the Church of the Nativity, one of the most famous pilgrimage sites in the world.

believed to be the burial site of Jacob's second wife and the mother of Benjamin. The modest, white-domed shrine was erected in the mid-19th century by the Anglo-Jewish philanthropist. The tomb attracts Jewish women who pray for fertility or a safe birth.

Immediately after the tomb there is a fork in the highway and the road to the right, Manger Street, leads into the heart of the town. Bethlehem is a very graceful, hilltop town with a tranquil, relaxing atmosphere. The residents are friendly and welcoming of tourists, not least because this is how they make their livelihood. But beneath the picturesque exterior, Bethlehem, though officially at peace and firmly in the hands of the Palestinians, has social tensions. About half of the town's 50,000 residents are Christian and half Muslim and the Christians fear their traditional hegemony over Bethlehem is being threatened. Moreover, the Christians have historically fought bitterly over the **Church of Nativity** which is owned jointly by the Roman Catholic, Greek Orthodox and Armenian Orthodox churches.

Located in Manger Square the Church of Nativity is one of Christianity's oldest, continually functioning churches. Originally built in the 4th century by Constantine the Great, the church was added to by Justinian the Great in the 6th century. From 1099 onwards the Crusaders elevated the church to cathedral status and used it for the coronations of their kings.

After the defeat of the Crusaders the church underwent centuries of neglect, not due to any fault of the town's Muslim masters but because the three churches who own various parts of the church always squabbled over who had the privilege of undertaking repairs.

The inter-church hostility reached its climax in the 19th century when a star placed by the Greek Orthodox in a part of the church claimed by the Catholics resulted in the Crimean War. The Ottoman Turks removed the star and the Russian Orthodox, backing their Greek

Inside the Church of the Nativity.

brethren, issued an ultimatum to the Turks to replace the star. When the Turks refused to do so, Russia went to war against Turkey.

The most sacred part of the nativity complex is the **Cave of the Nativity** beneath the front of the church. A star marks the very site where it is believed that Christ was born and bears the Latin inscription, "Here Jesus Christ was born of the Virgin Mary". Adjacent to the church is **St Catherine's Church**, a modern Catholic establishment from where midnight mass is broadcast around the world each year.

Although the three owners of the church agree that this was the exact site where Christ was born, each celebrates Christmas on a different date. The Catholics on 25 December, the Greek Orthodox according to 25 December on the Julian calendar (6 January on our Gregorian calendar) and the Armenians on 14 January.

Milk Grotto Church. Other sites of interest in Bethlehem include the **Milk Grotto Church**, just down Milk Grotto street running eastwards from Manger Square. Legend has it that the floor is white because some of Mary's milk splashed to the floor while she was feeding the infant Jesus. Not surprisingly, Christian women having difficulties breastfeeding their babies visit the church to help their lactation. In addition, Manger Square is a pleasant place to browse through souvenir shops and lounge around enjoying a meal in one of the restaurants.

On the eastern fringes of Bethlehem is the village of **Beit Sahur** (Arabic for "House of the Shepherd"). It is claimed that in one of the fields by the village, called **The Shepherd's Field**, the angel appeared before the shepherds "watching their flocks by night" and announced the birth of Christ. Another field on the west of the village is supposedly where Boaz courted Ruth.

There are many important sites worth visiting to the south and east of Bethlehem but before doing so it is worth checking on the security situation. De-

spite the peace process there still can be periods of tension.

Situated on highway 356 south of Beit Sahur, **Herodion** was a lavish desert fortress and palace built by Herod. This is an impressive site distinguishable from afar because it looks like the mouth of a volcano; it also offers a commanding view of the surrounding desert. The Jewish historian Josephus described this, Herod's famed artificial mountain, as having the shape of a breast, and it's one to which this strange king retreated and clung when he was feeling especially paranoid in Jerusalem. Upon it, he constructed an impressive palace, which was later converted into a synagogue by the Jews during the War against the Romans. It is said that Herod is buried here, but even if you have no desire to check out his grave, you will not want to miss the breath-taking view from the mountaintop: Like Herod, you can feel like the master of all you survey.

To the east of Beit Sahur is the **Mar Saba** monastery. This desert monastery is well worth seeing, perched as it is on the edge of a cliff overlooking the Kidron stream in splendid isolation amid the Judean Desert, a breathtaking sweep of billowing, barren rocks leading down to the Dead Sea. Established by St Saba in 492, the monastery was rebuilt by its Greek Orthodox owners after an earthquake in 1834.

However, before visiting Mar Saba it should be borne in mind firstly that women are not admitted to the monastery, though the stunning location still makes a visit worthwhile. Secondly, the monastery is literally in the middle of nowhere and though maps make access seem straightforward, it is easy to take the wrong turn in several Arab villages en route. Only the adventurous are advised to undertake this trip without a guide or on a formal tour.

Likewise **Hebron**, 16km (10 miles) south of Bethlehem, is only for the brave. This ancient city has been at the very heart of the Israeli-Palestinian conflict in the 20th century and was the last major city on the West Bank to come under Palestinian rule. Even so the **Cave of Machpelah (The Tomb of the Patriarchs)** and several neighbourhoods nearby remain under Israeli control. The Cave, which is closed more than it is open, due to the security situation and various festivals, contains the tombs of Abraham and Sarah, Isaac and Rebecca and Jacob and Leah. Hebron can reached either via Bethlehem or directly from Jerusalem via a series of new tunnels and a bridge starting in Gilo.

Jericho and the Dead Sea

This excursion down to the lowest point on earth, 400 metres (1,300ft) below sea level, through inspiring desert terrain, includes Jericho, the beautiful biblical oasis which was settled over 8,000 years ago. Floating in the nearby highly salty Dead Sea is also a special experience that should not be missed.

The road down to the Dead Sea passes through the stirring rocky and rugged

landscape of the Judean Desert. Just after the junction with highway 458, at the peak of a hill, is the **Inn of the Good Samaritan** where Christians believe that Christ's encounter with the good Samaritan took place. The vastness and stark tranquility of the desert has drawn monastics and hermits for centuries and it is easy to understand the attraction.

A detour to Jericho via the old Roman road rather than along the main highway, follows **Wadi Kelt**, an attractive ribbon of lush green amid the arid brown and yellow hues of the desert. This route can be reached by turning left immediately before Mitspe Yerikho and following the orange signs. About 4km (2½ miles) down the narrow desert road is a staircase leading down to **St George's Monastery** (Monday to Saturday 8am–5pm) first built in the 5th century. The present edifice clinging to the side of the canyon cliff was completed by the Greek Orthodox in 1901. Surrounded by palm trees, the location is idyllically remote. The monastery includes a 6th-century mosaic floor and an ossiary containing the skulls of dozens of martyred monks.

The road leads down to **Jericho**, a broad expanse of green in the desert which has been a Palestinian autonomous zone since 1994. Jericho is located in the Great Syrian African Rift Valley and while the town is pleasantly warm in the winter, especially after the chilly mountain climate of Jerusalem, it is blisteringly hot in the summer. Jericho claims to be the oldest town in the world on the basis of wooden walls carbon dated as 8,000 years old. These can be found at **Tel Jericho** (daily 8am–5pm) which is near the northern entrance to the town. Nearby is **Hisham's Palace**, an 8th-century winter palace with exceptionally well preserved mosaics. Another Jericho attraction is the **Monastery of the Temptation** (Quarantel), located half way up the mountainside behind Tel Jericho. The Greek Orthodox monastery offers a breathtaking panorama of the Jordan Valley, Jericho

and the Dead Sea. According to Christian tradition Christ was brought here by the Devil, who tempted him with control over all that he saw.

Several kilometres east of Jericho the **Allenby Bridge** leads over the River Jordan, in fact nothing more than a broad stream, into the Hashemite Kingdom of Jordan.

Several kilometres south of Jericho is the **Dead Sea**, so named because the excessive amount of salt in the water has killed off marine life. The Dead Sea is in fact a lake some 77km (49 miles) long and 10km (6 miles) across at its widest point. Visitors love to be photographed floating in the sea and the nearest place to be able to enter the water (with showers nearby) is at the **Kalya** water park. The showers are mandatory because the water is slimy and smelly and the salt will cause agonising stinging over any wounds. Menstruating women should not enter the water.

It is worth travelling further south to the **Ein Fashka** nature reserve (daily

Left, a Dead Sea facial. **Right**, peace at the lowest point on earth.

8am–5pm; closes 4pm in the winter) to take a dip. These freshwater pools are a favourite spot for ornithologists especially in the spring and autumn when birds migrating between Europe and Africa stop off making their way along the rift valley.

Though the water does feel very uncomfortable, the Dead Sea is actually extremely healthy. The minerals in the sea include bromine which acts as a sedative to soothe the nerves and iodine and magnesium which smooth the skin and are especially beneficial for conditions like psoriasis, rheumatism and arthritis. Treatment programmes are offered by medical professionals at **Ein Gedi** and at the hotels in **Ein Bokek** which usually involve being covered in Dead Sea mud. The medicinal properties of the region are recognised by physicians and some European national health plans offer subisidised trips to the Dead Sea. A further advantage of the area is that evaporating gases from the sea filter out many of the sun's harmful rays reducing the risk of sunburn despite searing summer temperatures.

Israel also mines these minerals and the Dead Sea Works near the site of the infamous biblical city of Sodom at the southern end of the sea exports $600 million worth of minerals annually.

Other sites of interest by the Dead Sea include **Qumran** (Saturday to Thursday 8am–5pm, closed Sunday) where in 1947, a Bedouin shepherd was looking for a goat which had strayed. He threw a stone into one of the caves in the cliff side and heard a sound of smashing pottery. Later, it transpired that he had made the most exciting archaeological discovery of the century: scrolls, dating to the first centuries BC and AD, preserved in earthenware jars.

The scrolls have revolutionised scholarship of the Second Temple period and thrown new light on the origins of Christianity, indicating that Jesus may have been an Essene, or at least was strongly influenced by the sect. The scrolls have revealed the mood of messianic fatal-

Visiting the caves at Ein Borek.

ism among the Jews of that time, explaining both the emergence of Christianity and the fervour of the Jewish rebels in their hopeless war against Rome. The scrolls have also disclosed much about the nature of the Essene way of life and the beliefs of the sect, as well as revealing details of temple ritual and worship.

The partly reconstructed buildings of Qumran are on a plateau some 100 metres (330 ft) above the shore and are worth a visit. Numerous caves, including those where the scrolls were found, are visible in the nearby cliffs, but these are not accessible to the tourist.

Ein Gedi, half way down the coast of the Dead Sea, has a health spa, and there are several interesting hikes here up mountain gorges including **Nakhal David**, which involves a 20-minute walk to **David's Spring** outside a cave where it is believed that David hid from Saul after they had argued. **Nakhal Arugot**, 1km (½ mile) to the south, involves a longer climb to a refreshing desert waterfall and icy cool pools for bathing.

Masada (daily from sunrise until 4pm) is an isolated peak at the southern end of the Dead Sea, more than 2 hours drive from Jerusalem. This is the most fabulous and, with the possible exception of the Western Wall, the most culturally resonant sight in all of Israel. Part of the line of cliffs which rise up to the Judean desert plateau, Masada is cut off from the surrounding area by steep wadis to the north, south and west.

It was on this desolate mesa that Herod the Great built an impregnable fortress as a retreat from his potentially rebellious subjects. Visitors to the site can wander through the magnificent three-tiered palace which extends down the northern cliff; the Roman bath house, with its ingenious heating system; the vast storehouses; the western palace with its fine mosaics and the huge water cisterns hewn in the rock. They can appreciate the remarkable desert landscape from the summit, which can be climbed easily from the west via the Roman ramp, ascended by cable-car from the east, or more ener-

Masada from the air.

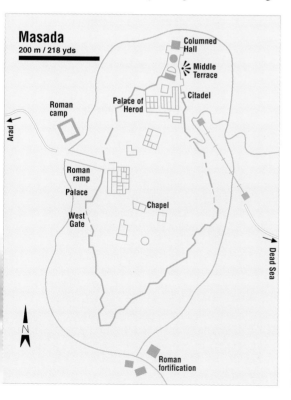

getically climbed via the "**Snake Path**", also from the east.

These features alone make the fortress worth a visit, but it is the story of the epic siege of the fortress in the Jewish War against Rome which has made Masada a place of pilgrimage second only to the Western Wall.

In AD 66, a group of Jewish rebels called the Sicarii – named after the *sica* (dagger) their favourite weapon – seized Masada from its Roman garrison, triggering the Jewish War against Rome. Securing their base there, the Sicarii proceeded to Jerusalem, where they took over the leadership of the revolt. In the bitter infighting between the rebel groups, their leader was killed and they returned to Masada to regroup.

The new Sicarii leader, Elazar Ben-Yair, waited out the war at Masada, joined from time to time by other groups. He was still in possession after the fall of Jerusalem in AD 70. In AD 73, the Roman Tenth Legion arrived to put an end to this last Jewish stronghold.

With its auxiliaries and camp followers, the legion numbered over 15,000. Defending Masada were fewer than 1,000 Jewish men, women and children. Herod's store rooms were still well supplied. The Romans destroyed the aqueduct feeding the cisterns from dams in the wadi, but the cisterns had enough water for a prolonged period and were accessible from the summit.

The legion constructed a wall around the rock, reinforced by camps, which blocked the main possible escape routes and then built an earth ramp, reinforced by wooden beams and shielded by stone, which pointed like a dagger at the perimeter wall of the fortress.

The final defences were set on fire, and when the blaze died down, the Romans entered Masada to discover the bodies of the defenders laid out in rows. Rejecting slavery, the men had first killed their own families and then themselves, drawing lots for a final 10 to carry out the act, one last electee killing the other nine before committing suicide.

This account in *The Jewish War* by Flavius Josephus has become one of the legends of modern Israel. Young soldiers being inducted into the armoured corps today swear their oath of allegiance atop the fortress and vow: "Masada shall not fall again!"

The excavations by Yigael Yadin in the 1960s uncovered the magnificence of Herod's fortress and palaces, but the most moving finds were of the Zealots' living quarters in the casement wall, their synagogue and ritual baths, the remains of the fire, and, in some cases, bits of their final meal. The skeletons of a man, woman and child were uncovered in the northern palace; more were found in a nearby cave, where they had apparently been thrown by the Romans.

The country caught its collective breath when the discovery was announced of a set of inscribed pottery shards, which might have been the lots cast by the defenders to decide which of them would kill the others. One of them was inscribed "Ben-Yai".

Left, the cistern at Masada. **Right**, camel at Qumran. **Overpage**, notes stuffed in cracks of Jerusalem's Western Wall.

INSIGHT GUIDES

TRAVEL TIPS

New Insight Maps

Maps in Insight Guides are tailored to complement the text. But when you're on the road you sometimes need the big picture that only a large-scale map can provide. This new range of durable Insight Fleximaps has been designed to meet just that need.

Detailed, clear cartography
makes the comprehensive route and city maps easy to follow, highlights all the major tourist sites and provides valuable motoring information plus a full index.

Informative and easy to use
with additional text and photographs covering a destination's top 10 essential sites, plus useful addresses, facts about the destination and handy tips on getting around.

Laminated finish
allows you to mark your route on the map using a non-permanent marker pen, and wipe it off. It makes the maps more durable and easier to fold than traditional maps.

The first titles
cover many popular destinations. They include Algarve, Amsterdam, Bangkok, California, Cyprus, Dominican Republic, Florence, Hong Kong, Ireland, London, Mallorca, Paris, Prague, Rome, San Francisco, Sydney, Thailand, Tuscany, USA Southwest, Venice, and Vienna.

✷ INSIGHT GUIDES
The world's largest collection of visual travel guides

CONTENTS

Getting Acquainted

The Place 222
History 222
Government & Economy........222
People................................223
Climate 223
Business Hours 224
Public Holidays 224

Planning the Trip

Passports and Visas 225
Customs 225
Health 226
Money Matters......................226
What to Bring 227
Tourist Offices 227
Getting There 227

Practical Tips

Media 228
Postal Services 229
Telecommunications 229
Embassies and Consulates....230
Travelling with Children.........230
Student Travel 230
Senior Citizens 230
Disabled Travel....................231
Security and Crime 231
Medical Services..................231
Etiquette 232
On Departure 232

Getting Around

By Road 233
Public Transport 233
Taxis 235
Domestic Flights 235
Driving................................235
On Foot 236

Where to Stay

Kubbutz Guest Houses 237
Christian Hospices 237
Bed & Breakfast..................237

Hotels 237
Holiday Flats & Apartotels 238
Camping & Youth Hostels 239

Where to Eat

What to Eat 239
Drinking Notes 240
Where to Eat 241

Culture

Archaeological Sites..............243
Museums.............................243
Cultural Centres 244
Art Galleries 244
Music, Dance & Theatre........244
Cinema 244
Nightlife 245

Festivals

Religious Festivals 245
Cultural Events.....................245

Outdoor Attractions

Parks & Gardens 246
Zoos 246
Hiking 246

Shopping

What to Buy 246
Shopping Areas....................246
Markets 247
Specialist Shops 247
Shopping Hours 247

Sports

Participant 247
Spectator 247

Language

Hebrew 248
Arabic 248

Further Reading

General 250
Other Insight Guides.............250

Getting Acquainted

The Place

Area: 108 sq. km (42 sq. miles)
Situation: Jerusalem lies 48 km (30 miles) east, as the crow flies, of Israel's Mediterranean coast at approximately 35°20' longitude and 31°80' latitude. To the east, north and south Jerusalem borders on the West Bank, captured by Israel from Jordan in 1967 and the subject of autonomy negotiations between Israel and the Palestinians. Some 40 km (25 miles) to the east of Jerusalem is the border with Jordan near the Palestinian town of Jericho.
Highest neighbourhood: Romema 830 metres (908 ft)
Population: 620,000
Language: Hebrew and Arabic
Religion: 66 percent Jewish, 28 percent Muslim, 6 percent Christian. Jerusalem is a holy city to Jews, Christians and Muslims.
Time zone: GMT plus two hours (plus three between April and September)
Currency: New Israel Shekel (NIS)
Weights and measures: Metric
Electricity: 220 volts AC, single phase, 50 cycles
International dialling code: 00 972 2

History

It was about 3,000 years ago that King David moved his capital from Hebron to Jerusalem, capturing the city from the Canaanite tribe called the Jebusites. It is unclear when the city, with its commanding military location on mountain peaks and underground water supply, was originally established. But Jews and Muslims believe that it was on the Temple Mount some 4,000 years ago that Abraham prepared to

sacrifice his son Isaac when God tested Abraham's obedience to him.

King David's son Solomon, consolidated Jerusalem's primacy by constructing the Temple. Subsequently, though Jerusalem remained a predominantly Jewish city with periods of Jewish independence, through conquest it came under the control of Assyrians, Babylonians, Persians, Greeks and Romans. Shortly after Christ was crucified in Jerusalem by the Romans, the Jews were exiled from the city which was re-named Aeolia Capitolina. The Holy City was ruled by Byzantine Christians, Arab Muslims, Crusaders, Mamelukes and Ottoman Turks before the British captured Jerusalem in 1917.

The emergence of Zionist claims meant that both Jew and Arab courted the British for control of the city. Though the United Nations ruled that Jerusalem should have an international status, the War of Independence in 1948, in which the Arab nations attacked the Jewish state resulted in the city being partitioned between Israel and Jordan. In 1967 Israel captured East Jerusalem from Jordan. During the negotiations with the Palestinians which began in 1993, the Israeli government's policy was that the issue of Jerusalem as the country's capital was not open to discussion, though they would try to accommodate all reasonable religious needs.

Government

All the major institutions of Israeli government are located in Jerusalem. Israel is a parliamentary democracy with a 120 single chamber called the Knesset elected every four years by proportional representation of all citizens over 18. The Prime Minister, who heads the government, is also directly chosen every four years by the electorate. The titular head of state is the president, who is elected every five years by secret ballot of Knesset members. Also located in Jerusalem's government district are the Supreme Court, which has the

power to interpret Knesset laws, and the Bank of Israel, through which the government can regulate the financial system. Jerusalem itself is run by a mayor and a local council elected every four years.

The Palestinian Arabs living in East Jerusalem have never recognized any of these Israeli government or municipal institutions. Though Arabs have the right to vote in government and local elections, the Palestinians have refused en masse to exercise these rights. In recent years though the New Orient House in the Sheikh Jarrah quarter of the city has emerged as a Palestinian quasi-government building, becoming a bone of contention in the negotiations between Israel and the Palestinians over the future status of Jerusalem.

Economy

Jerusalem is one of the poorest cities in Israel with average per capita incomes less than half that of Tel Aviv and Haifa. Not that Jerusalem is impoverished. Most Jerusalemites enjoy a comfortable standard of living with average monthly incomes of more than US$1,000 a month. Generally speaking, the ultra-orthodox and Arab communities have less well developed economic infrastructures.

Even among the mainstream Jewish sector of the city, there is relatively little industry in the country's capital. Israel exports more than $15 billion worth of goods each year, but the exports of Jerusalem companies amount to little more than $500 million annually, mainly from Intel Electronics (semiconductors), Teva Pharmaceuticals and some other smaller high-tech concerns. Being the capital, Jerusalem's largest employer is the Israeli government, and the city's biggest foreign currency earner is tourism. More than 80 percent of the 2 million people who come to Israel each year spend some time in the city. The Hebrew University, with over 20,000 students, also attracts many people to the city. Jerusalem also has many religious educational institutions and world Jewish national organizations.

People

Jerusalem is Israel's largest city with a population of 620,000. This comprises about 10 percent of the country's total population of 5.5 million. Arabs number about 180,000 of the city's population, of whom about 150,000 are Muslims. The remainder are Christians and include Orthodox, Catholic and Armenian communities. An estimated 25 percent of Jerusalemites are ultra-orthodox Jews, who live in separate communities and can be distinguished by the black hats and coats worn by the men.

Greater Jerusalem – stretching from the Jewish communities of Ma'ale Adumim and Givat Ze'ev in the east and west, and the Arab towns of Ramallah and Bethlehem in the north and south – has a population approaching 1 million. Greater Tel Aviv, with more than 2 million residents, is the country's largest metropolis.

Climate

Much of the Middle East swelters through a long, very hot summer followed by a short, mild winter. Spring and fall are barely noticed. But Jerusalem, because of its altitude, enjoys four clearly distinct seasons.

Make no mistake: winter in Jerusalem is cold. True, the thermometer rarely dips much below zero centigrade, but the Holy City's hilltops are buffeted by strong winds and a substantial rainfall of 600mm (24 inches) is concentrated in heavy bursts from late November to early March. Hotels are well heated, but homes, although they generally have central heating, can be less comfortable with their stone floors and walls designed more for summer than winter.

Despite the cold, nothing is more romantic or magical than a snow-

Average Temperatures

(Minimum – Maximum)

	January	April	July	October
Jerusalem				
(°C)	6–11	12–21	20–29	16–26
(°F)	43–53	53–69	66–84	60–78
Tel Aviv				
(°C)	9–18	12–22	21–30	15–29
(°F)	49–65	54–72	70–86	59–84
Tiberias				
(°C)	9–18	13–27	23–37	19–32
(°F)	48–65	56–80	73–98	65–89
Eilat				
(°C)	10–21	17–31	25–40	20–33
(°F)	49–70	63–87	78–103	69–92

Annual Rainfall: 600 mm (24 inches).

storm in Jerusalem. There are brief snowfalls most years but not every year. And then suddenly the weather changes and, after a day or two of sunshine and clear blue skies, even the heaviest snow has melted. For Jerusalem winters are not all grey and gloom. Every so often there is a mild stretch of warmth and sunshine, though the nights remain cold.

The blossoming of almond trees in late winter heralds the coming of spring as the hills and valleys around the city are ablaze with delicate hues of pink and white. Early spring, Passover and Easter, is the best time to be in Jerusalem. The heavy winter rains combine with the spring sunshine to bring forth a variety of colourful flowers. Red anemones, pink cyclamen, yellow mustard, blue orchids and brown irises bring the countryside alive. Spring weather is unpredictable. It can be cold one day, followed the next by a *hamsin* wind blowing in off the Sahara desert which sends temperatures soaring to nearly 40°C (104°F). The body becomes confused and vulnerable, and colds and flu abound.

Summer is the least interesting of seasons in Jerusalem. The only

question is whether it is going to be hot or very hot. The sun hovers oppressively overhead, blindingly bright, burning and dehydrating hapless tourists not used to its power in such southerly latitudes. But, unlike Tel Aviv and the Mediterranean coast, humidity is low, making conditions more comfortable, and from early evening through to dawn it can be deliciously cool.

Visually speaking, there is no autumn in Jerusalem, no glorious reds, browns and golds. But the weather turns much milder and the sun becomes more benign as it moves south of the equator. Late October and early November is a particularly pleasant time to be in Jerusalem. There can be heavy rainfalls and cold snaps but generally speaking the weather remains agreeable until the second half of December. Then suddenly the air develops that crisp, cold winter bite, always in time to greet the Christmas pilgrims.

Elsewhere in Israel, just short distances from Jerusalem, the weather can be very different. Tel Aviv and the coastal plain, only a 50-minute drive from Jerusalem, has comparable temperatures in the summer, but the much higher humidity makes it more uncomfortable than Jerusalem, especially at nights. However, in the winter Tel Aviv has much more sunshine and warmth. The Galilee has an identical climate to Jerusalem but Tiberias, the Dead Sea, Negev and Eilat are hotter.

In any event, beware of the sun because Jerusalem is considerably further south than destinations like Spain, Italy and Greece.

Business Hours

Banks: Sunday and Thursday from 8.30am–1pm and 4–6pm. Monday, Tuesday and Wednesday 8.30am–1pm only. Friday and eves of holy days 8.30am–12 noon. Branches in the leading hotels usually offer convenient additional banking hours.
Offices: Sunday–Thursday 8am– noon.
Stores: Sunday–Thursday 8am–7pm or later, Friday mornings only and sometimes Saturday night. Some smaller stores may, however, take a siesta.

Public Holidays

Saturday is the Jewish sabbath and it is difficult to find anything open in Jewish West Jerusalem and

elsewhere in Israel on that day except for some non-kosher restaurants and most museums. But in Arab East Jerusalem everywhere is open on Saturday, including restaurants, stores and moneychangers.

A five-day week operates in Israel from Sunday to Thursday with Sunday being a regular day. Friday is rather like Saturday in Europe or America, with all stores, some banks and most services open but government offices closed. Because the sabbath begins at sundown, most stores and restaurants will begin closing by early afternoon on a Friday. The same is true on the day prior to a festival.

The Jewish calendar is a lunar-solar calendar. Each month lasts from new moon to new moon (28/29 days) with leap months added every few years to allow for the solar year. Therefore Jewish festivals will fall on a different date in the Gregorian calendar each year within a band of about four weeks. The following holidays are the major festivals (everything is closed, as on the sabbath).

Jewish Holidays
Rosh Hashanah (Jewish New Year), two days in September
Yom Kippur (Day of Atonement), one day in September/October

Succot (Tabernacles), one day in September/October
Simchat Torah (Rejoicing of the Law), one day in October
First day Pesach (Passover), one day in March/April
Last day Pesach (Passover), one day in March/April
Independence Day, one day in April/May
Shavuot (Pentecost), one day in May/June

Minor festivals include:
Tu B'Shvat (New Year for the Trees), January/February
Purim, February/March
Lag B'Omer, April/May
Hanukkah, eight days in December.
On **Holocaust Day** (April/May), **Memorial Day** (April/May) and **Tisha B'Av** (July/August), all restaurants (outside of hotels) and places of entertainment are closed.

Muslim Holidays
The Muslim sabbath is Friday. While many Arabs will attend special morning prayers at mosques, only a few stores and businesses are actually closed. Muslims observe a lunar year with 12 months so that each festival falls earlier each year and rotates backwards through the seasons. Muslim holidays when Arab stores are likely to be closed:

Ten Facts about Jerusalem

1 The city has many names. The Jews call it Yerushalaim, the Arabs Al Kuds and in Roman times it was re-named Aeolina Capitolina.
2 Many orthodox Jews will not set foot on the Temple Mount for fear of entering the unknown former site of the Holy of Holies, the part of the ancient Temple where the High Priest spoke to God and which was strictly off limits to anybody but the High Priest.
3 The Christian Holy Sites were identified in the 4th century by Queen Helena, mother of Roman Emperor Constantine the Great.
4 The keys to the Church of the Holy Sepulchre are held by a

Muslim because the denominations that own various parts of the church do not trust each other.
5 The Dome of the Rock is not a mosque but a shrine.
6 Jerusalem and the Judean Mountains form a continental divide with rainfall running down westwards to the Mediterranean (Atlantic Ocean) and eastwards to the Syria-Africa Rift Valley (Indian Ocean).
7 The Old City has seven gates, still functioning. There is an eighth gate – the Golden Gate – facing the Mount of Olives, that is now bricked up. It is believed that the

Messiah will enter Jerusalem through this gate.
8 Mount Zion was inadvertently left outside the Old City walls when Suleiman the Magnificent had them constructed in the 16th century. Rumour has it that as a result the Ottoman ruler executed his chief engineer.
9 The Jerusalem Forest to the west of the city has six million trees representing the Jews who perished in the Holocaust.
10 The entrance to the Knesset was switched from the south to the north side just before it was opened in 1966 for fear of Jordanian artillery near Bethlehem.

Ayd Al Fitr – marking the end of Ramadan a month of fasting from sunrise to sunset.
Ayd Al Adha – the feast of the sacrifice which falls at the end of the pilgrimage to Mecca (Haj) and commemorates Abraham's offering of Isaac as a sacrifice.
Muslim New Year and the **Prophet Mohammed's Birthday**.

Christian Holidays

Outside of the Christian Quarter of the Old City of Jerusalem and nearby Bethlehem there is almost no outward indication that it is Christmas or Easter. Jews and Muslims don't recognise these Christian days. In fact, Jerusalem enjoys three Christmases and two Easters. The Western churches celebrate Christmas on 25 December, but the Orthodox churches still mark the festival according to the Julian calendar, 12 days later on 6 January. The Armenian Orthodox church celebrates Christmas another week later on 14 January. Nor is there any agreement on the date of Easter. Some years the churches concur on the same date but often the Orthodox church will commemorate Good Friday a week after the Western churches.

Planning the Trip

Passports & Visas

Visitors are required to hold a valid passport, while stateless persons must have a valid travel document with a return visa to the country of issue. Tourists from the United Kingdom and other European Union countries do not require a visa. Citizens of the United States, Canada, Australia and many other countries do require a visa but this is granted free at the port of entry. Citizens of other countries should check with their nearest Israeli consulate. A knowledgable travel agent can provide accurate information.

Citizens of many countries in Africa, Asia and Eastern Europe will require a visa before departure. Visa fees are only several dollars. If you visit Israel on a cruise ship, you will be given a Landing For the Day card, which permits you to remain in the country as long as your ship is in port, and you need to apply for a visitor's visa.

Visitor's visas are usually valid for three months only. An extension can usually be obtained from the nearest district office of the Ministry of Interior. The Jerusalem office is located in downtown West Jerusalem, 1 Shlomzion Hamalkah Street, tel: 629 0222. Extending a visa costs $25 and office hours are Sunday–Thursday from 8am–midday. There are usually long lines so be prepared to wait.

Anyone wishing to enter Israel for an extended period of work, study or permanent settlement should apply while still abroad to an Israel consular mission for the appropriate visa.

For all visitors it is essential to have a ticket for the next

destination after Israel. Officials at Israel's port of entry have been known to turn away travellers with a one-way ticket and/or insufficient funds with which to maintain themselves during their stay.

Some Arab and Muslim countries will refuse entry to anybody who has Israeli entry stamps in their passport. But Israeli officials will, if asked, refrain from stamping Israel in passports. However, if you enter from Egypt, the Egyptian stamp which specifies the crossing point will indicate that you have been to Israel.

Customs

Customs regulations enable you to bring into the country without paying duty the following items: eau de cologne or perfume not exceeding a quarter of a litre (half-pint); 2 litres (3ˇ pints) of wine and 1 litre (2 pints) of spirits; 250 cigarettes or 250 grams (9 oz) of tobacco; and gifts not exceeding $200 in value.

The following items may be brought in duty-free, providing they are taken out on departure: typewriters, computers, cameras, video cameras, tape recorders, jewellery, binoculars, baby carriages, musical instruments, etc. These regulations were formulated many years ago during more austere times in Israel when there was a fear of visitors smuggling in consumer goods to give or sell to Israelis tax free. In practice, visitors are no longer troubled by the customs authorities unless bringing in conspicuously unnecessary objects like colour television sets or fax machines. Customs authorities are empowered to demand a deposit for expensive items which is returnable when the visitor and the particular item leave the country.

The red and green channel system used in the European Union is also used at Ben Gurion International Airport. Passengers uncertain about the regulations are advised to pass through the red channel and make enquiries about the matter in doubt.

Health

There are no vaccination requirements for tourists entering Israel except if arriving from an infected area. Likewise there are no major diseases in Israel that the visitor may wish to be innoculated against. As elsewhere, Aids is a growing cause for concern in Israel and the numbers contracting the disease are growing. Nevertheless, the numbers of Aids cases is considerably lower in Israel than in North America and Western Europe despite comparably liberal sexual behaviour.

Water

Tap water is as healthy as any in Western Europe or North America, and for the extra fussy there is plenty of mineral water available. The most common health problems are upset stomachs, usually caused by a change of diet and spicy foods rather than unsanitary conditions. A lack of respect for the sun can result in sunburn and sunstroke, while dehydration plagues those who over-exert themselves sightseeing. Tourists should acclimatise to the sun gradually, apply high factor suntan lotions and keep indoors altogether or in the shade between 10am and 4pm, especially between April and October. Wear light comfortable clothes that cover arms and legs and don a hat and a pair of sunglasses.

Most important, it is vital to drink continually even if you do not feel thirsty. Research shows that the body can need as much as a litre (2 pints) each hour to replace the liquid lost by sweat during summer exertions. Bear in mind that tea, coffee and alcohol have diminished value in replenishing body liquids. Stick to water and soft drinks. Symptoms of dehydration can mislead, making you think you have another problem. These symptoms include headaches and migraines, upset stomachs and nausea and even fever, diarrhoea and vomiting. When sightseeing arrange your day sensibly, visiting outdoor sights in the early morning and late afternoon, while resting or taking in museums during the middle of the day.

Money Matters

The Israeli currency is the New Israeli Shekel (NIS) which officially succeeded the old Israeli shekel in 1985 during a period of hyper-inflation. The NIS is relatively stable and floats freely against the world's major currencies with a revised exchange rate each day according to supply and demand. The NIS is divided into 100 agorot, small change comes in 5 agorot, 10 agorot and half shekel brass coins. There are silver coins for a shekel, 5 shekels and 10 shekels, and notes are issued in four denominations: 20 NIS (grey with portrait of former Prime Minister Moshe Sharett); 50 NIS (purple with portrait of Nobel Literature Prize winner, Shmuel Agnon); 100 NIS (grey with portrait of former President Yitzhak Ben Zvi); and 200 NIS (reddish brown with portrait of former President Zalman Shazar).

Tourists may bring an unlimited amount of foreign currency into Israel whether in cash, traveller's cheques, letters of credit or State of Israel Bonds. Tourists are not required to declare the amount of foreign currency in their possession upon arrival and foreign currency exchanges during their stay are not recorded. Tourists can also bring in and take out an unlimited amount of shekels. Shekels can be purchased before your visit in banks outside Israel but this can be problematic because few banks keep NIS in stock and it may take several days for notes to be ordered.

Exchange rates are the same in all banks but queues are shorter at Bureaux de Change. There are moneychangers in East Jerusalem and the West Bank who may offer slightly different rates. Vendors are prepared to accept the world's better-known currencies but often offer inferior exchange rates. Hotels and specially approved tourist stores will sell goods free of 17 per-cent VAT if payment is made in foreign currency.

Visa, MasterCard/EuroCard, American Express and Diners Club are honoured virtually everywhere. The cash machines outside almost every Israeli bank will dispense money against these cards. This can save waiting around in crowded banks and enable the visitor to obtain cash outside banking hours. Should your credit card be lost or stolen, telephone one of the following numbers immediately: **American Express**, tel: 03-524 2211.
Diners Club, tel: 03-572 3572.
Visa, tel: 03-572 3572.
EuroCard/MasterCard, tel: 03-576 4444.

Traveller's cheques are widely accepted, though banks take a commission on each cheque so it is probably cheaper to bring higher denomination cheques. Eurocheques are also honoured by banks.

There are many banks in Israel. Banking hours are usually Sunday and Thursday 8.30am–1pm and 4pm–5.30pm or 6pm, Monday, Tuesday and Wednesday 8.30am–1pm and Friday 8.30am–noon.

The following are special tourist branches of banks in Jerusalem:
American Israel Bank, 14 Hillel Street, tel: 02-625 7181.
First International, Dan Pearl Hotel, tel: 02-6257311.
Hapoalim, 16 King George Street, tel: 02-6207676.
Hapoalim, Zion Square, tel: 02-62-7171.
Israel Discount, 11 Ben Yehuda, tel: 02-675 4444.
Leumi, 17 King David Street, tel: 02-620 1811.
Mercantile Discount, 64 Jaffa Road, tel: 02-625 4241.
United Mizrachi, 12 Ben Yehuda Street, tel: 02-620 8922.

Tour Operators

United Kingdom tour operators specialising in Israel:
AMG, 70 Edgware Way, Edgware, Middlesex., tel: 0181-958 5636.
All Abroad, 26 Temple Fortune Parade, London NW11, tel: 0181-458 2666.
Expert Travel, 784/6 Finchley Road, London NW11, tel: 0181-922 1234.
Goodmos Tours, Dunstan House, 14A St Cross Street, London EC1N 8XA, tel: 0171-430 2230.
Longwood Holidays, 182 Longwood Gardens, Clayhall, Ilford, Essex IG5 0EW, tel: 0181-551 4494.
Peltours, Sovereign House, 11–19 Ballards Lane, Finchley, London N3 1UX, tel: 0181-346 9144/0181-343 0590. Manchester office: 27–29 Church Street, Manchester, tel: 0161-236 0006.
West End Travel, 341 Oxford Street, London W1R 1HB, tel: 0171-409 0630.

•**Car Rentals:**
USA: Eldan, toll free: 1-800-938-5000.
UK: London: 0181-951-5727.

What to Bring

Comfortable, durable walking shoes will make sightseeing less arduous. In the cold months (November–March) bring warm and waterproof clothing, and if staying in Jerusalem even in the summer bring a cardigan, sweater or jacket for chilly evenings.

In the warm, hot summer (April–October), but in the winter too, come armed with dark sun glasses, a broad-brimmed hat, and light-weight clothes, preferably loose fitting and cotton. Women will need modest dress (covering arms and legs and low necklines) for visiting holy sites. Keeping all parts of the body covered for both men and women might be a good idea any-way to minimise skin damage from the sun. It is worth bringing a swimsuit even in winter and suntan lotion is mandatory for those wishing to sunbathe. For hiking in hot weather a water canteen is necessary.

Tourist Offices

Canada
Suite 700, 180 Bloor Street West, Toronto, Ontario, tel: 416-964-3784.
United States
Wabash Avenue, Chicago, Illinois, tel: 312-782-4306/7/8.
6380 Wilshire Boulevard, Los Angeles, California, tel: 213-658-7462/3.
Suite 326, 420 Lincoln Road, Miami Beach, Florida, tel: 305-673-6862.
350 Fifth Avenue, 19th floor, New York, New York, tel: 212-560- 0650.
Suite 550, 220 Montgomery Street, San Francisco, California, tel: 415-775-5462/3/4.
3514 International Drive NW, Washington DC, tel: 202-364-5500.
United Kingdom
180 Oxford Street, London W1N 9DJ, tel: 0171-299 1111; fax: 0171-299 1112.

Getting There

By Air
Ben Gurion International Airport is situated near Lod alongside the Jerusalem–Tel Aviv highway 35 minutes by car from Jerusalem. The airport is 50 km (30 miles) west of Jerusalem and 20 km (12 miles) southeast of Tel Aviv. Facilities include a Government Tourist Office (tel: 03-971 1485). Banks, post offices and restaurant facilities are all open 24 hours a day except on the sabbath and holidays. El Al lost and found department, open 24 hours a day can be reached on tel: 03-971 2484.

El Al Israel Airlines carries over 40 percent of the 6 million passengers who use the airport each year. Other major airlines with regluar flights to Ben Gurion Airport include Air France, Alitalia, Austrian Airlines, British Airways, Delta, Iberia, KLM, Lot, Lufthansa, Malev, Olympic, Sabena, SAS, South African Airlines, Swissair and TWA. Regular charter flights are organized by El Al, Arkia (another Israeli carrier), Monarch and Tower.

The following airlines have offices in Jerusalem:
Air France, 3 Shlomzion Hamalka Street, tel: 02-625 2495.
Alitalia, 23 Hillel Street, tel: 02-625 8653.
British Airways, 33 Jaffa Road, tel: 02-625 6111.
El Al, 12 Hillel Street, tel: 02-624 6725/6/7.
KLM, 33 Jaffa Road, tel: 02-625 1361.
Lufthansa, 16a King George Street, tel: 02-624 4941.
Sabena, 23 King David Street, tel: 02-623 4971.
SAS, 14 Azzahara Street, tel: 02-283235.
Swissair, 31 Haneviim Street, tel: 02-623 1373.
Tower Air, 14 Hillel Street, tel: 02-255137.
TWA, 34 Ben Yahuda Street, tel: 02-624 1576.

Jerusalem has its own airport at Atarot, north of the city. But as a consequence of the non-recognition of Jerusalem's status by the international community internation-al flights are not allowed to land there. Private international flights can land at Atarot, however, and there are daily internal flights to all parts of Israel.

By Sea
Israel's main ports are Ashdod and Haifa. The Stability Line and Sol Line offer regular sailings from Europe to Haifa port and many Mediterranean cruises include Israel in their itinerary. Official ports of entry for foreign yachts and boats include these two cities as well as the marinas as Tel Aviv and Eilat. Marinas will be opened at Haifa, Herzliya and Ashkelon.

By Road
Bus Services
There are services from Cairo to Tel Aviv and Jerusalem and to the Taba border point near Eilat.

Land Travel from Jordan & Egypt

From Jordan

Following the signing of a peace agreement between Israel and Jordan in 1994, communications between the two countries have improved considerably (Israel now recognises Jordanian stamps in passports and visas and vice versa). Visitors can now choose between several border crossings: the Allenby Bridge, the Jordan River Crossing (near Bet Shean) and the Arava Checkpoint (between Eilat and Aqaba). **Note:** You should check the situation before travelling. Israel's Ministry of Tourism can provide the latest information, tel: 02-754 8111.

Allenby Bridge, near Jericho, some 40 km (25 miles) from Jerusalem, is the main crossing point. For information, tel: 02-994 1038

The visa requirements are the same as those at any other point of entry into Israel (it is not possible to get an Israeli visa upon arrival at the Bridge and, as yet, it is still not possible to get one in Jordan).

The Bridge is open Sunday to Thursday 8am–4pm and on Friday and the eves of holidays 8–11am. It is closed on Saturday and on Jewish holidays. At Allenby Bridge a Tourist Information Office is open at the same time as the Bridge. Other facilities are: currency exchange, post office, public telephones, cafeteria, toilets, porters and *sherut* (service) taxis to Jerusalem, Jericho, Bethlehem, Hebron, Ramallah and Gaza.

For opening hours and restrictions at other points of entry between Jordan and Israel check the latest details with Israel's Ministry of Tourism, or contact the border itself:
Jordan River (near Bet She'an), tel: 06-6586448.
Arava Checkpoint (near Eilat), tel: 07- 633 6812.

From Egypt

Points of entry open between Israel and Egypt are Nizzana, Rafiah, and Taba, open 363 days a year (exceptions are Yom Kippur and the first day of Id el Adha).

Nizzana, which is the main point of entry, is about 60 km (37 miles) southwest of Beersheba, and is open between 8am–4pm.

Rafiah, 50 km (30 miles) southwest of Ashkelon, is open between 8.30am–5pm.

Taba, just south of Eilat is open 24 hours a day.

There are also services from Amman to the three border crossings with Israel which meet up with buses from Jerusalem and Tel Aviv. A direct service is planned between Amman and Israeli cities.

Car Travel

Israel has good roads but most of them are packed with traffic. Drivers, as elsewhere in the Mediterranean, are fast and discourteous and specialise in overtaking on the inside. Pedestrians tend to meander in the road. Car hire is expensive and is probably not necessary for travelling in the centre of the country which has good bus and taxi services. Parking is difficult and expensive in the city centres. However, it is worth hiring a car for touring the Galilee or Negev.

Practical Tips

Media

Print

Israelis and Palestinians are prolific newspaper readers. In fact, all four Hebrew-language daily newspapers are printed in Tel Aviv. The only daily Jewish journal printed in Jerusalem is the English-language daily, the *Jerusalem Post*. Published six days a week (except Saturday) the *Jerusalem Post* offers poor value for money but will enable tourists to keep up with events. Founded in 1932, the *Jerusalem Post* was owned by the Histadrut Trade Union movement and traditionally pursued a left-of-centre editorial policy. But in 1990 it was sold to the Canadian based Hollinger Corporation which also owns the *Daily Telegraph* and *Sunday Telegraph* in Britain. Under new mangement, the *Post* supports the right-wing Likud.

A much better value publication is the *Jerusalem Report*, an English-language bi-weekly magazine which gives comprehensive news and feature insights into Israel, the Jewish world and the Middle East. The *International Herand Tribune* is published daily in Tel Aviv, together with an English translation of the Hebrew daily *Ha'aretz*.

Jerusalem is the focal point of the Palestinian press, with several dailies and weeklies supporting Palestinian positions both inside and outside the PLO, as well Jordanian interests. The PLO-backed newspaper *Al Fajr* is also printed in English.

In addition, Israeli daily newspapers are available in Russian and weekly journals in French, Spanish, Amharic, Hungarian, Romanian and other languages.

Postal Services

Israel's post offices can be identified by a logo of a white stag leaping across a red background. Post boxes are red for out of town and international mail and yellow for mail in Jerusalem. Letters take a week or so to reach Western Europe and North America, five days if sent express and three days if sent EMS express. Central post offices will exchange foreign currency and accept Eurocheques and enable money to be received or transferred abroad via Western Union Inc. All post office branches offer fax services. Telegrams and telexes can also be sent from post offices or by telephone on: 171.

Post offices in the centre of Jerusalem are open 8am–7pm. Sunday through Thursday and 8am–1pm Friday and the day before a public holiday.

Post Office branches:
Jerusalem Central Post Office, 23 Jaffa Road, tel: 02-629 0647. Poste restante service available.
East Jerusalem Branch 2 Salah A Din Street, tel: 02-290686.
Jaffa Gate branch (just inside Jaffa Gate), tel: 02-628 2965.
Jewish Quarter, 5 Hakotel, tel: 02-626 0259.
Mahane Yehuda branch, 4 Meni Eliahu Street, tel: 02-624 1963.
Rehavia branch, 8 KKL Street, tel: 02-624 2290.
Shamai branch (town centre), 6 Shamai Street, tel: 02-241672.
Jerusalem Theater branch, 7 Chopin Street, tel: 02-561 9026.
Mea Shearim branch, 1 Habakbuk Street, tel: 02-537 1194.
Agrippas, 42 Agrippas, tel: 02-624 7533.
Hapa'amon, 3 King George Street, tel: 02-624 0260.

Telecommunications

In the 1980s the Israeli phone system left much to be desired, but today the country's telecommunications infrastructure is excellent, with mobile phones and faxes as ubiquitous as anywhere in the world.

Public telephones can be found in the street, public places or in restaurants and stores. These phones are either operated by inserting telephone cards or cash coins. At major tourist sites some phones accept credit cards and this can be a convenient way of phoning abroad.

Many private companies lease out mobile, cellular phones and as elsewhere this is a highly competitive business so shop around. Avoid hotel phones because many hotels will charge treble the real cost of the call. Fax machines are available in all post offices.

Domestic calls are at their most expensive between 8am and 6pm. There is a 25 percent reduction from 6–10pm and a 50 percent reduction from 10pm–8am. There is also a 50 percent reduction from 1pm on Fridays through Saturday.

Israel is divided into the following area codes:

Jerusalem	02
Tel Aviv	03
Haifa	04
Mobile phones	05
The north	06
The south	07

Radio & Television

The Israel Broadcasting Association (IBA) has its headquarters in Jerusalem and has two television channels and six radio networks. In addition, Channel Two is an independent commercial station and there are some 50 more channels available through cable television including CNN, Sky, and the BBC as well as English-language stations from some of Israel's neighbours such as Jordan and Lebanon.

News in English is broadcast daily on Channel 1 at 6.15pm. Israel Radio has English language news on 575, 1170 and 1485 khz. at 7am, 1pm, 5pm, and 6pm.

BBC World Service radio can be received on 1322 khz and the Voice of America on 1260 khz.

Ashdod, Rehovot 08
Herzliya, Netanya 09

Overseas calls can be made from all phones through direct dialling, or booked through a special office behind the Jerusalem Central Post Office at 3 Koresh Street, tel: 02-624 9858, or the international operator 188, or via private companies like Solan International Communications, 2 Luntz Street, tel: 02-625 8908.

Alternatively, using the 177 toll-free number can connect you to an operator abroad who can place reverse charge (collect) calls, or debit credit card and subscriber accounts:
Canada: tel: 177-430-2727.
United Kingdom (British Telecom): tel: 177-440-2727.
United States: AT&T – tel: 177-100-2727; MCI – tel: 177-150-2727; Sprint – tel: 177-102-2727

Three Israeli telecom companies offer international calls: Golden Lines; Barak; and Bezeq. To phone abroad first dial 012 (for Golden Lines), 013 (for Barak) or 014 (for Bezeq), then the country code (44 for Britain, 1 for the US and Canada etc.), then the area code (but omitting any initial zeros) followed by the number.

Each of the three companies offers flat-rate tariffs 24 hours a day, seven days a week. However, tariffs, thoughu relatively inexpensive, vary considerably from company to company and it is worth using the following toll-free numbers to clarify which telecom provider is cheapest. Barak, for example, offers the cheapest calls to the UK, while Golden Lines is cheapest to the US.
Golden Lines, tel: 1-800-012-012
Barak, tel: 1-800-013-013
Bezeq, tel: 188
These numbers will also give details of discounts for frequent callers.

Useful Numbers

Directory Enquiries	144
Overseas Operator	188
Direct Dialling Information	195
Telegrams	171

Internet Information

Israel's Ministry of Tourism has an excellent site offering information about the country, accommodation, restaurants, transport etc. at: http://www.israelmfa.gov.il/sites.html (under *"sites"* choose *"tourism"*).

Information about Israel can be found from the Foreign Ministry's site. URL:http//www-mfa.gov.il

Alternatively information about Israel and Jerusalem can be found at the following Jewish net sites: http://-www1.huji.ac.il/jeru/moreinfo.html and http://www1.huji.ac.il//-jerusalem.html

Embassies & Consulates

With the exception of Costa Rica, Honduras and El Salvador, all countries maintain their embassies in Tel Aviv because Jerusalem's status as Israel's capital is not recognised internationally. This may change if a comprehensive settlement is reached with the Palestinians.

Many countries, however, do maintain a consulate in Jerusalem and some, like the US and UK, even have two consulates, in line with the pre-1967 status-quo when the city was divided, though only one consulate is used for receiving the public.

Consulates in Jerusalem:
Belgium, 5 Biber Street, tel: 02-582 8263.
Denmark, 5 Bnei Brith Street, tel: 02-625 8083.
France, 5 Emile Botha Street, tel: 02-625 9481.
Greece, 31 Rachel Imenu Street, tel: 02-561 9584.
Italy, 16 29th of November Street, tel: 02-563 1236.
Spain, 53 Rambam Street, tel: 02-5633473
United Kingdom, 19 Nashashibi Street, tel: 02-582 8281
United States, 27 Derekh Shekhem, tel: 02-628 2452.

Travelling with Children

There are few special facilities for children such as changing rooms for babies, but this is in part because children are easily accepted everywhere. In restaurants, hotels and in the street they will be indulged by passing adults with smiles, candy and possibly even kisses and hugs. Restaurants may not have a children's menu but will be happy to provide a special children's portion if you ask.

Most hotels and restaurants will provide high chairs. Children are even allowed in pubs and bars and even small children will often be seen out at midnight with their parents. Children under five travel for free on buses provided they sit on their parent's lap. Children under four must be strapped into a special car seat (except in taxis), so if renting a car remember to specify the age of your small children.

Student Travel

Students can receive concessions on buses (10 percent), on trains (25 percent) and at museums provided they have a valid international student card. The Israel Student Travel Association (ISTA) offers low-priced tours and programmes of interest to student travellers and also issues international student cards. ISTA, 5 Elissar Street, tel. 02-225288. Also if you have a student card ask your travel agent about cheaper flights before leaving for Israel. By some European definitions you can remain a student until age 31.

Senior Citizens

El Al Israel Airlines offers discounts for senior citizens on some flights to Israel so check with your travel agent. Senior citizens receive discounts on buses, trains and at museums. In general Israelis and Jerusalemites in particular have much respect for the elderly and will give up their seat on a bus if no other seats are available.

Women Travellers

Israeli men can behave in an extremely familiar manner with women, especially those unaccompanied by males, and their attentions can often verge on sexual harassment. But remember several things so that the situation does not escalate unnecessarily. It is normal in Israeli society for strangers to touch each other when talking and to have eye to eye contact. However familiar men get in terms of verbal suggestions and touching on shoulders or arms, they are almost certain not to go beyond this unless encouraged. The best way to deal with unwelcome advances is to ignore them. Lack of dialogue, or a curt, cold response will usually nip over-enthusiastic and unwanted sexual attention in the bud.

But unlike elsewhere in the Middle East, women can dress in Western-style clothing and in West Jerusalem frequent restaurants and even bars and discos without having to be accompanied by men.

In Arab East Jerusalem, more conservative habits predominate and women dress modestly and do not visit the night spots. In ultra-orthodox Jerusalem, women who do not cover their arms and legs have even been known to have stones thrown at them. Although scant attire is acceptable in most of Jerusalem, it is probably more sensible for women to cover up as much as possible in case of inadvertently wandering into an orthodox neighbourhood or holy site, to prevent stimulating local gigolos, and reduce the incidence of sunburn.

Disabled Travel

Ben Gurion International Airport has a special lift for the boarding and disembarking of passengers in wheelchairs. Folding wheelchairs can be hired, free of charge but a charitable donation would be appreciated, from Yad Sarah, 43 Haneviim Street, Jerusalem, tel: 02-644 4444. Many facilities are designed for wheelchair access but many more are not. Getting around Jerusalem can be especially problematic for the disabled because the city is built on hills.

The Gay Scene

Jerusalem has a modest but by no means completely closeted homosexual community. Homosexuals have been known to hang out occasionally at the bottom of Independence Park near the Muslim Cemetery.

Religious Services

There are synagogues, churches and mosques of every shape, size, colour and denomination in Jerusalem. Some of them advertise the times of their services in the Jerusalem Post. Here is a small sampling of places of worship.

Jewish

Jerusalem Great Synagogue, 56 King George Street, tel: 02-624 7112.
Chabad Synagogue, 16 Yirmiyahu Street, tel: 02-581 4755.
Centre for Conservative Judaism, 4 Agron Street, tel: 02-622 3539.
The Union for Progressive Judaism, 13 King David Street, tel: 02-623 2444.

Christian

St George's Cathedral (Anglican), 20 Nablus Road, tel: 02-628 3302.
Southern Baptist Convention, 4 Narkiss Street, tel: 02-622 5942.
Notre Dame (Catholic), Paratroopers Road (opposite the New Gate), tel: 02-628 9723.
Church of the Redeemer (Lutheran), 2 Muristan Road, tel: 02-628 2543.

Tipping

Western-style tipping rather than Middle Eastern *baksheeh* is the rule of thumb in Israel.

Many restaurants will add 10 percent service charge to the bill, in which case a tip is not necessary. If there is no service charge then a 10–15 percent gratuity is the norm. In hotels chambermaids and porters/bell hops expect small tips for their exertions.

Taxi drivers are not tipped by locals but tend to expect a small tip from tourists.

St Andrews Church of Scotland (Presbyterian), Rakevet Street, tel: 02-671 7701.
Brigham Young Centre (Mormons), Mount Scopus, tel: 02-627 3181.
Seventh Day Adventists, 4 Abraham Lincoln Street, tel: 02-622 1547.
Greek Orthodox, Greek Patriarchate Road, tel: 02-628 4917.

Muslim

Al Aqsa Mosque, Temple Mount, tel: 02-628 1248.

Security & Crime

Jerusalem, like all of Israel, has a high rate of non-violent crimes (theft of homes, cars, property, pickpocketing etc.) but little violent crime (mugging, murder and rape). Avoid leaving valuables in hotel rooms or cars, and do not leave wallets and purses temptingly sticking out of pockets. Do not imagine that being in a holy site brings with it protection against thievery.

In terms of violent crime the security situation is the most pressing problem, but here too incidents are few and far between. Media headlines tend to exaggerate the problem but check with tourist information offices before venturing to West Bank towns like Bethlehem and Jericho.

Loss of Belongings

Report any lost belongings to the nearest police station and ask for a certificate of loss for insurance purposes. If you lose your passport contact your consulate as quickly as possible.

Jerusalem Central Police Station, Russian Compound, tel: 02-639 1111.
Egged Bus Company Lost Property 195 Jaffa Road, tel: 02-630 7666.
El Al Lost Property (Ben Gurion Airport), tel: 03-971 2541.

In the event of losing credit cards these are the numbers to telephone:
American Express: tel: 03-524 2211.
Diners Club: tel: 03-572 3572.
Visa: tel: 03-572 3572.
EuroCard and **MasterCard**: tel: 03-576 4444.

Drugs and Other Offences

Hashish is illegal but prosecutions are rarely brought. Because neighbouring Lebanon supplies much of the world's hashish, the drug is widely available in Israel with peddlars usually frequenting bars. Heroin is also grown in Lebanon but here the Israeli authorities are less likely to turn a blind eye if you are caught in possession.

If you end up needing a lawyer contact your local embassy or consulate. They can probably suggest a lawyer who has immigrated to Israel from your home country.

Medical Services

Visitors should have ample medical insurance because treatment can be expensive. Israel has a well developed infrastructure often compared, for better or worse, with Britain's national health system. With over 26,000 physicians in a population of six million, Israel easily has the highest number of doctors per capita in the world.

A private consultation with a doctor (ask for a recommendation at your hotel reception) should cost no more than $40 and could be half that price. Ambulances can be summoned by dialling 101 and there is a doctor on night duty at the Magen David Adom First Aid Station, 7 Hamag Street, Romema, tel: 02-652 3133.

Emergency Numbers

- **Police**, tel: 100
- **Ambulance**, tel: 101
- **Fire Brigade**, tel: 102.
- **Nursing Service**, tel: 02-563 6505
- **Yad Sarah** (for loan of medical equipment), tel: 02-644 4444

The city's main hospitals are:
Hadassah Ein Kerem, tel: 02-642 7427.
Hadassah Mount Scopus, tel: 02-584 4111.
Shaare Zedek, tel: 02-655 5111.
Remember to ask for a receipt in order to get back expenditure from insurance. Holders of Blue Cross-Blue Shield insurance are eligible for pre-paid medical treatment at Hadassah.

If you find yourself without insurance try one of the hospitals in Arab East Jerusalem. The standard is high but the fees are much lower:
Augusta Victoria Hospital, tel: 02-628 2401.
Mokassid Hospital, tel: 02-628 8133.

In the emergency rooms of Israeli hospitals treatment is given first to the most urgent cases. Patients who sit there in stoic silence despite being in terrible pain may be mistaken for milder cases. So if in agony be expressive about it lest you be overlooked for other patients behaving more melodramatically.

See Golden Pages phone books for dentists, while the *Jerusalem Post* will tell you which pharmacy is on night or weekend duty. In general pharmacists speak excellent English and are very helpful. Most pharmacists will sell routine prescription drugs like antibiotics over the counter even though this is strictly speaking illegal.

Etiquette

After receiving some service or purchase, it is polite to say *toda* (thanks) or *toda raba* (thanks very much). Often the response will be *bevakasha* (please) or *alo davar* (it's nothing). The standard hello or goodbye is *shalom*. "How are you?" is *Ma Shlomcha?* to a man or *Ma Shlomech?* to a woman. "See you" is *lehitra'ot*.

But generally Israelis can be curt, not bothering to say please or thank you, though increasingly greater efforts are being made to be polite to tourists. This is all part of the Israelis' famous informality Do not judge them harshly by their lack of courtesy. If you are really in trouble, Israelis will surprise you by their painstaking and generous efforts to help.

Israelis can be very physical, looking strangers hard in the eye and doing a lot of touching. This is usually out of friendliness rather than sexual forwardness but the situation can be confusing for a female tourist coming into contact with a strange man.

Of obvious sensitivity is religious etiquette. When visiting holy sites, women should dress conservatively (no bare legs or shoulders), and men should wear shirts and pants. When visiting Jewish shrines or memorials it's also standard for men to cover their heads; if you don't have a *kepah* or hat, a cardboard substitute is often provided. In some religious neighbourhoods, especially in Jerusalem, these conservative rules of dress apply as general practice. While not all Israelis are observant, you should be aware that religious Jews see the Sabbath as a holy day and smoking or other behaviour can be considered offensive.

On Departure

By Air
You must confirm your scheduled departure with your airline at least 72 hours in advance.

Departing passengers should arrive at the airport 2–3 hours prior to their departure time and prepare the following documents: a valid passport, flight tickets and money (Israeli currency preferred) for payment of the airport tax, which is obligatory for every passenger over the age of 2. This tax is usually included in the ticket price.

Baggage check-in: The Israel Airports Authority offers a day-before check-in service for your baggage which saves the hassle of security checks at Ben Gurion Airport. Your suitcases are transported to the airport and instead of arriving two and a half hours before your flight you need only arrive one hour 15 minutes before your flight. A charge of about $2.50 per person is made for this service. You can hand your baggage in the day before at 7 Kanfei Nesharim St., Givat Shaul, Jerusalem. For information about opening hours and the appropriate time to take in your baggage, tel: 03-9723388.

Security Checks: These are for your protection. Be prepared to unlock your luggage and submit yourself and carry-on bags to a careful but courteous examination. To avoid spoiling any precious records of your visit, make sure to empty your camera of film.

Getting to the Airport
From Tel Aviv: By United Tours Bus No. 222 from Railway Station, Rehov Arlosorov to Ben-Gurion Airport every hour, year round, from 4am–noon. For further information and details tel: 03-754 3410.

By Egged Buses, every 15 minutes, 6am–11.30pm.
From Jerusalem: By Egged Buses, from 6.15am–7pm, approximately every 20 minutes.

By Nesher *sherut* taxi: book in advance at 21 Rehov Hamelech George, tel: 02-257227.
From Haifa: By Egged Buses, from 7am–6pm, approximately every 45 minutes.

By Aviv *sherut* taxi service, 5 Rehov Allenby, tel: 04-666333, approximately every hour between 6am–5pm.

Getting Around

By Road

From Tel Aviv to Jerusalem: The *sherut* shared taxi from either the new or old central bus stations is cheaper than the bus costing only $5. There is a bus to Jerusalem every 15 minutes from the New Central Bus Station and a bus every 20 minutes from the Central Railway Station at Arlozorov Street. The train service is sporadic, there are only one or two trains each day, and is designed more for sightseeing (some stretches of the route have magnificent scenery) rather than speed. While the bus takes 50 minutes, the train takes more than 2 hours.

From Haifa to Jerusalem: *Sherut* shared taxis should be booked in advance. There is an express bus hourly the Central Bus Station. The journey takes about 2 hours.

From Eilat to Jerusalem: There are four or five buses daily and the journey takes about four hours.

From the Allenby Bridge to Jerusalem: The *sherut* shared taxi is the best bet costing only $9. There is no direct bus service to Jerusalem.

From Nizzana and Rafiah Egyptian border points to Jerusalem: Travellers should have a pre-paid bus ticket from Cairo to Jerusalem or Tel Aviv.

Public Transport

The most popular form of public transport in Israel is buses, run principally by the Egged Bus Cooperative. This is one of the largest cooperatives worldwide and one of the world's largest bus companies. The railways are non-existent except for a good coastal service between Tel Aviv and Haifa.

BUSES

Buses are modern, airconditioned, frequent, punctual and reasonably cheap but can be crowded and are driven far too fast by sometimes, reckless drivers. Egged runs both the inter-urban and urban services except in the Greater Tel Aviv region. From East Jerusalem to Arab destinations on the West Bank, buses are run by private Arab companies that range in quality from excellent to distinctly Third World.

Urban services in Jerusalem charge a flat fare of about $1 regardless of whether you are travelling just one stop or right across the city. Passengers can save money and the inconvenience of searching for small change every journey by buying multi-ride tickets – i.e. 22 rides for the price of 20.

There are also tickets enabling you to ride wherever and whenever you want in Jerusalem for a month for a reasonable price. Such tickets can also be acquired for nationwide travelling on Egged buses for periods of 7, 14, 21 or 28 days. Egged offers discounts to students and pensioners. Children under five travel for free providing they can sit on a parents lap. In other words one parent and two children under five must pay two fares.

Buses do not run from an hour before the entrance of the sabbath on Friday afternoon until after sundown of Saturday except some limited services in Arab districts. During the week city bus services start at 5am and finish at about midnight. Inter-city bus services commence after 6am and finish fairly early in the evening except for the Tel Aviv–Jerusalem bus which continues through to midnight.

For further information contact urban and inter-urban services, tel: 02-530 4704.For details about Egged excursions, tel: 02-5304883.

Inter-Urban Bus Services

Buses leave from Jerusalem's Central Bus Station near the western entrance to the city and include the following services. Note that a new Jerusalem Central Bus Station is currently under construction, scheduled for completion in late 1999/early 2000. While building is underway the bus station has been moved to a site 400 metres eastwards along Jaffa Road (Yafo) and can be found opposite 208 Jaffa Road between Yafo and Shderot Ben-Zvi.

400	Bnei Braq/Givataim
404	Holon, Bat Yam
405	Tel Aviv New Central Bus Station
415/420	Bet Shemesh
423	Petah Tikvah
428	Netanya
432/433	Rishon Le Zion
434/435	Rehovot
437/448	Ashdod
438	Ashkelon
444	Dead Sea/Eilat
446/470	Beer Sheva
487	Ein Gedi
940	Haifa express
945	Haifa via Ben Gurion Airport, Petah Tikvah, Netanya, Hadera
947	Haifa via Ben Gurion Airport

From the Airport

Ben Gurion Airport is 50 km (30 miles) west of Jerusalem and a 40 to 50-minute drive by road.

By far the easiest way of getting from the Airport to Jerusalem is by the *sherut* **shared taxi** which can be found outside the departure building. This taxi will drop you off at your required destination in Jerusalem for less than $10 a person. A **private taxi** to Jerusalem should cost no more than $30.

There is also a regular **bus** service from the airport to Jerusalem Central Bus Station.

Car rental companies located at the airport include Avis, Hertz, EuroCar, InterRent, Budget, Rent-a-Car, Kopel, Thrifty and Eldan.

Urban Bus Services

1 Western Wall, Jewish Quarter, Yemin Moshe, Mea Shearim, Central Bus Station.

2 Har Nof, Givat Shaul, Central Bus Station, Kiryat Zans, Old City, Yemin Moshe.

3 Mea Shearim, Romema, Kiryat Zans.

4 Malkah Shopping Mall, Katamonim, German Colony, Rehavia, Downtown West Jerusalem, Ramat Eshkol, French Hill.

4A same as 4 but continues to Hadassah – Hebrew University Mount Scopus.

5 Shmuel Hanavi, Malkhei Yisrael, Mea Shearim (this route runs through ultra-orthodox neighbourhoods and is for men only)

6 Talpiot, Abu Tor, Yemin Moshe, Downtown West Jerusalem, Mahane Yehuda, Central Bus Station, Bet Hakerem, Givat Mordechai, Malkah Shopping Mall.

7 Romema, Central Bus Station, Mahane Yehuda, Downtown West Jerusalem, Rehavia, Abu Tor, Talpiot, Ramat Rahel.

8 Central Bus Station, Mahane Yehuda, Downtown West Jerusalem, Rehavia, Abu Tor, Haas Sherover Promenade, East Talpiot.

9 Central Bus Station, Hebrew University Givat Ram, Knesset, Israel Museum, Rehavia, Downtown West Jerusalem, Ma'alot Dafna, Hadassah Hebrew University Mount Scopus.

10 Har Hotzvim, Ramot Shlomo

11 Har Nof, Givat Shaul, Central Bus Station, Mahane Yehuda, Downtown West Jerusalem, Mea Shearim.

12 Kiryat Menachem, Kiryat Hayovel, Malkah Shopping Mall.

13 Givat Masua, Kiryat Menachem, Kiryat Hayovel, Bet Hakerem, Central Bus Station, Mahane Yehuda, Downtown West Jerusalem, Jaffa Gate, French Hill, Pisgat Ze'ev East.

14 Bet Hakerem, Kiryat Moshe, Central Bus Station, Downtown West Jerusalem, Rehavia, German Colony, Talpiot Industrial Zone.

15 Har Nof, Givat Shaul, Central Bus Station, Geula, Downtown West Jerusalem, Rehavia, Talbieh, Jerusalem Theatre, Hapalmach.

16 Bayit Vegan, Bet Hakerem, Kiryat Moshe, Givat Shaul, Central Bus Station, Romema, Har Hahotzvim, Ramot.

17/ 17A Ein Kerem, Bayit Vegan, Bet Hakerem, Central Bus Station, Mahane Yehuda, Downtown West Jerusalem, Rehavia, Israel Museum, Givat Mordechai, Malkah Shopping Mall.

18 Kiryat Hayovel, Bayit Vegan, Bet Hakerem, Central Bus Station, Mahane Yehuda, Downtown West Jerusalem, Yemin Moshe, German Colony, Katamonim, Malkah Shopping Mall.

19 Hadassah Ein Kerem, Kiryat Hayovel, Ramat Danya, Rehavia, Downtown West Jerusalem, Jaffa Gate.

20 Jaffa Gate, Downtown West Jerusalem, Mahane Yehuda, Central Bus Station, Bet Hakerem, Kiryat Hayovel, Kiryat Menachem, Ir Ganuy.

21 Ramat Sharett, Bayit Vegan, Bet Hakerem, Central Bus Station, Mahane Yehuda, Downtown West Jerusalem, Yemin Moshe, Baka, Talpiot.

22 Pisgat Zeev, French Hill, Downtown West Jerusalem, Rehavia, San Simon, Katamonim, Pat.

23 Hadassah–Hebrew University Mount Scopus, Rockefeller Museum, Downtown East Jerusalem, Jaffa Gate.

24 Katamonim, German Colony, Hapalmach, Israel Museum, Knesset, Bet Hakerem, Kiryat Hayovel, Malkah Shopping Mall.

25 Neveh Yaakov, Pigat Zeev, Ramat Eshkol, Downtown West Jerusalem.

26 Hadassah–Hebrew University Mount Scopus, Ramat Eshkol, Central Bus Station, Bet Hakerem, Biblical Zoo.

27 Damascus Gate, Downtown East Jerusalem, Beit Yisrael, Mahane Yehuda, Kiryat Moshe, Bet Hakerem.

28 Hadassah–Hebrew University Mount Scopus, Ramat Eshkol, Central Bus Station, Hebrew University Givat Ram.

29 Central Bus Station, Givat Shaul (Har Menuhot) Cemetery.

30 Gilo, Talpiot, Abu Tor, Jaffa Gate.

31 & 32 Gilo, Katamonim, Rehavia, Downtown West Jerusalem, Mahane Yehuda, Central Bus Station.

33 Har Nof, Bayit Vegan, Malkah Shopping Mall.

34, 35 & 36 Ramot, Har Hahotzvim, Central Bus Station, Mahane Yehuda, Downtown West Jerusalem.

37 Central Bus Station, Romema, Ramot Shlomo.

38 Western Wall, Jewish Quarter, Yemin Moshe, Rehavia.

39 Bayit Vegan, Bet Hakerem, Kiryat Moshe, Central Bus Station, Ramat Eshkol

41 Central Bus Station, Jerusalem (Atarot) Airport.

42 Jerusalem City Hall, Mount of Olives

45 Central Bus Station, Pisgat Ze'ev, Neve Yaakov.

46 Neve Yaakov, Pisgat Zeev, Hadassah–Hebrew University Mount Scopus

Urban Bus Services contd.

48 Pisgat Zeev, French Hill, Ramat Eshkol, Central Bus Station, Downtown West Jerusalem, Rehavia, Abu Tor, Talpiot Ind. Zone.

99 **Tourist sightseeing bus.** For a $10 one-day ticket you can travel as many times as you like. The bus takes a circular route from the Central Bus Station to Mount Scopus, Mount of Olives, Old City, East Talpiot, Downtown Jerusalem, Israel Museum, Knesset, Mount Herzl, Hadassah.

151 Downtown West Jerusalem, Central Bus Station, Bet Zait.

152 Central Bus Station, Even Sapir.

154/ Downtown West Jerusalem,
155 Central Bus Station, Mevas- seret Zion.

156/ Downtown West Jerusalem,
157 Central Bus Station, Motza, Kastel.

160 Central Bus Station, Kiryat Arba.

161 Central Bus Station, Gush Etzion.

162 Central Bus Station, Mount Gilo.

166 Central Bus Station, Tekoah.
167 Central Bus Station, Efrata.
171 Jerusalem Ramot, Givat Ze'ev.
174/ Central Jerusalem, Ma'aleh
175 Adumim.
183 Downtown West Jerusalem, Central Bus Station, Kesalon.
184 Central Bus Station, Meta.
185 Downtown West Jerusalem, Central Bus Station, Abu Ghosh, Kiryat Yearim.
186 Central Bus Station, Bet Meir.
187 Downtown West Jerusalem, Central Bus Station, Har Adar.
188 Downtown West Jerusalem, Ein Nekuba, Ein Rafah.

Inter-Urban Bus Services contd.

953	Afula via the Jordan Valley
961	Tiberias
963	Kiryat Shmona via Tiberias
964	Safed via Tiberias

TRAINS

Jerusalem's railway station was built early this century by the Ottoman Turks. The Jerusalem line was closed during 1998 for extensive repairs and it is unclear when it will re-open. Before the closure there was only one train a day to Tel Aviv and sometimes two during the holiday season. The train is a worthwhile, but not very fast, way of seeing the Jerusalem hillsides. Jerusalem Station, David Remez Square, near Liberty Bell Park, tel: 02-673 3764 (buses numbers 6, 7, 8 and 21).

Taxis

As in many cities of the world, taxis are plentiful until you actually need to hail one. Drivers prefer not to put on their meter for tourists, offering a pre-negotiated fare which is usually slightly higher than the measured price would be. This is illegal and visitors should insist on their right to have the meter on. Drivers would rather not use the meter because it also means they can avoid income tax.

That said, taxis are relatively cheap and journeys around Jerusalem should certainly not cost more than three or four dollars. Even long-haul journeys to Tel Aviv or Haifa are not exorbitant. It should cost no more than $50 to hire a taxi to Tel Aviv. Inter-city prices are fixed and should be quoted in advance.

In addition, there is the *sherut* shared taxi which leaves from Zion Square or the Central Bus Station for Tel Aviv. To arrange for the Nesher shared taxi to pick you up from your hotel or place of residence to take you to Ben Gurion Airport, tel: 625 7227.

The following list includes taxi stations in Jerusalem:
Hapisgah, tel: 02-642 1111.
Hatzomet, tel: 02-582 6666.
Jerusalem, tel: 02-625 5233.
Rehavia, tel: 02-625 4444.
Smadar, tel: 02-566 4444.
Yisrael, tel: 02-625 2333.

Domestic Flights

There are daily flights from Jerusalem's Atarot airport (tel: 02-585 0980) to Haifa, Eilat and Galilee. If you want to view Jerusalem from the air – well worth doing if you have the money to burn – try Kanfei Jerusalem, tel: 02-583 1444.

Driving

Israel has a good road infrastructure which is overburdened by heavy traffic. Israelis in general and Jerusalemites in particular drive with Mediterranean creativity, including lots of horn honking, overtaking on the inside and general improvisation.

In spite of the ostensible chaos, laws are strictly enforced, and it is necessary to wear seat belts by law in both the front and back seats. Children under 4 must be fitted into appropriate seats.

Speed limits vary between 50 and 70kph (30–40mph) in the city and be sure to have your passport and driving licence with you at all times. Police tend to be lenient with tourists but are entitled to take you in front of a judge for the immediate imposition of a fine. Theft of cars and contents is widespread so keep your vehicle locked.

Most garages in Israel sell 91, 96, 98 and lead-free fuels at prices about 20 percent cheaper than in Britain, though considerably more expensive than in the United States. The major oil companies – names like Paz, Delek, Sonol, Dor, Gal and Alon are unfamiliar because the Arab boycott did not allow the major multinational oil corporations to operate in Israel.

Car Rental

Many of the world's principal car hire companies such as Hertz and Avis operate nationwide networks of offices in Israel, as well as large local companies like Eldan who also have offices overseas. Renting a car in Israel will cost about $300 a week and possibly less between October and March. The cheapest way of hiring a car is to book it abroad as part of the overall package, when hire prices can be as low as $200 a week. An overall package also has the convenience of enabling visitors to pick up and leave the car at the airport. For tourists intending spending most of their time in Jerusalem, it is probably cheaper and less hassle, considering the heavy traffic, difficulties in parking etc, simply to take taxis.

Avis, 22 King David Street, tel: 02-624 9001/3.
Eldan, 24 King David Steeet, tel: 02-625 2151–3.
Eurodollar, 8 King David Street, tel: 02-623 5467.
Europcar, 8 King David Street, tel: 02-624 8464.
Hertz, 18 King David Street, tel: 02-625 6334.
Reliable, 14 King David Street, tel: 02-624 8204/5.
Sa-Gal, 14 King David Street, tel: 02-624 1516
Splendid, 14 King David Street, tel: 02-624 2488,
Petra, Shuafat, tel: 02-682 2668.

Road Distances in km (miles)

	Jerusalem	Tel Aviv	Haifa
Arad	104 (65)	158 (98)	255 (158)
Ashdod	66 (41)	42 (26)	139 (86)
Beersheba	84 (52)	113 (70)	210 (130)
Eilat	312 (194)	354 (220)	451 (280)
Haifa	159 (99)	95 (59)	—
Hebron	35 (22)	97 (60)	194 (120)
Jerusalem	—	62 (39)	159 (99)
Metula	221 (137)	196 (122)	120 (75)
Nablus	63 (38)	57 (35)	93 (58)
Nazareth	157 (97)	102 (63)	35 (22)
Netanya	93 (58)	29 (18)	66 (41)
Rehovot	53 (33)	24 (15)	121 (75)
Rosh Hanikra	201 (125)	137 (85)	42 (26)
Tel Aviv	62 (39)	—	95 (59)
Tiberias	157 (97)	132 (82)	69 (43)

West Bank by Car

It is not advisable to travel by car in the West Bank with yellow Israeli number plates. The car may be stoned. However, a car rented from Petra, a Palestinian company, will be less liable to suffer such damage.

Parking

Finding a parking space is very difficult in parts of the city, especially in Downtown West Jerusalem where even the parking lots are full between 11am and 1pm. Parking in a car park generally costs about $1.50 per hour. If a kerbside is marked blue and white, you need a ticket which can be purchased in batches of five from kiosks or stores (these tickets can also be used in Tel Aviv and Haifa). Each ticket cost $1 and allows you to park for an hour. Alternatively you can put coins into a parking meter (in the city centre) or buy a ticket from a vending machine. Tickets must be displayed or meters fed from 8am-7pm. If you fail to display a ticket you are liable to a fine of $20. Do not ignore kerbsides marked red and white. This means no parking and you are liable to be clamped or towed away.

On Foot

Pedestrians

Drivers cannot be relied upon to stop at pedestrian crossings. The safest place to cross is at traffic lights when the pedestrian light is green. Police will hand out fines – usually only a warning to tourists – to pedestrians who cross on a red light. Take extra care at at right turn filters where the pedestrian light is green but traffic may still pass.

Hiking

The Jerusalem region is ideal for hiking in the cooler months (October–March) or during early mornings and late afternoons in the summer.

Hitchhiking

Israel is a hitchhiker's paradise. The only problem is that it is so popular that there are often long lines of hitchhikers at major junctions where there are usually special hitchhiking stations. Priority is given to soldiers at hitchhiking stations. It is even acceptable to hitch in town but to hitch successfully it is advisable to be assertive, waving at cars rather than simply putting up a thumb and trying to catch the driver's eye. Hitching is not advisable in the West Bank and unaccompanied women should be selective about whom they accept lifts from.

Most Israeli youngsters backpack their way around the world, usually just after their national army service, and so backpackers are seen as respectable and conventional rather than undesirable hippies. Hitchhiking is a legitimate form of travel and youth hostels abound. Youth hostel representatives will often hang around bus stations touting for customers. Cheap meals can be had at *falafel* stalls where you can usually stuff as much salad as you want into a pitta bread.

Where to Stay

Choosing Accommodation

There is a very diverse range of accommodation available in the Jerusalem region. Options include conventional hotels ranging from de luxe down to more modest establishments and very rudimentary youth hostels charging $10 or $15 a night. In addition, there are kibbutz guest houses (relatively expensive rural retreats), Christian hospices (more luxurious than they sound, usually with a 19th-century European ambience) and bed and breakfast possibilities. This guide begins with the latter options, which offer the visitor a more uniquely Israeli and Holy City experience.

Kibbutz Guest Houses

Tourists wanting a quintessentially Israeli experience should try a kibbutz guest house. As kibbutzim are rural settlements, the following list are of guest houses just a short bus ride (no more than 20 minutes) from Jerusalem. Visitors need not worry about being asked to work or wash their dishes while staying on a kibbutz worker's collective. All guest houses are good class hotels (with relatively expensive prices) with country club type amenities such as swimming pools and tennis courts.

Hare Yekuda
Neve Ilan. Tel: 02-534 8111; fax: 02-534 8197. Pleasant hillside country club atmosphere, 20 minutes from Jerusalem. **$$**

Kibbutz Kiryat Anavim
Kiryat Anavim. Tel: 02-534 2770. Seven miles to the west of the city nestling in a pine forest in the Judaean Hills. **$$**

Kibbutz Ma' aleh Hahamisha
Ma'aleh Hahamisha. Tel: 02-534 2591. Adjoining Kibbutz Kiryat Anavim with slightly better and more modern facilities. **$$**

Kibbutz Ramat Rachel
Mitzpeh Rachel. Tel: 02-670 2555; fax: 673 3155. Actually within the city limits near the south eastern suburb of Talpiot. Modern attractive setting with superb view of the Judaean Desert. **$$**

Price Guide

Price for a double room (normally quoted in US dollars), usually including breakfast. Holidaymakers can save up to 33% on hotel prices given here by booking a package deal overseas.

$	under US$90
$$	US$90–150
$$$	above US$150

Christian Hospices

Guests needn't worry about being placed in a cell and made to wear sackcloth and ashes. On the contrary, these establishments, mainly founded in the second half of the 19th century, have been renovated and made into comfortable accommodation with amenities comparable to hotels but with the charm of a bygone age. Nor do you have to be a devout Christian to stay in these hospices, which welcome all paying guests whether Jew, Muslim, atheist or Christian.

Notre Dame
Paratroopers Road, tel: 02-628 1223; fax: 02-628 2397. Ideally located for pilgrims opposite the New Gate of the Old City. Luxurious accommodation, splendid 19th-century architecture and one of Jerusalem's best restaurants. Taken over in the 1970s by the Vatican from the Assumptionists and extensively renovated. **$$**

Our Sisters of Zion
PO Box 17105, Ein Kerem, tel: 02-641 5738; fax 02-643 7739. De-lightful Provence-style pension in the nearby village of Ein Kerem. Spacious gardens filled with olive trees and grape vines. **$$**

St Andrew's Scots Memorial Hospice
Rakevet Street, tel: 02-673 2401. Intimate guest house offering mulled wine, mince pies and haggis to its Christmas guests adjacent to the Holy City's only Calvinist church. But don't expect kippers for your breakfast. Superb location overlooking the Old City. **$**

YMCA
King David Street, PO Box 294, tel: 02-625 3433. Stylish 1930s building opposite the King David Hotel. Recently refurbished. **$**

Bed & Breakfast

A comprehensive range of B&B accommodation can be booked through a central office called "Good Morning Jerusalem", located in the Jerusalem International Congress Centre (Binyanei Ha'Ooma) opposite the Central Bus Station, tel: 02-651 1270. Prices range up to a maximum of $54 a night per couple.

Hotels

Prices are high if you simply turn up. It is much cheaper to book a package deal from overseas. Whereas a luxury hotel can charge $100 or even $150 a night, a two-week package including flight and a luxury hotel from Britain can cost just $1,000 or $1,500 from America's East Coast. This said, hotels in Jerusalem do cater for a most pockets.

Hotel rates are generally quoted in dollars and include a 15 percent service charge. If you pay in foreign currency you are exempt from 17 percent VAT. High season is July and August and Christmas, Easter, Passover and the Jewish High Holydays (September/early October).

American Colony, Nablus Street, tel: 02-628 5171; fax: 02-627 9779. Jerusalem's oldest hotel has much character and charm and is the favoured haunt of the foreign press corps because of its "neutral" location on the border between the Arab and Jewish parts of the city. Good food and an intimate atmosphere. **$$$**

Caesar Hotel
208 Yafo, tel: 02-5005656; fax: 02-5382802. Right opposite the Central Bus Station, this modern, unexceptional hotel is ideally located for tourists who want to travel around Israel. **$**

Dan Pearl
Tzahal Square, tel: 02-6226666; fax: 02-6226649. All the luxury of a top class hotel with rooms overlooking the Old City walls and Jaffa Gate. **$$$**

Hilton
1 King David Street, tel: 02-6211111; fax: 02-6211000. This recently opened hotel is attractively designed and well appointed near the Jaffa Gate and downtown Jerusalem. **$$$**

Holiday Inn Crowne Plaza, Givat Ram, tel: 02-658 8888; fax: 02-651 4555. Formerly a Hilton, this high-rise hotel is the landmark by the entrance of the city. Far from the centre of town but close to the Central Bus Station and adjacent to the Jerusalem International Conference Centre. Has an excellent Indian restaurant. **$$**

Holyland Hotel
Bayit Vegan, tel: 02-6437777; fax: 02-6437744. Away from town with an interesting view and close to the Model of the Second Temple. **$$**

Hyatt Regency, 32 Lehi Street, Mount Scopus, tel: 02-533 1234; fax: 02-532 3196. A stylish design which blends into the hillside (not so easy for a 600-room hotel). Hyatt's usual interior of waterfalls and splendour. Beautiful view of the Old City but far from town. **$$$**

Itzik
141 Yafo, tel: 02-6233730; fax: 02-6243879. Interesting location in the heart of the Mahane Yehuda market and close to the Central Bus Station. Otherwise fairly basic accommodation. **$**

Jerusalem Gate, 43 Yermiyahu Street, tel: 02-383101. For the budget conscious but not those on a very tight budget. Right by the Central Bus Station. **$**

Jerusalem Tower, Hillel Street, tel: 02-252161. Clean, comfortable, compact and smack in the middle of Downtown West Jerusalem. **$**

King David
23 King David Street, tel: 02-620 8888; fax: 02-623 2303. Israel's premier hotel where political leaders, the rich and famous stay. Built in the 1930s, it has a distinctive style and charm but in terms of quality of service and value for money its less prestigious rivals try harder. Tends to rely on its reputation but has beautiful gardens overlooking the Old City. **$$$**

Laromme, Jabotinsky Street, tel: 02-675 6666; fax: 02-675 6777. A lot of character for a hotel built in the 1980s. Excellent location by the attractive Yemin Moshe with its windmill. **$$$**

Price Guide

Price for a double room (normally quoted in US dollars), usually including breakfast. Holidaymakers can save up to 33% on hotel prices given here by booking a package deal overseas.

$	under US$90
$$	US$90–150
$$$	above US$150

Lincoln Hotel, 24 King David Street, tel: 02-234351. Opposite the King David. Very pleasant, modern, intimate and inexpensive. **$**

Mount Zion, Hebron Street, tel: 02-672 4222; fax: 02-673 1425. Originaly an ophthalmology hospital built a century ago, this was converted into a luxury hotel in the 1980s. Commands an excellent view of Mount Zion and the Old City Walls. **$$**

Palatin Hotel, corner Agrippas Street and King George Street, tel: 02-231141. Small and basic with budget prices right in the noisiest section of Downtown West Jerusalem. **$**

Radisson Moriah, Keren Hayesod Street, tel: 02-569 5695; fax: 02-623 2411. Tranquil atmosphere for such a large hotel. Slightly cheaper than most other luxury hotels and conveniently located near Yemin Moshe. **$$$**

Reich Hotel
Bet Hakerem, tel: 02-6523121; fax: 02-6523120. Basic accommodation located in the salubrious, leafy lanes of Bet Hakerem which are pleasant but far from the centre of town. **$**

Renaissance, 6 Wolfson Street, tel: 02-528111. Very large and luxurious. Has the country's biggest banqueting facilities but otherwise unexceptional. **$$$**

Ron, Zion Square, tel: 02-625 3471; fax: 02-625 0707. Located in the heart of the New City, this hotel has all the delightful charm of a central European pension. **$**

Sheraton Plaza, 37 King George Street, tel: 02-259111. An ugly concrete block in the heart of Jerusalem, but the lap of luxury and very central for both the Old and New cities. Its "Cow on the Roof" (in the basement) is one of the finest and most expensive restaurants in town. **$$$**

Seven Arches, Mount of Olives, tel: 02-627 7555; fax: 02-627 1319. Formerly the Inter-Continental. Built on a desecrated Jewish graveyard by the Jordanians, making it unkosher for Jews. Very stylish with breathtaking view of the Old City. **$$**

Windmill, 3 Mendele Street, tel: 02-566 3111; fax: 02-561 0964. Opposite the Moriah but less luxurious and less expensive. Great location for a relatively economicaly priced hotel. **$**

Holiday Flats & Apartotels

Lev Jerusalem, 18 King George Street, tel: 02-530 3333. Service options include two restaurants that will deliver food to your apartment, health club and babysitting service. Located in the heart of West Jerusalem.

Apartotel
214 Jaffa Street, tel: 02-538 1221. Much more basic with few services, but close to the Central Bus Station.

Camping

Israel is an excellent country for camping and there are a number of sites near Jerusalem where visitors can put up a tent and enjoy full sanitary facilities, available electricity and nearby shops and restaurants as well as shaded picnic and camp fire areas with round the clock security.

• **Bet Zayit**
Tel: 02-534 6217. Three miles (5 km) west of the city just off the Jerusalem-Tel Aviv highway.

• **Ramat Rachel**
Tel: 02-670 2555. To the southeast of the city with a more regular bus service into town.

Youth Hostels

Bernstein Youth Hostel
1 Keren Hayesod Street, tel: 02-258286. Belongs to the Israel Youth Hostel Assocation. Clean and friendly but closes 9am–5pm and requires guests to be in before 11pm. $11 for a bed.

Ein Kerem, P.O. Box 17013, Jerusalem, tel: 02-641 6282. Belongs to the Israel Youth Hostel Association. For those who prefer fresh country air within close proximity to Jerusalem. Same closing hour restrictions as the Bernstein hostel.

Jaffa Gate Youth Hostel
El Khattab Square, tel: 02-589 8480. As the name implies, close to the Jaffa Gate next door to the Christian Information Centre. Dormitory bed $4; private room $15.

King George Hostel
15 King George Street, tel: 02-622 3498. Dirty and noisy but popular. Hang-out for hippy types. $8 a bed.

Where to Eat

What to Eat

Dining is a national pastime in Israel – engaged in as much and as often as possible On the street, at the beach, in every public place and certainly in every home, day and night – you'll find Israelis constantly eating.

The Biblical residents of the Land of Canaan were nourished by the fertility and abundance of a land "flowing with milk and honey". Milk was mainly from sheep and goats, and the honey from dates, figs and carobs. Much depended on the sun, the rains and the seasons. Food was simple; feast predictably followed famine.

Times have changed – at least in the culinary sense. Just as Israel is a blend of cultures coming from all over the world, so its cuisine is a weave of flavours and textures, contrasts and similarities. There is no *definite* Israeli fare, just as there is no definitive Israeli. Rather, there is an unique merging of East and West, and the results are a profusion of culinary delights.

Holy Day Foods

If there are jelly doughnuts (*sufganiot*) it must be *Chanu-ka* – the occasion also for *potato latkes* (pancakes). On *Purim*, you'll find *oznay haman* (*hamentashen* or filled triangular cookies).

If you're in Israel around holy day time, try to experience some holy day fare. Any self-respecting Israeli will tell you that holy days are especially important occasions and special food is integral to them.

The predominant foodstyle, however, reflects the country's geographical location – somewhere between the Middle East and the Mediterranean. Dining out? Don't be led astray by signs that say "oriental" food. This will not mean Far Eastern food.

In Israel, "oriental" refers to the Middle East. "Oriental" Jews are those of Sephardic (Spain, Italy, various Arab countries) heritage. Each Jewish ethnic group, whether Moroccan, Libyan, Tunisian, Yeminite, Iraqi or native-born (*Sabra*) Israeli, has its own special dish and holy day fare.

Their food is similar yet distinct from each other. Basic herbs and spices include cumin, fresh and dried coriander, mint, garlic, onion, tumeric, black pepper, and sometimes cardamom and fresh green chilli pepper. Dark fruity olive oil brings out tantalising fragrances.

Arabic food is also considered "oriental" and both Arabic and Jewish meals begin the same way – with a variety of savory salads. *Humus*, a ground chickpea concoction seasoned with *tahina* (sesame paste), lemon juice, garlic and cumin, is probably the most popular dip, spread and salad rolled into one. *Tahina* itself, prepared likewise, comes next.

Here you'll also find one of the most astounding varieties of eggplant salads you've ever seen; eggplant in *tahina*, fried sliced eggplant, chopped eggplant with

At Passover, it's time for *matzo-brie*, coconut macaroons and sponge cake. *Shavuot* is strictly for dairy delights. *Sukkot* and *Tu B'shvat* are celebrated with dried fruits and nuts. Every Friday afternoon, there are special braided *challahs* for the Sabbath. And every Sabbath there is *cholent* (*hamin* if you're Sephardic), a baked bean and meat stew set to bake on Friday for lunch on the Sabbath.

vegetables, chopped liver-flavoured eggplant and more. Assorted pickled vegetables are considered salads as well.

While the waiters may show some sign of disappointment, you can order the salads as a meal itself. Or follow them with *kebab* (grilled ground spiced sauce), *shashlik* (grilled sliced lamb or beef with lamb fat), *seniya* (beef or lamb in *tahina* sauce), stuffed chicken or pigeon, chops or fish.

Don't expect pork in either a *kosher* or traditional Muslim restaurant. Both religions prohibit its consumption. Seafood, while forbidden by Jewish and permissible by Muslim law, is widely available. Shrimps and calamari are the predominant varieties.

Do try the fish, especially in the seaside areas of Tiberias, Tel Aviv, Jaffa and Eilat (there are no fish in the Dead Sea!). Trout, grey and red mullet, sea bass and St Peter's fish are generally served fried or grilled, with a piquant sauce sometimes added. Authentic North African restaurants will also feature *harimeh*, a hot and spicy cooked fish, fragrant with garlic, tomatoes, cumin and hot pepper.

And if you still have room, there's dessert. In Arabic restaurants, this may mean *baklava* (filo dough sprinkled with nuts and sweet syrup), and some other rich sweet or fruit. In typical Jewish oriental restaurants, it could mean

caramel creme custard, chocolate mousse or an egg white confection laced with chocolate syrup and, for some unknown reason, called Bavarian creme. Turkish coffee or tea with fresh mint seals the meal. If you do not want sugar, inform the waiter in advance.

Meat and Poultry
Those who prefer fowl will find the chicken and turkey, and in more elegant restaurants, the goose and mullard duck (an Israeli hybrid), excellent choices. While much beef is imported, all fowl is domestically raised.

Fruits and Vegetables
The country's produce is legendary. Fruits and vegetables arrive at market stall hours after picking, and a trip to the open-air Mahane Yehudah in Jerusalem or the Carmel market in Tel Aviv, will reveal a sumptuous array of everything from apples to artichokes, *kohl-rabi* to celery. Sub-tropical fruits include kiki, mango, persimmon, loquat, passion fruit, cheromoya and papaya. Fresh dates, figs, pomegranates and the world's largest strawberries are seasonal attractions.

Produce is sold by the kilo or gram, and is most reasonably priced and freshest at open-air markets. Avoid supermarket produce as they tend to be second-rate. Wash everything well before you eat.

Kosher Food
The Hebrew word *kosher* means food conforming to Jewish dietary laws. Pork and shellfish are prohibited, and meat and dairy foods cannot be served together. While *kosher* food is the rule in Israel, many restaurants and some hotels – and, of course, Arab establishments – are non-*kosher*.

Drinking Notes

Water
You can drink the water in Israel safely, though bottled water is also available.

Soft Drinks
All the usual carbonated drinks are available. As in Britain, "soda" refers to soda water and not a flavoured carbonated drink. Diet and regular soft drinks are available. The most delicious and healthiest drinks to try are the wide range of fruit drinks available. For a few dollars, street vendors will squeeze you an orange, carrot, grapefruit, kiwifruit or a dozen other fruits.

Tea and Coffee
Tea connoisseurs will be out of luck. Most Israeli establishments dip a feeble tea-bag into hot water. But, as throughout the Middle East, Israelis take their coffee seriously. Most popular are Middle Eastern coffee (*botz*), Turkish coffee, Viennese coffee (*cafe hafuch*) and filter coffee. Instant coffee western style is known as *nes* (as in Nescafé). Cafés, like bars in Europe, are often the centre of social life.

Alcohol
Israel has a wide selection of wines, both red and white. During the 1980s many good-quality wines were produced, but they can be expensive. There are several local beers, both bottled and draft, and a range of imported beers – but ale specialists will probably turn up their noses. There are both home-distilled and imported spirits and liquors. The local speciality is *arak*, very similar to Greece's *ouzo*.

Dairy Products

In days of old, water was scarce and not very palatable, so milk became a major component of the Biblical diet. Goat's milk was considered the richest and most nourishing. Next came sheep's milk, cow's milk and, finally, camel's milk.

Today Israel continues the "land of milk and honey" tradition with a wealth of more familiar cheeses (like Swiss, Camembert, Brie and Gouda), double-rich cottage cheese, and a wide variety of goat and sheep yogurt and cheeses

(special types of which are found in some health food stores and the Arab villages).

A visit to the supermarket will reveal uniquely Israeli white cheeses; wrapped in paper or sold in tubs, all marked with labels signifying fat content. Try *Tov Ta'am*, a soft spreadable 5 percent fat, white cheese wrapped in paper – if you want something low on fat. Or taste *leben* or *eshel* – cultured milk products with approximately the same fat content as yogurt.

Although Israel has none of the alcoholic inhibitions of its Islamic neighbours, most Israelis consume relatively small amounts of alcohol compared to Europeans and Americans. Excessive drinking is viewed with suspicion by society at large. A person who drinks, say, six bottles of beer (3 pints) every day is likely to be branded an alcoholic.

There are plenty of bars and pubs, and all restaurants and cafés serve alcohol. Israelis will often go to a pub and spend the entire night nursing just one or two drinks. By the same token it is acceptable to sit at a streetside café chatting for several hours over just a coffee and cake.

Where to Eat

Jerusalem's restaurants reflect the diversity of its population. The Arab restaurants of East Jerusalem serve excellent food, especially a sophisticated array of salad starters (*mezze*), after which the meat *entrée* is often a disappointment with no room left in the sated diner's stomach anyway. West Jerusalem has a concentration of meat eateries in Agrippas Street near Mahane Yehuda market. Here the local delicacy is the *Meurav Yerushalmi* – a Jerusalem mixed grill of different cuts of beef.

From Indian and Chinese to Argentinian and Mexican, Jerusalem has a broad selection of restaurants. You can eat very cheaply at the *falafel* stalls in Mahane Yehuda or Downtown West Jerusalem. In fact, as a general rule the more expensive the restaurant the greater the disappointment. The sloppy, informal service and the quality of food in the most expensive of establishments never quite matches the billing.

Many of these listed restaurants listed here can get very busy and it is often worthwhile to reserve a table.

ORIENTAL (MIDDLE EASTERN)

Abu Shukri
67 Ha-Gai Street, tel: 02-627 1538. Located on the Via Dolorosa, this canteen-like institution serves the city's best *humus* and *ful* (beans). Mop it up like the locals with pitta bread. **$**

Azzahra
13 Azzahra Street, tel: 02-628 2447. Located in East Jerusalem and specialising in Arab cuisine, try the *mezze* salads and stuffed lamb. **$$**

Eucalyptus
7 Horkanos Street (off Halleny Hamalka Street), tel: 02-624 4331; fax: 02-622 2922. Billed as a restaurant offering the ancient recipes of the Land of Israel. The owner/chef has a way with herbs and spices. **$$**

Ima (kosher)
189 Agrippas Street, tel: 02-624 6860. Does interesting *mezzes* and soups but the *entrée* can be a disappointment. **$$**

Price Guide

Price per person for a three-course meal excluding wine and service.

$	under NIS80
$$	NIS80–250
$$$	over NIS250

Niss Mesadonet
10 Rabbi Akiva Street, tel: 02-623 3880. Kurdistani home cooking at inexpensive prices. Try the soups – especially *kubbe*, a doughy, meaty dumpling served in beef soup. Charming old stone building with a beautiful garden for dining out in the summer. **$$**

Philadelphia
9 Alzahara Street, tel: 02-628 9770. The best known and most prestigious restaurant in East Jerusalem though prices are modest. Has an excellent *mezze*. Have the stuffed vegetables with your entrée. Also try the lamb kebabs and round things off with sweet *bakhlawa* con-

Bars & Pubs

• **Finks**, on the corner of King George and HaHistadrut Streets, tel: 02-623 4523. Jerusalem's oldest-established watering hole is very small and caters to a mature clientele. Also serves good food.

• **Glasnost**, Helena Hamalkah Street 15, tel: 02-256954. In the very heart of Jerusalem's nightlife quarter in the Russian Compound.

fectioneries. Offers a free shuttle service from your hotel. **$$**

Shipudei Hagefen (kosher)
74 Agrippas Street, tel: 02-625 3267. Pleasant restaurant in the heart of this street's restaurant district. Try the mixed Jerusalem grill. **$$**

Sima (kosher)
82 Agrippas Street, tel: 02-623 3002. Well-known eatery serves good value steaks and grilled meats at break-neck speed. Waiters will not let you linger over your food. **$**

The Yemenite Step (kosher)
10 Yoel Salomon Street, tel. 02-624 0477. Traditional Yemenite food such as *malawah* is said to be both very healthy and full of spices that act as aphrodisiacs. Judge for yourself. Located in one of Jerusalem's most charming streets. **$**

FISH

Ocean
7 Rivlin Street, tel: 02-623 3859. Delightful location with outdoor seating. Local specialties are baked and grilled fishes plus forbidden unkosher foods like calamari. **$$$**

Sea Dolphin
21 Al Rashadiah Street, tel: 02-628 2788. East Jerusalem's premier fish restaurant. Popular among Jerusalemites for many years. **$$**

ARGENTINIAN

El Gaucho (kosher)
22 Rivlin Street, tel: 02-625 6665. For those who like their steaks very big. Don't order too many courses unless you have a huge appetite.

Staff dress like Argentinian *gauchos.* $$

ARMENIAN

Armenian Tavern
79 Armenian Patriarchate Road, tel: 02-6273854. Authentic Armenian food served in a converted underground cistern near the Jaffa Gate. $

CHINESE

Ten Li Chow (kosher)
8 Ramban Street, tel: 02-566 5956. Reasonable but unexceptional food in an attractive location near Rehavia's restored windmill, next to the King's Hotel. $$
Yosi Peking (kosher)
5 Shimon Ben Shetach Street, tel: 02-625 0817. Pleasant location in the centre of the city. Good food. $$

FRENCH AND CONTINENTAL

Arcadia
10 Agrippas Street, tel: 02-624 9138. This is one of the city's best restaurants despite the shabby alleyway near the entrance. Try the goose and liver. $$$
American Colony Hotel
Nablus Road, tel: 02-627 9777. Very reasonable *à la carte* menu supervised by the hotel's Swiss chef. $$
Cardo Culinarium (kosher)
The Cardo, Jewish Quarter, tel: 02-6264155. You've got to be in the mood for a laugh. Diners are compelled to wear togas and laurel wreaths. The restaurant was actually built in Roman times. $$
Cow On The Roof (kosher)
Sheraton Plaza Hotel, tel: 02-622 8133. Elegant western dining. Very expensive and exclusive. By reservation only. $$$
Mishkenot Sha'ananim
Yemin Moshe behind the Windmill, tel: 02-625 4424. Excellent French cuisine with glorious panorama of the Old City walls. Try the fillet steak. $$$
Notre Dame
8 Shivtei Yisrael Street, tel: 02-628 8018. Situated in the magnificent Notre Dame hospice complex.

Reputed to be one of the finest restaurants yet prices are not too expensive. $$$

HUNGARIAN

Csardas (kosher)
11 Shlomzion Hamalka Street, tel: 02-6243186. Classic Hungarian cuisine. Very good service with wholesome tasty food and gypsy violinist thrown in on busy evenings. $$
Europa (kosher)
42 Jaffa Road, tel: 02-622 8953. Unpretentious atmosphere, central location at Zion Square with a variety of Hungarian specialties including stuffed chicken and goulash. Popular with locals. $

INDIAN

Tandoori (kosher)
Holiday Inn Crowne Plaza, Giuat Ram, tel: 02-658 8867. One of a chain of Kosher Indian restaurants (do not expect yogurt on your Tandoori) with an excellent selection of vegetarian dishes. $$

Price Guide

Price per person for a three-course meal excluding wine and service.

$	under NIS80
$$	NIS80–250
$$$	over NIS250

ITALIAN

Mamma Mia (kosher)
38 King George Street, tel: 02-624 8080. Introduced good quality, tasty home-made pasta and pizza to the Jerusalem palate. Very reasonable prices but sometimes very, very busy. $
Valentino's (kosher)
Hyatt Regency Hotel, 32 Lehi Street, tel: 02-533 1234. More upmarket environment than Mamma Mia. Also excellent pastas and antipastas. $$

NORTH AFRICAN

Darna (kosher)
3 Horkenos Street, tel: 02-624 5406. North African food and

Dairy & Light Meals

Anna Ticho House
Off 9 Harav Kook Street, tel: 02-624 4186. Very pleasant garden restaurant which is quiet but in the heart of Jerusalem. The house salad with crushed nuts and cheese is recommended. $

Moroccan atmosphere including authentic implements and ceremonial service. $$$
El Marakkesh (kosher)
4 King David Street, tel: 02-625 1208. Moroccan cuisine including delightful Moroccan cigars (mince meat stuffed in dough) and stuffed vine leaves). $$$

VEGETARIAN

Jan's Tea House (kosher)
5 Chopin Street, tel: 02-5612054. Located beneath the Jerusalem Theatre, this trendy restaurant serves vegetarian dishes Bedouin style. $$

CAFÉS AND PATISSERIES

Café Alno
17 Ben Yehuda Street, tel: 02-625 3821. Well-liked Ben Yehuda institution with excellent patisserie.
Café Atara (kosher)
7 Ben Yehuda Street, tel: 02-562 5014. Jerusalem's oldest café, founded 65 year ago, recently moved to a new location further up the street.

Culture

Jerusalem is a paradise for culture vultures. From archaeological, historical and religious sites through to museums and art galleries, every corner of the city is redolent with culture.

Archaeological Sites

Those who are really enthusiastic about archaeology might want to participate in a dig for a few weeks. If so contact Marta Retig, Department of Antiquities and Museums, Ministry of Education, PO 586 Jerusalem 91004, tel: 02-629 2627. Many of the museums listed have an archaeological focus.
City of David and Warren's Shaft. Open Sunday–Thursday 9am–5pm, and Friday to 1pm. Shows the underground water system established by engineers 3,000 years ago. An illuminated model explains the function and structure of the shaft.

Cardo, Jewish Quarter, Old City. Remains of the original main north–south Roman thoroughfare through Jerusalem.
Ophel Archaeological Garden. Open standard times. Near the Western Wall. Remains of many civilizations dating back to Solomon's time three millennia ago.

Museums

Ammunition Hill Museum, Ammunition Hill (near Ramat Eshkol), tel: 02-582 9132. Commemorating the Six Day War in 1967. Open Sunday–Thursday 9am–4pm, Friday 9am–1pm.
Armenian Art and History Museum, Armenian Quarter, Old City. A 150-year-old museum with frescoes, paintings, ritual objects and manuscripts dating back to the 7th century. Also chronicles the genocide of the Armenians by the Turks in 1915. Open Monday–Saturday 10am–5pm. Closed Sunday.
Bible Lands Museum, Granot Street (opposite Israel Museum), tel: 02-611066. Exhibits archaeological artifacts from Middle Eastern cultures during the biblical period. Open Sunday–Tuesday and Thursday 9.30am–5.30pm, Wednesday 1.30–9.30pm, Friday 9.30am–2pm. Closed Saturday.

Bloomfield Science Museum, Rupin Boulevard, tel: 02-561 8128. Focuses on science and technology, making the subject accessible to children with hands-on exhibits. Open Monday, Tuesday and Thursday 10am–6pm, Wednesday 10am–8pm, Friday 10am–1pm, Saturday 10am–3pm. Closed Sunday.
Burnt House of Kathros, 13 Tiferet Yisrael Street, Jewish Quarter, Old City. The home of a Jewish family during the Second Temple period circa AD70. Open Sunday–Thursday 9am–5pm, Friday 9am–1pm.
Islamic Art Museum, 2 Hapalmach Street, tel: 02-566 1291. Exhibits art from Islamic lands with emphasis on metal work, ceramics, jewellery, carpets and miniatures. Open Sunday–Thursday 10am–1pm and 3.30–6pm, Friday 10am–1pm.
Islamic Museum, Temple Mount. Shows Islamic craftsmanship at its most ornamental and exquisite. Open Saturday–Thursday 8am–noon. Closed Friday.
Israel Museum, Ruppin Street, tel: 02-670 8811. The country's national museum. As well as the Dead Sea Scrolls, the museum contains major exhibitions of archaeology, art, sculpture and Jewish ethnography. Open Sunday–Thursday 10am–5pm, Tuesday

Religious Sites

There are so many sites of religious significance to Jews, Christians and Muslims that it would be impossible to list them all. Here are the most sacred of the sites.
Western Wall. Believed by Jews to be the only remaining wall of the Temple destroyed by the Romans.
Temple Mount. Site of the Temple itself which today houses the Dome of the Rock and the Al Aqsa Mosque.
Dome of the Rock. Resplendent Muslim Shrine with gold dome built by the Caliph Abd Al-Malik in 691 on the Temple Mount, on the site from where Mohammed is said to have ascended to heaven. The

rock inside the shrine is also where Abraham was alleged to have prepared to sacrifice his son Isaac. Open to non-Muslims daily except Friday.
Al Aqsa Mosque. This beautifully decorated 8th-century silver domed mosque also stands on the Temple Mount. King Hussein's grandfather King Abdullah was assassinated here.
Church of the Holy Sepulchre. A complex church in the Old City on the site where Orthodox and Catholic Christians believe Christ was crucified, buried and resurrected. Contains the last five stations of the Via Dolorosa. Open dawn until after sunset.

Via Dolorosa. Believed to be the route Christ took from his condemnation by Pilate through to his crucifixion in the Church of the Holy Sepulchre.
Garden Tomb. In East Jerusalem very close to the Arab bus station. Often called the Protestant Holy Sepulchre. British officer General Gordon institutionalised the notion in the 19th century that this might have been the site of the crucifixion. Open Monday–Saturday 8am–1pm, 3.30–5pm. Closed Sunday.
Church of the Nativity, Manger Square, Bethlehem. Church and crypt alleged to be the very stable in which Christ was born.

4pm–10pm, Friday 10am–2pm, Saturday 10am–4pm.

Palestinian Arab Folklore Centre, Obeid Ibn Jarrah Street, East Jerusalem. Features various aspects of Palestininan traditions, especially dress. Open Saturday–Thursday 9am–5pm. Closed Friday.

Rockefeller Museum, Suleiman Street, tel: 02-628 2251. Important archaeological exhibits from the Middle East and surrounds. Open Sunday–Thursday 10am–5pm, Friday and Saturday 10am–2pm.

Second Temple Model, next to Holyland Hotel, tel: 02-678 8118. Scaled model of Jerusalem 2,000 years ago before the destruction of the Temple realistically conveys how it must have looked. Open Sunday–Thursday 8am–9pm, Friday and Saturday 8am–5pm.

Tower of David Museum of the History of Jerusalem, Jaffa Gate, tel: 02-627 4111. Archaeological excavations of this fortress built 2,000 years ago and a state-of-the-art exhibition about Jerusalem's history. Open Sunday–Thursday 10am–4pm, Friday and Saturday 10am–2pm.

Yad Vashem – Holocaust Memorial and Museum, tel: 02-675 1611. All too vividly documents the rise of Nazism and the attempt to exterminate the Jewish people. Open Sunday–Thursday 9am–4.45pm, Friday 9am–2pm. Closed Saturday. Free.

Cultural Centres

American Cultural Centre, 19 Keren Hayesod Street, tel: 02-625 5755.
British Council Library, 3 Shimshon Street, Baka (Off Bethlehem Street), tel: 02-625 0513.
The Jewish National and University Library, Givat Ram campus of the Hebrew University.

Art Galleries

Artists House, 12 Shmuel Hanagid Street, tel: 02-625 2636. Exhibitions of local arts and crafts.
Bezalel National Art Museum, Zacks-Abramov Pavilion for Modern Art within the Israel Museum.

Entertaining Children

Visiting historical, archaeological and religious sites can be very wearing for smaller children, especially in the heat. However, the **Israel Museum** has an excellent Youth Wing and the **Bloomfield Science Museum** is also worth visiting (see *Museums* listings for details).

In addition there are several parks and zoos that will appeal to children, notably the **Liberty Bell Park**, which has a playground, and the **Kibbutz Tzova children's zoo** (see *Outdoor Attractions: Parks & Gardens* and *Zoos*).

•Israelis are very "child friendly" and strangers are likely to indulge your children with all manner of sticky and sweet things.

Ticho House, Off 9 Harav Kook Street, tel: 02-624 4186. Exhibition of the paintings and drawings of Anna Ticho, Jerusalem's best-known 20th-century landscape artist.

There are also art exhibtions in the Jerusalem Centre for Performing Arts (see *Music, Dance & Theatre*) and the Jerusalem Cinemathèque (see *Cinema*). In Yad Vashem Holocaust Memorial there is an exhibtion of Holocaust art (see *Museums*).

Music, Dance & Theatre

Jerusalem Centre for the Performing Arts, Marcus Street, tel: 02-561 0011. This complex includes the Jerusalem Theatre, the Henry Crown Auditorium and the Rebecca Crown Theatre. Though Jerusalem has no theatre company of its own there are regular performances here by the Tel Aviv-based Habimah and Carmeri theatre companies and the Haifa Municipal Theatre Company. These performances are in Hebrew but simultaneous translations are usually available in English. There are also frequent performances by overseas theatre companies, especially during the Israel Festival.

In dance and music, there are often performances by the Bat Dor and Inbal dance companies and the Israel Opera. The Henry Crown Auditorium is home of the Jerusalem Symphony Orchestra which gives regular performances.

Sultan's Pool Ampitheatre. It is a must to see a concert – it could be anything from Dire Straits or Bob Dylan to Placido Domingo or the Israel Philharmonic Orchestra – at this venue. Beneath the walls of the Old City there can be few such romantic ampitheatres anywhere in the world. Open only in the summer and even then take a sweater for chilly evenings.

Khan Theatre, 2 David Remez Square, tel: 02-671 8281. Smaller, more intimate theatre in old stone building opposite the station shows the work of fringe theatre and smaller companies.

Pargod Theatre, 84 Bezalel Street, tel: 02-625 8819. Not so much a theatre as a basement hall for jazz and other musical performances.

Cinema

There are many cinemas in Jerusalem and all are modern with sophisticated sound systems. The largest is an eight-cinema complex at the Malkah Shopping Mall. In the Talpiot industrial zone there is also a seven-cinema complex.

Worth a visit is the Cinemathèque in Derech Hebron overlooking the Old City walls. It occupies a stylish building and is frequented by Jerusalem's secular high-brow society. Even if you don't want to watch a movie, have a coffee there and enjoy the atmosphere. The Cinemathèque shows golden oldies donated to their archives, sometimes of poor technical quality.

As well as the latest Hollywood epics and British and Australian releases, Israeli cinemas show the best movies from France, Italy, Germany, Hungary, Spain and elsewhere, usually with English as well as Hebrew subtitles (but check at the box office first). Israel also makes about 12 movies a year, offering an insight into local culture though not often very memorable cinema.

Nightlife

Although lower profile than that of Tel Aviv's, Jerusalem has a vibrant nightlife. This is especially true between April and October when it is warm enough to stroll through the streets and sit outside at cafés and restaurants. The city's nightlife really gets going after 10pm and the streets remain packed until well after midnight.

The **Ben Yehuda Street Mall** and adjacent pedestrian precincts like Salomon Street and Rivlin Street are the busiest between 10pm and midnight. After midnight the focus switches to the bars and pubs of the **Russian Compound**. Also busy at night is the **Malkah Shopping Mall**.

The **Talpiot Industrial Zone** is where most of the discotheques are located, but if you're over 30 you'll feel out of place. More mature revellers should stick to the discos in some of the large hotels like the Holiday Inn.

Casinos
Gambling is illegal in Israel but a casino is accessible at the Oasis south of Jericho (technically in a Palestinian autonomous zone). This is a 30-minute drive east of Jerusalem. Take your passport.

Festivals

Religious Festivals

Jewish Holy Days
Israel observes a lunar year in accordance with Jewish religious tradition. So Jewish holy days fall on different dates in the general calendar each year. New Year occurs in September/October, with the holiday of Rosh Hashana. But the standard Gregorian system is also in daily use everywhere. All Jewish holy days commence at sundown on the preceding day and end at nightfall.

	Date (Hebrew/Gregorian)
Rosh Hashana	Sep/Oct
Yom Kippur	Sep/Oct
Succot	Sep /Oct
Simchat Torah	Sep/Oct
Chanukah	Nov/Dec
Tu B'Shvat	Jan/Feb
Purim	Feb/Mar
Pesach	Mar/Apr
Independence Day	Apr/May
Lag Ba'Omer yar	Apr/May
Jerusalem Liberation Day	May/Jun
Shavuot	May/Jun
Tisha B'Av	July/Aug

Muslim Holy Days
Friday is a holy day for Muslims and places of worship are closed during prayers on that day, as they are on all holy days. Muslim holy days are decided on in accordance with the appearance of the new moon, thus falling on different dates in the general calendar each year.

The most important are: **Id el Adha** (Sacrificial Festival – 4 days); **New Year**; **Mohammed's Birthday**; **Feast of Ramadan** (1 month); **Id el Fitr** (Conclusion of Ramadan – 3 days).

Druze Holy Days
Id el Adha, Sacrificial Festival; **Nabi Shu'eb**; **Nabi Sablan**.

The Sabbath

From sunset Friday to sunset Saturday everything shuts down for the Jewish Sabbath, or "Shabbat". All Jewish shops, businesses, institutions, offices and public places of entertainment (with the exception of a few restaurants and clubs) are closed and most public transport ceases. Some shops and all places of entertainment reopen with the termination of the Sabbath at nightfall, and public transport resumes.

•The working week runs from Sunday to Thursday; most businesses are also open Friday mornings.

Cultural Events

Jerusalem International Book Fair: every two years, in March. At the Jerusalem International Conference Centre.
Israel Festival: every May/June. Takes place mainly in Jerusalem and brings to Israel first-class theatre, dance and music companies from around the world.
Jerusalem Film Festival: every June/July. Good movies from around the world shown at the Jerusalem Cinemathèque.
Jerusalem International Puppet Festival: every August. Great for kids.
Liturgica: Just prior to Christmas. This international festival combines church and Israeli choirs.

Outdoor Attractions

Parks & Gardens

Jerusalem is a city with relatively large areas given over to parkland. The main parks and gardens in the city and surrounds are:

Sacher Park. Jerusalem's largest park stretches beneath the Knesset and is a favourite with soccer players. Sacher Park links up to the Valley of the Cross to the south, a landscape of biblical significance from where it is believed the wood for the crucifix was taken.

Liberty Bell Park (by the Laromme Hotel). Includes playgrounds, sports facilities, trampolines, an ampitheatre and train theatre.

Independence Park. Pleasant area of greenery right in the middle of downtown West Jerusalem.

Wohl Rose Garden. Adjacent to the Knesset, this garden is best visited in spring or autumn when the roses are blooming.

Jerusalem Forest. Stretching out westwards from the city this forest is said to contain 6 million trees in memory of the Jews who perished in the Holocaust. Unfortunately most are pine trees which limits the appeal of the forest. But with luck you may catch a glimpse of some gazelles. In spring the region is ablaze with flowers like red anemones, pink cyclamen and purple orchids.

Botanical Gardens. Attractive area of gardens beneath the Hebrew University's Givat Ram campus. Includes greenhouse for tropical plants, artificial lake and pleasant lakeside café.

Haas Promenade. Very attractive gardens and walkway on the slopes of the mountain, stretching from Abu Tor to East Talpiot in the southeast of the city, with magnificent view of Jerusalem's Old City and the Judaean Desert.

Zoos

Biblical Zoo, Malkha, tel: 02-643 0111. Open Sunday–Thursday 9am–5pm Friday 9am–3pm, Saturday 10am–2pm. The Biblical Zoo moved to new premises in 1993 in Malkah, near the shopping mall. It is beautifully landscaped into the mountainside and well worth visiting. Most of the animals are mentioned in the Bible, though unfortunately, many of them are now extinct in this region.

Kibbutz Tzova, Judaean Hills, tel: 534 7711. This kibbutz has a good little zoo for small children. Reach the kibbutz by taking the left hand turn after Ein Kerem or catching bus number 183 from Davidka Square or opposite the Central Bus Station.

Hiking

There are many interesting hikes that can be taken within close proximity to Jerusalem. The best of them is down **Wadi Kelt** to the east of the city, continuing to Jericho. It's a dramatic gorge cut into the rocks of the Judaean Desert, with spring water running along the canyon and making beautiful line of rich green in the arid landscape. St George's Monastery is perched precariously on the cliffside. The hike is about 10 km (6 miles) long. Wadi Kelt can be reached by turning left from the Jerusalem–Jericho highway about 10 km out of Jerusalem. Follow the orange signposts.

If you prefer hiking in forest land, there are many good walks in the **Sorek Valley** to the south west of the city out past Ein Kerem. Continue onto the Sorek Caves with their fascinating stalagtite and stalagmite formations.

For details of these walks and information about organised hikes, contact the **Society for the Protection of Nature (SPNI)**, 13 Helena Hamalka Street, tel: 02-623 2936.

Shopping

What to Buy

Most items are much more expensive than in America and 10–20 percent more expensive than in Western Europe (notably excepting **leather goods** and **diamonds**).

In the Arab market visitors may want to buy **ceramics**, hand-made **Hebron glass, embroidered clothes, olive wood, mother of pearl** (especially religious icons) and **jewellery**. There are dozens of shops selling exactly the same thing so compare prices as well as bargaining. As you walk away, shopkeepers will often shout a lower price.

Shopping Areas

When it comes to shopping Jerusalem offers both the eastern and western models. Visitors can bargain in the Arab market or shop in the air-conditioned comfort of the shopping mall. The major shopping areas are Downtown West Jerusalem (the triangle between King George, Jaffa and Ben Yehuda Streets), the Talpiot Industrial Zone, and the Malkah Shopping Mall. The latter is completely enclosed and air-conditioned or heated according to the season.

Try the stores in Downtown West Jerusalem for diamonds and leather goods. For Jewish ritual and religious objects, ultra-orthodox Mea Shearim has the best selection. There are large clusters of art galleries, antique stores, and leather and tourist-oriented clothing stores in King David Street, Hutzot Hayotzer (opposite the Jaffa Gate), and at the House of Quality opposite the Cinemathèque.

Markets

No tourist should miss the Arab bazaar (called the *suq* in Arabic or *shuk* in Hebrew). Enter the Old City from either the Jaffa or Damascus Gate and enjoy a bustling, sensuous mixture of colours, noises and smells. This is not a place for people who suffer from claustrophobia. And don't forget to bargain for everything. Being bashful can mean paying double or even more for your vacation gifts.

For those who like food markets try Mahane Yehuda, located between Downtown West Jerusalem and the Central Bus Station. The array of fruit and vegetables in season will tempt most of all.

Malls & Department Stores

Hamashbir LeZarchan
28 King George Street, tel: 02-624 0511.
Malkah Shopping Mall
Tel: 02-6793261.

Consumer Advice

• **Export Procedures:** Everything can be taken abroad except archaeological artifacts that do not have a certificate given by the seller. At special tourist stores you can pay in foreign currency and purchase items exempt of 17 percent VAT.

• **Complaints:** Shopkeepers will often argue over faulty goods, but if you persist they will usually be reasonable. Otherwise contact the Ministry of Trade and Industry's Consumer Council, 76 Mazeh Street, Tel Aviv, tel: 03-560 4611.

Specialist Shops

Books and Maps
Steimatsky
39 Jaffa Road (Yafo), tel: 02-625 0125. There are smaller branches throughout the city.

Diamonds
National Diamond Centre
143 Bethlehem Street, tel: 02-673 3770. Israel is the world's largest producer of cut and polished diamonds, and this is the largest national retail chain.

Fashion
Castro
18 King George Street, tel: 02-625 5421. Leading chain for casual women's fashions. There is also a branch in Mevasseret Zion.
Roberto
58 Jaffa Road (Yafo), tel: 624 7098. Jerusalem fashion chain for men. There is another branch in the Malkah mall.

Souvenirs
Arieh Klein
3 Ziv Yosef Street (off Bar Ilan Street, Sanhedria), tel: 02-538 9992. Large warehouse with an excellent selection of olive wood items.
Hatzorfim
5 Kanfei Nesharim Street, Givat Shaul, tel: 02-651 4026. Judaica and Jewish ritual items in silver. There is a branch in Geula near Mea Shearim and also branches throughout the country.
Jerusalem House of Quality
12 Hebron Street, tel: 02-672 5111. Contains a range of stores selling antiquities and Judaica.
Karakashian Armenian Pottery
Via Dolorosa, near the Sixth Station, tel: 02-6261587. Tasteful tiles and pottery in distinctive Armenian style. Allow a few days to order personalised tiles and items.

Shopping Hours

Shops open 8am–7pm on Sunday–Thursday and 8am–2pm on Friday. Stores are closed on Saturday during daylight hours but often open up after sunset until 11pm or even midnight. The Arab market is open all day Friday and Saturday. Some stores close for a siesta 1–4pm but most remain open throughout the day.

Sport

Jerusalem is quite poorly equipped with sports facilities. The ultra-orthodox Jews view sport as a Hellenistic abomination and fought against the construction of a national soccer stadium, which was finally completed in Malkah in 1992. Many secular Jews look down on sport as a non-intellectual pursuit. The Arab sector has been denied "luxury" public amenities for sports by the Jewish municipality.

Participant Sports

All the large hotels have swimming pools and most have tennis courts. Try also the **Jerusalem Tennis Centre**, Katamonim, tel: 02-679 2796.

Spectator Sports

Football (soccer)
Betar Jerusalem, the city's best-known soccer team, were league champions in 1997 and 1998, and thus participated in the European Cup. The team plays at the Malkah stadium near the Shopping Mall.

Basketball
Hapoel Jerusalem, one of Israel's leading basketball teams, play in Malkah at the Goldberg Sports Hall.

Health Spas

The **Dead Sea** is a little over an hour's drive out of Jerusalem. Try the hot water sulphur springs at Ein Gedi. The sea contains minerals beneficial for skin and circulatory problems and arthritis. As the Dead Sea is 400 metres below the sea level, a unique mist also filters out some of the sun's harmful rays.

Language

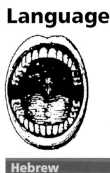

Hebrew is the most widely spoken language in the country (Hebrew and Arabic are the two official languages). Although other languages, especially English, are also fairly widely spoken it is a good idea to know some basic Hebrew words and phrases before coming to Israel. Here are some basic words which may help you find the language a little less daunting:

All-purpose greeting *shalom* (literally "peace")
good morning *boker tov*
good evening *erev tov*

yes *ken*
no *lo*
please *bevakasha*
thank you *toda*
very much *raba*

good *lov*
bad *ra*
big *gadol*
little *katan*
more *yoter*
less *pahot*
many *harbey*

I *ani*
you (singular, masc/fem) *ata/at*
    (plural, masc/fem) *atem/aten*
we/us *anahnu*
them (masc/fem) *hem/hen*

want (masc/fem) *rotseh/rotsa*
how much? *kama?*
too dear *yakar midai*
cheaper *yoter zol*

stop, wait a minute! *rega!*
restaurant *mis'ada*
water *mayim*

food *okhel*
bill *heshbon*
hotel *malon*
shop *hanut*
newspaper *iton'*
post office *do'ar*
bank *bank*

Where is? *eyfo?*
when? *matai?*
taxi *monit*
train *rakevet*
bus *autoboos*
station/bus stop *tahana*
cinema *kolno'a*

white *lavan*
black *shahor*
red *adom*
blue *kahol*

right, correct *nahon*
wrong *lo nahon*
straight *yashar*
right *yemin*
left *smol*

doctor *rofe*
hospital *bet cholim*
ambulance *ambulantz*
police *mishtara*
policeman *shoter*

one *ehad*
two *shtayim*
three *shalosh*
four *arba'*
five *hamesh*
six *shesh*
seven *sheva'*
eight *shmoney*
nine *taysha'*
ten *esser*
hundred *me'a*
thousand *elef*

Sunday *Yom rishon*
Monday *Yom shani*
Tuesday *Yom shlishi*
Wednesday *Yom reviyi*
Thursday *Yom chamishi*
Friday *Yom shishi*
Saturday *Shabbat*

PLACE NAMES

As of yet, there is no standardised spelling of Israeli place names. Thus one has: "Acre", "Akko" and "Acco"; "Nathanya" "Natanya" and "Netanya"; "Elat", "Elath" and "Eilat"; "Ashqelon" and "Ashkelon"; "S'fat", "Zefat", "Tzfat" and "Safed", etc. As if to purposely confuse the visitor, all are used freely.

PRONUNCIATION

a	as in	look
í	as in	see
ya	as in	Soraya
ai	as in	eye
ay	as in	may
aw	as in	away
kh	as in the Scottish loch	
gh	as in the Parisian r	
dh	as in	the

Try to pronounce double consonants twice as long. An apostrophe ' indicates a glottal stop.

GREETINGS

Hello *Márhaba, ahlan*
(reply) *Marhabtáyn, áhlayn*
Greetings *As-salám aláykum* (peace be with you)
(reply) *Waláykum as-salám* (and to you peace)
Welcome *Áhlan wasáhlan*
(reply) *áhlan fíkum*
Good morning *Sabáh al-kháyr*
(reply) *Sabáh an-núr* (a morning of light)/*Sabáh al-wurd* (a morning of the smell of flowers)
Good evening *Masá al-kháyr*
(reply) *Masá an núr*
Good night *Tisbáh al-kháyr* (wake up well)
(reply) *Wa ínta min áhlu* (and you are from His people)
Goodbye *Máa Saláma* or *alla Máák* (with peace or God be with you)/*Ya'atik aláfia* (may God give you health)
How are you? *Káyf hálak?* (to a man)/*Káyf hálik?* (to a woman)
Well, fine *Mabsút* or *mneeh* (for a man)/*Mabsúta* or *mneeha* (for a woman)

Please *min fádlak* (to a man)/*min fádlik* (to a woman)
After you *Tafáddal* (to a man)/*Tafáddali* (to a woman)/*Afáddalu* (to more than one)
Excuse me *Samáhli* or *Idha láwu samánt* (to a man)/*Samáhili* or *Idha láwu samánti* (to a woman)
Sorry *Áfwan* or *mutaásif* or *ásif* (for a man)/*Áfwan* or *mutaásifa* or *ásifa* (for a woman)
Thank you (very much) *Shúkran (jazilan)*
Thank you, I am grateful *Mamnúnak* (to a man)/*Mamnúnik* (to a woman)
Thanks be to God *Al-hámdu li-Ilá*
God willing (hopefully)*I nshá allá*
Yes *Náam* or *áiwa*
No *La*
Congratulations! *Mabrúck!*
(reply) *Alláh yubárak fik*

USEFUL PHRASES

What is your name? *Shú ismak?* (to a man)/*Shú ismik?* (to a woman)
My name is... *Ismi...*
Where are you from? *Min wáyn inta?* (for a man)/*Min wáyn intí?* (for a woman)
I am from:
...England *Ána min Ingíltra*
...Germany *Ána min Almánia*
...the United States *Ána min Amérika*
...Australia *Ána min Ustrália*
Do you speak English? *Btíhki inglízi?*
I speak:
...English *Bíhki inglízi*
...German *Almámi*
...French *Fransáwi*

a free room *ghúrfa fádia*
single room *ghúrfa munfárida*
double room *ghúrfa muzdáwija*
hot water *mái súkhna*
bathroom, toilet *hammám, tuwalét*
shower *dúsh*
towel *bashkír*
How much does the room cost per night? *Adáysh al-ghúrfa al-láyl?*

I do not speak Arabic *Ma bíhki árabi*
I do not understand *Ma báfham*
What does this mean? *Ya'áni esh?*
Repeat, once more *Kamán márra*
Do you have...? *Ándkum...?*
Is there any...? *Fí...?*
There isn't any... *Ma fí...*
Never mind *Ma'alésh*
It is forbidden... *Mamnú'a*
Is it allowed...? *Masmúh...?*
What is this? *Shú hádha?*
I want... *Bídi...*
I do not want *Ma bídi*
Wait *Istánn* (to a man)/*Istánni* (to a woman)
Hurry up *Yalla/bi súra'a*
Slow down *Shwáyya*
Finished *Khalás*
Go away! *Imshí!*
What time is it? *Adáysh as-sáa?/kam assáa?*
How long, how many hours? *Kam sáa?*

VOCABULARY

General
embassy *sifára*
post office *máktab al-baríd*
stamps *tawábi'a*
bank *bank*
hotel *otél/fúnduq*
museum *máthaf*
ticket *tádhkara*
ruins *athár*
passport *jiwáz as-sáfar*
good *kuwáys*
not good, bad *mish kuways*
open *maftúh*
closed *musákkar/múghlik*
today *al-yáum*
tonight *hadhi-l-láyl*
tomorrow *búkra*

Eating and Drinking
restaurant *máta'am*
food *ákl*
fish *sámak*
meat *láhma*
milk *halíb*
bread *khúbz*
salad *saláta*
delicious *záki*
coffee *áhwa*
tea *shái*
cup *finján*
with sugar *bi súkkar*
without sugar *bidún súkkar*
wine *nibíd*

beer *bíra*
mineral water *mái ma'adaniya*
glass *kubbaiya*
bottle *ázaja*
I am a vegetarian *Ána nabbáti* (for a man)/*nabbátiya* (for a woman)
the bill *al-hisáb*

zero *sifir*
one *wáhad*
two *itnín*
three *taláta*
four *árba'a*
five *khámsa*
six *sítta*
seven *sába'a*
eight *tamánia*
nine *tísa'a*
ten *áshara*
eleven *hidáshar*
twelve *itnáshar*

Getting Around
Where...? *Wáyn...?*
downtown/city centre *wást al bálad*
street *shária*
Amir Mohammed Street *Shária al-amir Mohammed*
car *sayára*
taxi *táxi*
shared taxi *servís*
bus *bas*
aeroplane *tayára*
airport *matár*
station *mahátta*
to *íla*
from *min*
right *yamín*
left *shimál*
straight *dúghri*
behind *wára*
near *aríb*
far away *ba'id*
petrol, super *benzín, benzín khas*

Days of the Week
Monday (*yáum*) *al-itnín*
Tuesday *at-taláta*
Wednesday *al-árba'a*
Thursday *al-khamís*
Friday *al-júma'a*
Saturday *as-sábt*
Sunday *al-áhad*

Shopping

market *súq*
shop *dukkán*
money *fulús*
cheap *rakhís*
expensive (very) *ghâli (jídan)*
receipt, invoice *fatúra, wásl*
How much does it cost?
Adáysh?/bi-kam?
What would you like? *Shú bidak?*
(to a man)/*Shú bidik?* (to a
woman)/*Shú bidkum?* (to more than
one)
I like this *Buhíbb hádha*
I do not like this *Ma buhíbb hádha*
Can I see this? *Mumkin ashúf
hádha?*
Give me *A'atíni*
How many? *Kam?*

Emergencies

I need help *Bídi musáada*
doctor *doctór/tabíb/hakím*
hospital *mustáshfa*
pharmacy *saidalíya*
I am ill, sick *Ána marídh* (for a
man)/*Ána marídha* (for a woman)
diarrhoea *ishál*
operation *amalíya*
police *shúrta*
lawyer *muhámmi*
I want to see... *Bídi ashúf...*

Further Reading

General

Agnon, Shai: *The Wedding Canopy.*
The only Israeli winner of the
Nobel prize for literature.
The Bible. This is where it all
happened.
Collins, Larry and LaPierre,
Dominique (1972) *O'Jerusalem.*
Pan, London. Well researched
book that brings alive the battle
for Jerusalem in 1948.
Encyclopedia Judaica (1972) Keter
Press, Jerusalem and Macmillan,
New York. Offers the most
comprehensive information about
Judaism and Israel.
Eilon, Amos (1971) *Fathers and
Sons.* Penguin, London.
Entertaining account of the
Zionist founding fathers.
Frank, Anne: *The Diary of Anne Frank.*
Helps the reader understand
what makes Israelis tick.
Herzl, Theodore: *Altneuland.* The
Zionist visionary's dream of what
a Jewish homeland might be like.
Hess, Moses: *Between Rome and
Jerusalem.* The 19th century
German Jew envisages a Jewish
State, anticipating Theodore
Herzl.
The Jewish Poets of Spain. Spanish-
Jewish poets from the late
Middle Ages, including Yehuda
Halevi and Ibn Gbrio I, pine for
Jerusalem.
Josephus: *The Jewish Wars.* An
account of Judea in Roman times.
Kollek, Teddy (1978) *For Jerusalem
– A Life.* Weidenfeld and
Nicholson, London. The former
mayor's autobiography.
Oz, Amos: *My Michael*; *To Know a
Woman*; *Elsewhere Perhaps* and
others. Oz is Israel's leading
contemporary novelist.
Uris, Leon: *Exodus.* Blockbuster
story of Israel's independence
subsequently made into a
famous movie.

Other Insight Guides

Among the 190 titles in the *Insight
Guides* series are companion
volumes on *Israel, Jordan, Egypt,
The Nile* and *Cairo.*

Insight Guide: Israel covers all
facets of the Holy Land, from
history and archaeology to people
and places. From the Dead Sea to
the Sea of Galillee, from Tel Aviv to
Eilat, it's all here.

Insight Guide: Jordan is the
definitive guide to this alluring
kingdom. From Petra to Wadi Rum,
from Crusader fortresses to scuba
diving.

Insight Guide: The Nile mixes
erudition with information and
entertainment to create the perfect
companion for one of the world's
great river trips.

ART & PHOTO CREDITS

Index

a

Abbasid Dynasty 38
Abd al-Malik, Caliph 38, 119
Abraham 23, 25, 184
Absalom's Pillar 141
Abu Tor 184
Agnon, S. Y. 80, 197
Aish Ha Torah Yeshiva 113, 114
Akiva, Rabbi 33
Al-Aksa Mosque 38, 120–123
Al-Hakim 38
al Husayni, Haji Amin 46, 47
al-Mamoon, Caliph 120
Al-Walid 38
Albright Institute 146
Alexander the Great 27, 146
Aliya (Immigration to Israel) 77
Allenby Bridge 18
Allenby, Edmund 42
Alliance Française 165
American Colony Hotel *145*, 146
Amichai, Yehuda 17, 80
Ammunition Hill 175
Anglican Compound 108
Apostle Paul 34
Arab Christians 68–69
Arafat, Yasser 51, 72, 74
Archaeological Seminars 112
archaeology 91
architecture 92–93
Ark of the Convenant 25
Armenian Museum 110
Armenian Quarter 41, 109–110
Arp, Jean 162
Art Museum 181
Artists' House Café 165
Ashkenazi 65
Augusta Victoria 185
Austrian Hospice 127
Avenue of the Righteous
    Among the Nations 181

b

ba'al teshuvah yeshivot 114
Balfour Declaration 42, 77
Bank Leumi 167
Barluzzi, Antonio 189
Basilica of Dominus Flevit 140
Bayit Vegan 178
BCE (definition of) 23
Begin, Menachem 47, 160

Beit Agron 162
Beit Ungarin Quarter 173
Beit Yoel 163
Bellow, Saul 18
Ben-Gurion, David *45*, 200, 201,
    202
Ben Gurion airport 18
Ben-Yehudah, Eliezar 80, 88, 170
Ben Yehudah House 170
Ben Yehudah Pedestrian Mall 163,
    164
Betar Jerusalem 183
Bethesda Pool 127
Bethlehem 87, 208–211
Bevingrad 169
Bezalalel Academy of Art and
    Design 165
Bezem, Naffali (sculptor) 181
Bible Lands Museum 178
Biblical Zoo 183
Billy Rose Art Garden 177, *178*
Binyenei Ha'Uma 81
Bloomfield Garden 159
Bloomfield Museum of Science
    178
B'nai Beitcha 176
Book of Isaiah 177
Botanical Garden 178
Brigham Young University 185
British Consulate 159
British rule 42, 169
Broad Wall 115
Broza, David 81
building boom 155
Bukharin Quarter *83*, 173–175
Burnt House, the 115

c

Café Atara *162*, 163
Cardo, the 91, *111*, 112
Cathilicon 130
Cave of Zedekiah 145–146
CE (definition of) 31
Cenaculum 135
Central Archives for Holocaust
    Studies 182
Central Bus Station 155
Central Post Office 167
Chagall, Marc *29*, 177, 189
Chagall Windows 189
Chamber of the Holocaust 135
Chanukah (meaning of) 28, 86
Chapel of Ascension 138
Children's Memorial 182
Christian community 68–69,
    86–87
Christian Information Centre 108
Christianity, origin of name 33

churches
    All Nations 140
    Christ Church 108
    Dormition, the 135
    Ethiopian Coptic 128
    Holy Sepulchre 30, *33*, 129, 133
    Holy Trinity 168
    Mary Magdalene 140
    Our Lady of the Spasms 128
    Pater Noster 138
    Redeemer, the 130
    Scotland 68
    St Anne 127
    St Chralampos, Chapel of 128
    St Helena, Chapel of 130
    St John the Baptist 189
    Visitation, the (Ein Kerem) 189
Cinemateque 158
Circle Line 155
Citadel of David, Old City 108
City Hall 167
City of David *22*, 25, 118
City Tower 165
Constantine the Great 34, 133
Crusades, the 41, 123
Czar Alexander II 168

d

Damascus Gate 42, *98–99*, 124,
    145
David, King 23–24, 160
Dead Sea 215–217
Dead Sea Scrolls 91, 177,
    215–217
Derek Hevron 158
diaspora (meaning of) 204
Diaspora Museum (Tel Aviv) 199,
    204–205
Diaspora Yeshivah 125
Dir Yasin 48
Dizangoff Centre (Tel Aviv) 200
Dome of the Chain 123
Dome of the Rock *39*, 92,
    104–105, 119–120, 123
    history of 38
Dung Gate 118

e

E-Tur 185
East Jerusalem 145–146
creation of 48
East Jerusalem Bus Station 145
Ecce Homo Arch 127
Eden Cinema 197
Ein Gedi 217
Ein Kerem 189
Einstein, Arik 81

Ein Yael Living Museum 183
El-Wad Street 124, 127
Eleona Church 138
Elijah Synagogue 114
Elon, Amos 91
Ethiopians 66–67
Ethiopian Church 170
Ethiopians' Street 170
Ethiopian Village 129
Ezra the Scribe 27

f

Farm Tool Museum 169
Fatimid Dynasty 38
Fefferberg's 164
festivals 81
Fifth Aliya 77
Finger of Og 168
Fink's 165
First Aliya 77
food 82–83
Fountain of Al Kas 123
Fourth Aliya 77

g

Gan Auster 167
Garden Tomb 145
Gate of Mercy 96–97, 139
Gate of Judgement 129
Gate of the Chain 123
Gaza 51
German Colony 166
German Probst Building 170
Gethsemane 32, 136–137, 140
Gihon Spring 25, 26
Givat Haananiah 184
Givat Ram 178
Golden Gate 96–97, 139
Goliath 23
Gordon, General 133, 145
Government Tourist Office 108, 165
Great Synagogue 165
Greek Orthodox Church 68
Greek Orthodox Patriarchate 130
Gulbenkian Public Library 111

h

Ha-Ari ("The Lion") 111
Haas Promenade 184
Habad House 112
Habad Road 112
Hadassah Hospital 185, 189
Hadrian, Emperor 33
Haganah 47
Haganah Museum Tel Aviv 198

Hall of Heroism 169
Hall of Names 181
Hall of Remembrance 182
Har Herzl 180
    haredim (Orthodox Jews) 62–63, 171, 172
Hasmoneans, the 28
Hassidic Jews 19
Hebrew language, the 80, 88–89
Hebrew Union College 161
Hebrew University 52, 170, 178, 185
Hechal Shlomo 23, 165
Hellenism 28
Henry Crown Symphony Hall 167
Heraclius, Emperor 34
Heritage House 114
Herod 25, 28, 159, 213
Herod's Family Garden 159
Herodian 111, 213
Herzl, Theodore 44, 45–46, 161, 180, 197
Herzl Museum 180
Herzl Street 197
Hess, Moses 45, 50
Hezekiah 26, 115, 118
Hill of Evil Council 183
Hillel, Rabbi 31
Hillel Street 162
Hinnom Valley 16, 26, 157
Hisham's Palace 215
Holy Sepulchre 129
Holyland Hotel 18, 178
House of Quality 158–159
House of Veronica 128
Hurvah Synagogue 112–113
Hutzot Hayotzer 156, 157
Hyrcanus John, 28

i

Idumeans, the 28
immigration 77
Independence Park 161, 162
IInternational Zionist Congress 46
Irgun, the 48, 160
Iron Gate 123
Isaiah 26
Islam 34, 37–38
Islamic Museum 123
Israel, creation of 48
Israel Centre 170
Israel Museum 93, 177
Israel Nature Preservation Society 169
Israeli Academy of Arts and Sciences 167
Israeli Arabs 71
Italian Synagogue 162

j

Jabotinsky, Vladimir 180
Jaffa 194–195
Jaffa Gate 108
Janusz Korczak Park 182
Jason's Tomb 166
Jebusites, the 23
Jeremiah 26
Jeremiah's Grotto 145
Jericho 213, 215
Jerusalem
origin of name 23
Persian sacking 34
Jerusalem Centre For the Performing Arts 167
Jerusalem Foundation 52, 159
Jerusalem Gate 171
Jerusalem International Conference Centre 178
Jerusalem Music Centre 157
Jerusalem Symphony Orchestra 80, 81
Jesus, birth of 28, 31
Jews, the 23–28, 33, 34
Jewish cemetery 139
Jewish Heritage Information Center 113
Jewish Necropolis 139
Jewish Quarter 41, 45, 93, 111–119
Jewish Quarter Museum 112
John F. Kennedy Memorial 189
Josiah 26
Judah (a tribe) 23, 25
Judah the Maccabbee 28
Judean Hills 185

k

Kauffmann, Richard 166
Kenyon, Dame Kathleen 91
Khan Theatre 159
kibbutz movement 82
Kibbutz Ramat Rahel 184
Kidron Valley 141
kings
Abdullah 123
Antiochus IV 28
Ataxerxes I 27
Cyprus 27
David, 23–24, 160
Herod, 25, 28, 159, 213
Hezekiah 26, 115, 118
Hussein 48, 123
Josiah 26
Manasseh 26
Nebuchadnezzar 26

Sargon II 26
Sennacherib 26, 115
Solomon 25, *27*
Zedekiah 26
King David Hotel 47, 160
King David Street 159–160
King David's Tomb 135
King George Youth Hotel 164–165
Knesset (Israeli parliament) 93,
176–177
Kollek, Mayor Teddy 51, 52, 183
kosher cooking 82
Kuzari 173

l

L. A. Mayer Museum of Islamic Art
167
language 88–89
Law of Return 185
League of Nations 168
Liberty Bell Garden 159
Lion's Gate 126
Liturgica 81
Lubatvitchers 63
Luria, Isaac 111

m

Ma'alot Dafna 175
Madaba map *20–21*
Madrassa Tankiziyya 124
Mahane Yehudah 164
Mahane Yehudah market *82*
Malkah 183
Mamelukes, the 41
Mameluke architecture 92,
123–124
Mamilla Pool 162
Mamilla Road 161
Manasseh, King 26
Mandelbaum Gate 170
Mary's Birthplace 127
Mary's Tomb 141
Masada 32, 91, *206–207, 217–218*
Mass Grave 139
Mawazzin 123
Mea She'arim Quarter 19, 62, 85,
171–173
Mendelsohn, Erich 166, 167
Menorah 177
Middle Synagogue 114
Military Cemetery 181
Mishkenot Sha'ananim 156–157
Mitchell Garden 157
Model of Jerusalem 109
Mohammed, Prophet 37
Mohammed Ali 42
Monastery of the Cross 176

Montefiore, Moses 15, 156
Montefiore Windmill *155*, 156
Moses 25
Mosque of Omar 130
Mount Herzl 180–181
Mount Moriah 25
Mount of Olives *19*, 32, 138–141
Mount Scopus 48, 184, 185
Mount Sinai 25
Mount Zion 134–135
Mughrabu Gate 120
Muristan Quarter 130
Museum of the History of Jerusalem
109
Muslims, the 17, 34
Muslim Cemetery 162
Muslim Quarter 123–124
Mussaieff, Shlome 174
Mussaieff House 174

n

Nachmanides 45
Nahalat Shiva 163, 172
Nahla'ot 164
National University Library 178
Natural History Museum 167
Nebi Samuel 176
Nebuchadnezzar, King 26
Nehemiah 27
Neve Tzedek Theatre 197
Neve Zedek 197
New Gate 130
New Orient House 131
Nikanor's Gate 179
Noguchi, Isamu 177
Northern Gate 173
Notre Dame de France 167

o

Old Protestant Cemetery 135
Old Yishuv Court Museum 111
Olmert, Ehud 51, 52
Omar, Caliph 37
Operation Magic Carpet 77
Ophel 108
Or Haim Street 111
Or Samayach Yeshivah 114, 175
Order of the Knights of the Temple,
124
Orthodox Jews 62–63, 86
Ottoman Empire 42
Oz, Amos 18, 80

p–q

Palace, The 174
Palestinian Authority (PA) 18
Palestinians 72–75
Pargod 164
Pargod Theatre 81
Peace Forest 184
Peel Commission 47
Peres, Shimon *47*, 52
Pesach (Passover) 31
Pharisees, the 28
Pilate, Pontius 31
Pilgrim's Reception Plaza 126
Pillar of Heroism 182
Pinsker, Leo 45, 77
Plaza-Sheraton Hotel 165
Poliker, Yehudah 81
population 59
President's Residence 167
Prime Minister's House 166
Prophet Mohammed 37
Queen Helena 34, 133, 146
Queen of Sheba 25, *27*, 170
Qumran caves 91, 177
Qumran Ruins 216–217

r

Rabbi Mocco ben Nachman 45
Rabin, Yitzhak 51, 61
Railway Station 159
Ramadan 17
Ramah 176
Ramat Eshkol 175
Ramban Synagogue 113
Ramot 176
Ramparts Walk 108
Rapaport, Nathan (sculptor) 181
Rasputin 168
Ratisbone, Monastery 165
Rav Kook House 164
Ravitz, Yehudit 81
Rehavia 166
Rehov HaNevi'im 169–170
religious groups 85–87
Rivlin, Rabbi Yosef 152, 162, 172
Rivlin Street 162
Robinsen's Arch 116
Rockefeller Museum 146
Roman Square Museum 145
Roth, Cecil 33
Roth, Phillip 135
Rothschild Boulevard (Tel Aviv) 197
Ruppin House 166
Russian Church 61
Russian Compound 167–169
Russian Jews 64–65

S

Sadducees, the 28
St Andrew's Church 159
St George's Cathedral 146
St James Cathedral 110
St Louis Hospice 167
St Stephen's Gate 126
Saladin 41
Salah ed-Din 146
Samaria 26
Samuel, Sir Herbert 46
Sanhedrin Tombs 175
Saul of Tarsus 33
Schick, Conrad 170
Schoken Library 166
Second Aliya 77
secular Jews 60–61
security 18
Seleucids, the 27
Selim I 42
Seljuks, the 38
Sennacherib, King 26, 115
Sephardic Jews 52, 63, 81
Sergei Building 169
Seven Arches Hotel 138
Shabbat Square 173
Shalom Tower 197
Shamir, Yitzak 47
Shamosh, Amnon, 80
Shams, Anton 80
Shavuoth (Feast of Weeks) 31
Sheba, Queen of 25, 27, 170
Sheik Jarrah 146
Sherover Walkway 184
Shmuel HaNavi 175
Shrine of the Book 177
Siloam pool 26, 118
Silwan 141
Simmon bar-kochba 33
Sisters of Zion Convent 189
Six Day War 48
Small Wall 123
Solomon, King 25, 27
Solomon's Stables 123
Sovier Jews 77
Spring of Gihon 118
Spring of the Vineyard 189
Spring of the Virgin 189
Stambouli Synagogue 114
Stations of the Cross 127–129
Stern House 161
story telling 19
Street of the Prophets 170
Sukenik, Eliezer 91
Sukkot (the feast of the
  tabernacles) 25, 31
Suleiman Street 145
Suleiman the Magnificent 41, 92,
120, 124, 126, 135, 157
Sultan's Pool 157
Supreme Court 93, 178
Suq Khan 124
Swedish Theological Seminary 170
Syrian Quarter 41

t–u

Talmud, the 17
Talpiot 184
Taxation Museum 161
Tel Aviv 192–193, 194–201
  meaning of 197
Temple Mount 118–119
Ten Lost Tribes of Israel 26
Terra Sancta College 165
Thabor House 170
Theodosius II 34
Third Aliya 77
Ticho, Abraham 163
Ticho, Anna 164
Ticho House 163
Tisha ba'Av 116
Tomb of Hezir 141
Tomb of the Kings 146
Tombs of the Prophet 139
Tomb of Simon the Just 146
Tombs of the Sanhedrin 175
Tomb of Vladimir Jabotinsky 181
Tomb of Zachariah 141
Torah, the 27, 80, 82, 91
tourism 17
Tourjeman-Post 170, 171
Tower of David 42, 108–109
Tower of David Museum 109
Train Theatre 159
Twain, Mark 108
ultra-Orthodox Jews 62–63
Umayyad Dynasty 38, 120
United Nations Headquarters 184

v

Valley of Hinnom 16, 26, 157
Valley of Jehosaphat 141
Valley of the Cross 176
Valley of the Lost Communities
  182
Van Leer Foundation 167
Vespasian Emperor, 32
Via Dolorosa 126–128
Vilna Gaon, the 172

w

Wadi Kelt 215
Wailing Wall 115–117
Walls, rebuilding of 42
War of Independence Memorial
  112
Warren, Charles 91
Warren's Shaft 118
Wax Museum (Tel Aviv) 197
Weizmann, Chaim 185
Well of Souls 120
West Bank 51
Western Wall 115–117
Wilson's Arch 116
Wohl Rose Garden 177
Wolfson Museum 165

y

Yad Vashem 181–182
Yadin, Yigael 91
Yarkon River 199
Yehoushua, A.B. 80
Yemenite Market (Tel Aviv) 197
Yemin Moshe 157
yeshiva (Jewish school) 80, 114
Yeshurun Synagogue 165
Yiddish, 171–172
YMCA tower, 160
Yohanan Ben-Zekkai, 114
Yom Kippur 85
Youth Hostel (Ein Kerem) 189

z

Zahal Square 167
Zedekiah, King 26
Zion Gate 135
Zion Square 95, 155, 156
Zionism 45–48, 62
origin of 45

A
B
C
D
E
F
G
H
I
a
c
d
e
f
g
h
i
j
k
l

The Insight Approach

The book you are holding is part of the world's largest range of guidebooks. Its purpose is to help you have the most valuable travel experience possible, and we try to achieve this by providing not only information about countries, regions and cities but also genuine insight into their history, culture, institutions and people.

Since the first Insight Guide – to Bali – was published in 1970, the series has been dedicated to the proposition that, with insight into a country's people and culture, visitors can both enhance their own experience and be accepted more easily by their hosts. Now, in a world where ethnic hostilities and nationalist conflicts are all too common, such attempts to increase understanding between peoples are more important than ever.

Insight Guides:
Essentials for understanding

Because a nation's past holds the key to its present, each Insight Guide kicks off with lively history chapters. These are followed by magazine-style essays on culture and daily life. This essential background information gives readers the necessary context for using the main Places section, with its comprehensive run-down on things worth seeing and doing.

Finally, a listings section contains all the information you'll need on travel, hotels, restaurants and opening times.

As far as possible, we rely on local writers and specialists to ensure that information is authoritative. The pictures, for which Insight Guides have become so celebrated, are just as important. Our photojournalistic approach aims not only to illustrate a destination but also to communicate visually and directly to readers life as it is lived by the locals. The series has grown to almost 200 titles.

Compact Guides:
The "great little guides"

As invaluable as such background information is, it isn't always fun to carry an Insight Guide through a crowded souk or up a church tower. Could we, readers asked, distil the key reference material into a slim volume for on-the-spot use?

Our response was to design Compact Guides as an entirely new series, with original text carefully cross-referenced to detailed maps and more than 200 photographs. In essence, they're miniature encyclopedias, concise and comprehensive, displaying reliable and up-to-date information in an accessible way. There are almost 100 titles.

Pocket Guides:
A local host in book form

However wide-ranging the information in a book, human beings still value the personal touch. Our editors are often asked the same questions. Where do *you* go to eat? What do *you* think is the best beach? What would *you* recommend if I have only three days? We invited our local correspondents to act as "substitute hosts" by revealing their preferred walks and trips, listing the restaurants they go to and structuring a visit into a series of timed itineraries.

The result: our Pocket Guides, complete with full-size fold-out maps. These 100-plus titles help readers plan a trip precisely, particularly if their time is short.

Exploring with Insight:
A valuable travel experience

In conjunction with co-publishers all over the world, we print in up to 10 languages, from German to Chinese, from Danish to Russian. But our aim remains simple: to enhance your travel experience by combining our expertise in guidebook publishing with the on-the-spot knowledge of our correspondents.

" I was first drawn to the Insight Guides by the excellent "Nepal" volume. I can think of no book which so effectively captures the essence of a country. Out of these pages leaped the Nepal I know – the captivating charm of a people and their culture. I've since discovered and enjoyed the entire Insight Guide series. Each volume deals with a country in the same sensitive depth, which is nowhere more evident than in the superb photography. **"**

Sir Edmund Hillary

The World of Insight Guides

400 books in three complementary series cover every major destination in every continent.

Insight Guides

Alaska
Alsace
Amazon Wildlife
American Southwest
Amsterdam
Argentina
Atlanta
Athens
Australia
Austria
Bahamas
Bali
Baltic States
Bangkok
Barbados
Barcelona
Bay of Naples
Beijing
Belgium
Belize
Berlin
Bermuda
Boston
Brazil
Brittany
Brussels
Budapest
Buenos Aires
Burgundy
Burma (Myanmar)
Cairo
Calcutta
California
Canada
Caribbean
Catalonia
Channel Islands
Chicago
Chile
China
Cologne
Continental Europe
Corsica
Costa Rica
Crete
Crossing America
Cuba
Cyprus
Czech & Slovak Republics
Delhi, Jaipur, Agra
Denmark
Dresden
Dublin
Düsseldorf
East African Wildlife
East Asia
Eastern Europe
Ecuador
Edinburgh
Egypt
Finland
Florence
Florida
France
Frankfurt
French Riviera
Gambia & Senegal
Germany
Glasgow
Gran Canaria
Great Barrier Reef
Great Britain
Greece
Greek Islands
Hamburg
Hawaii
Hong Kong
Hungary
Iceland
India
India's Western Himalaya
Indian Wildlife
Indonesia
Ireland
Israel
Istanbul
Italy
Jamaica
Japan
Java
Jerusalem
Jordan
Kathmandu
Kenya
Korea
Lisbon
Loire Valley
London
Los Angeles
Madeira
Madrid
Malaysia
Mallorca & Ibiza
Malta
Marine Life in the South China Sea
Melbourne
Mexico
Mexico City
Miami
Montreal
Morocco
Moscow
Munich
Namibia
Native America
Nepal
Netherlands
New England
New Orleans
New York City
New York State
New Zealand
Nile
Normandy
Northern California
Northern Spain
Norway
Oman & the UAE
Oxford
Old South
Pacific Northwest
Pakistan
Paris
Peru
Philadelphia
Philippines
Poland
Portugal
Prague
Provence
Puerto Rico
Rajasthan
Rhine
Rio de Janeiro
Rockies
Rome
Russia
St Petersburg
San Francisco
Sardinia
Scotland
Seattle
Sicily
Singapore
South Africa
South America
South Asia
South India
South Tyrol
Southeast Asia
Southeast Asia Wildlife
Southern California
Southern Spain
Spain
Sri Lanka
Sweden
Switzerland
Sydney
Taiwan
Tenerife
Texas
Thailand
Tokyo
Trinidad & Tobago
Tunisia
Turkey
Turkish Coast
Tuscany
Umbria
US National Parks East
US National Parks West
Vancouver
Venezuela
Venice
Vienna
Vietnam
Wales
Washington DC
Waterways of Europe
Wild West
Yemen

Insight Pocket Guides

Aegean Islands★
Algarve★
Alsace
Amsterdam★
Athens★
Atlanta★
Bahamas★
Baja Peninsula★
Bali
Bali Bird Walks
Bangkok★
Barbados★
Barcelona★
Bavaria★
Beijing★
Berlin★
Bermuda★
Bhutan★
Boston★
British Columbia★
Brittany★
Brussels★
Budapest & Surroundings★
Canton★
Chiang Mai★
Chicago★
Corsica★
Costa Blanca★
Costa Brava★
Costa del Sol/Marbella★
Costa Rica★
Crete★
Denmark★
Fiji★
Florence★
Florida★
Florida Keys★
French Riviera★
Gran Canaria★
Hawaii★
Hong Kong★
Hungary
Ibiza★
Ireland★
Ireland's Southwest★
Israel★
Istanbul★
Jakarta★
Jamaica★
Kathmandu Bikes & Hikes★
Kenya★
Kuala Lumpur★
Lisbon★
Loire Valley★
London★
Macau★
Madrid★
Malacca
Maldives
Mallorca★
Malta★
Mexico City★
Miami★
Milan★
Montreal★
Morocco★
Moscow
Munich★
Nepal★
New Delhi
New Orleans★
New York City★
New Zealand★
Northern California★
Oslo/Bergen★
Paris★
Penang★
Phuket★
Prague★
Provence★
Puerto Rico★
Quebec★
Rhodes★
Rome★
Sabah★
St Petersburg★
San Francisco★
Sardinia
Scotland★
Seville★
Seychelles★
Sicily★
Sikkim
Singapore★
Southeast England
Southern California★
Southern Spain★
Sri Lanka★
Sydney★
Tenerife★
Thailand★
Tibet★
Toronto★
Tunisia★
Turkish Coast★
Tuscany★
Venice★
Vienna★
Vietnam★
Yogyakarta
Yucatan Peninsula★

★ = Insight Pocket Guides with Pull out Maps

Insight Compact Guides

Algarve
Amsterdam
Bahamas
Bali
Bangkok
Barbados
Barcelona
Beijing
Belgium
Berlin
Brittany
Brussels
Budapest
Burgundy
Copenhagen
Costa Brava
Costa Rica
Crete
Cyprus
Czech Republic
Denmark
Dominican Republic
Dublin
Egypt
Finland
Florence
Gran Canaria
Greece
Holland
Hong Kong
Ireland
Israel
Italian Lakes
Italian Riviera
Jamaica
Jerusalem
Lisbon
Madeira
Mallorca
Malta
Milan
Moscow
Munich
Normandy
Norway
Paris
Poland
Portugal
Prague
Provence
Rhodes
Rome
St Petersburg
Salzburg
Singapore
Switzerland
Sydney
Tenerife
Thailand
Turkey
Turkish Coast
Tuscany

UK regional titles:
Bath & Surroundings
Cambridge & East Anglia
Cornwall
Cotswolds
Devon & Exmoor
Edinburgh
Lake District
London
New Forest
North York Moors
Northumbria
Oxford
Peak District
Scotland
Scottish Highlands
Shakespeare Country
Snowdonia
South Downs
York
Yorkshire Dales

USA regional titles:
Boston
Cape Cod
Chicago
Florida
Florida Keys
Hawaii: Maui
Hawaii: Oahu
Las Vegas
Los Angeles
Martha's Vineyard & Nantucket
New York
San Francisco
Washington D.C.
Venice
Vienna
West of Ireland